Bureaucratic Discretion

Pergamon Government and Politics Series

Series Editors:
Richard A. Brody
Stanford University
Norman J. Ornstein
American Enterprise Institute for Public Policy Research
Paul E. Peterson
The Brookings Institution
Nelson W. Polsby
University of California, Berkeley
Martin M. Shapiro
University of California, Berkeley

Pergamon Titles of Related Interest

Pergamon Government & Politics Series

Bureaucratic Discretion

*Law and Policy
in Federal Regulatory Agencies*

Gary C. Bryner
Brigham Young University

PERGAMON PRESS

NEW YORK · OXFORD · BEIJING · FRANKFURT
SÃO PAULO · SYDNEY · TOKYO · TORONTO

U.S.A.	Pergamon Press, Maxwell House, Fairview Park, Elmsford, New York 10523, U.S.A.
U.K.	Pergamon Press, Headington Hill Hall, Oxford OX3 0BW, England
PEOPLE'S REPUBLIC OF CHINA	Pergamon Press, Room 4037, Qianmen Hotel, Beijing, People's Republic of China
FEDERAL REPUBLIC OF GERMANY	Pergamon Press, Hammerweg 6, D-6242 Kronberg, Federal Republic of Germany
BRAZIL	Pergamon Editora, Rua Eça de Queiros, 346, CEP 04011, Paraiso, São Paulo, Brazil
AUSTRALIA	Pergamon Press Australia, P.O. Box 544, Potts Point, N.S.W. 2011, Australia
JAPAN	Pergamon Press, 8th Floor, Matsuoka Central Building, 1-7-1 Nishishinjuku, Shinjuku-ku, Tokyo 160, Japan
CANADA	Pergamon Press Canada, Suite No. 271, 253 College Street, Toronto, Ontario, Canada M5T 1R5

Copyright © 1987 Pergamon Books, Inc.

First printing 1987

Library of Congress Cataloging in Publication Data
Bryner, Gary C., 1951–
Bureaucratic discretion.
(Pergamon government and politics series)
Includes index.
1. Administrative discretion—United States.
2. Administrative procedure—United States.
I. Title.   II. Series: Pergamon government &
politics series.
KF5407.B79 1987   353   86-30526
ISBN 0-08-034494-1 Hardcover
ISBN 0-08-034493-3 Flexicover

Printed in Great Britain by A. Wheaton & Co. Ltd., Exeter

This book is dedicated to Jane, Benjamin, Nicholas, and Jonathan.

 CONTENTS

Preface   ix

List of Figures   xii

List of Tables   xiii

PART 1: COMPETING THEORIES
OF ADMINISTRATIVE RULE MAKING

Chapter

1   The Problem of Bureaucratic Discretion   1
        The Theory of Bureaucratic Discretion   3
        Discretion and Administrative Rule Making   9
        The Rest of the Book   17

2   Administrative Law and Administrative
        Procedures   19
        The Evolution of Administrative Procedures   19
        Evaluating Administrative Law and Administrative
            Procedures   30

3   Scientific and Economic Analysis in
        Administrative Rule Making   41
        Decision Making Rules and Scientific Analysis   42
        The Assumptions Underlying Scientific and
            Economic Analysis   55
        Evaluating Economic and Scientific Analysis   58

4   Political Oversight of Administrative
        Rule Making   65
        Presidential Review of Administrative Activity   65
        Congressional Control of Administrative Activity   73
        Assumptions Underlying Political Accountability
            of Rule Making   78
        Evaluating Political Oversight of Rule Making   81

PART 2: CASE STUDIES

5   The Environmental Protection Agency   91
     The EPA's Statutory Authority   92
     Rule-Making Procedures in the EPA   94
     Regulating Ozone: A Case Study of the
        Rule-Making Process   105
     Evaluating EPA Rule-Making Procedures   108

6   The Occupational Safety and Health
     Administration   119
     The Rule-Making Process at OSHA: Statutory
        Provisions   121
     The Cotton Dust Standard: A Case Study of OSHA
        Rule Making   134
     Evaluating the OSHA Standard-Setting Process   140

7   The Consumer Product Safety Commission   146
     Statutory Authority of the CPSC   147
     UFFI: A Case Study of CPSC Rule Making   157
     Evaluating CPSC Rule Making   166
     The Consequences of Mismatching Responsibili-
        ties and Resources   172

8   The Food and Drug Administration   174
     Regulation of Food Safety   175
     FDA Rule Making and Food Safety Regulation   182
     Drug Regulation and Congressional Intent   192
     Assessing the FDA's Regulatory Efforts   198

PART 3: CONCLUSION

9   The Prospects for Limiting Bureaucratic
     Discretion   203
     Remedies and Reforms   209

Notes and References   219

Index   247

About the Author   250

PREFACE

The dramatic growth of the regulatory power of the federal government during the New Deal generated demands to reduce and limit the discretion of administrative agencies which had received broad delegations of power, and ultimately resulted in passage of the Administrative Procedure Act in 1946. The great expansion of the federal government's regulatory reach in the late 1960s and the early 1970s produced a corresponding effort to structure this power and reduce the discretionary authority it created. Congresses, presidents, and federal courts have created a variety of procedural devices and approaches to limit administrative discretion and make agencies more accountable to democratic, constitutional, and legal expectations.

Have these efforts achieved their purposes? Has the problem of administrative discretion been resolved? Have administrative procedures, objective analysis and expertise, oversight of administrative decisionmaking, and other reforms of the late 1970s and early 1980s succeeded in limiting and shaping the power of regulatory agencies? How should we think about administrative discretion? Are the remedies worse than the disease? The purposes of this book are to explore answers to these questions and raise other ones, to consider alternative ways of thinking about regulatory power and administrative processes, and to encourage further debate concerning ways to structure governmental power.

Concern with the distribution of governmental power is particularly timely in 1987, as we celebrate the bicentennial of the Constitution. The Constitution provides the basic framework and decisionmaking processes for the national government. It reflects the ideal of the rule of law—the concept that the authority of the state should be exercised through clear rules applicable to all citizens, with minimal discretion in their application. Its provisions are aimed at limiting, checking, and refining the powers of the federal government. The expectations engendered by the Constitution, however, run counter to political incentives and to ideas of administrative government that champion discretion and independence.

Much of this book focuses on how administrative decisionmaking can satisfy the competing expectations held for it and how regulatory agencies, in particular, might better pursue the conflicting and contradictory goals held for them. The approach pursued here is a practical one. New ways of thinking about and responding to the problem of administrative discretion are sought, ways that can lead to more efficient and effective achievement of policy goals and can also be more consistent with constitutional expectations and values.

It is important to indicate to the reader what this book does not attempt to do. It does not attempt to develop quantitative measures of administrative processes and regulatory decisions, nor does it rely on a methodologically sophisticated analysis of administrative behavior. It seeks to develop a conceptual analysis, focusing on how we have come to think about and accept administrative discretion, and the direction our thinking ought to take in the future. Unlike many studies of regulation, it does not address the important question of when there should be government regulation—when government intervention in economic and social activity, to alter or direct private decisions, should occur. I plan to engage in that debate elsewhere. This book assumes that at least in the near future, if not in the long run, some government intervention in economic and social affairs will continue to take place, with regulatory agencies issuing and enforcing rules binding on the behavior of individuals and organizations. The primary concern here is to consider how to improve the ability of administrative agencies to accomplish the tasks delegated to them, in a way that also satisfies other important values and expectations concerning the exercise of public power.

I am greatly appreciative of and indebted to a number of individuals and institutions for their help and support in pursuing this study. I have relied heavily on the work of a variety of scholars in law, political science, economics, and other disciplines who have written about administrative law, regulation, public administration, constitutional law, and democratic theory, whose work I have cited in the references. While I write from the perspective of political science, I have sought to synthesize and integrate ideas from a variety of sources and perspectives.

A number of scholars have been most generous with their time and have read parts of this manuscript in its various stages over the past few years. I appreciate and have gained much from their criticisms and suggestions and only wish that I could have responded more effectively to their comments. They include Martha Derthick, Arch Dotson, Alfred Kahn, Robert Katzmann, Isaac Kramnick, Paul E. Peterson, and Martin Shapiro. I am particularly indebted to Theodore Lowi for what I have learned from his work in this area and for the opportunity to discuss these ideas with him. I appreciate very much the willingness of a number of officials in regulatory agencies to be interviewed for this study. I have benefitted greatly from the opportunity to try out and discuss these ideas with students at Brigham Young University, in my courses in public policy and public administration. I am also most grateful for the financial support received from Brigham Young University, the Brookings Institution, and Cornell University.

It has also been a delight to be able to work with Lynn Rosen, Christina Lombardi, and others at Pergamon Press. I appreciate very much their professionalism and expertise as well as their personal interest in and support of this project and the attention they have given to it.

 LIST OF FIGURES

3.1 The Environmental Protection Agency's Process for Establishing and Revising National Ambient Air Quality Standards 51

3.2 Risk Management and Assessment in Federal Agencies 53

3.3 Availability of Information concerning the Health Effects of Selected Chemicals 60

3.4 Public Perception of U.S. Annual Death Rates from Selected Causes 63

5.1 The Environmental Protection Agency (organizational chart) 100

6.1 The Occupational Safety and Health Administration (organizational chart) 123

7.1 The Consumer Product Safety Commission (organizational chart) 153

8.1 The Food and Drug Administration (organizational chart) 176

8.2 Drug Development and Approval under the FDA 194

 # LIST OF TABLES

1.1	Statutory Constraints on Administrative Rule Making	14
3.1	Decision-Making Criteria for Health and Safety Agencies	45
3.2	Generic Guidelines for Scientific and Economic Analysis: The Federal Government's Experience	47
3.3	Government Agencies Involved in Environmental and Health Risk Assessment	52
3.4	Kinds of Data Used in Risk Assessment	54
5.1	EPA Enabling Statutes: Substantive and Procedural Provisions	92
5.2	The EPA Rule-Making Process	99
5.3	Analytic Support Documents in EPA Rule Making	101
5.4	The Public Docket in EPA Rule Making	104
6.1	Steps in OSHA's Rule-Making Process	124
6.2	OSHA Health Standards	141
7.1	Organization of CPSC Project Teams	154
7.2	CPSC Rules: The First Decade	167
8.1	Selected FDA Food Additive Bans	187
9.1	Rule-Making Procedures: A Comparison	206

Part 1

Competing Theories of Administrative Rule Making

Chapter 1   THE PROBLEM OF BUREAUCRATIC DISCRETION

The delegation of broad, policy making powers to administrative agencies has become one of the most important characteristics of contemporary American government. Federal administrative agencies have been empowered to issue rules and regulations that affect virtually every area of economic activity. The great explosion in the number of agencies and programs created in the late 1960s and the 1970s rested on optimistic expectations concerning the ability of government to accomplish an increasingly wide range of public purposes. Some of these policies are pursued under broad statutory statements of general purpose that offer little more guidance than to serve the "public interest," while other statutes give specific, detailed instructions to administrative agencies.

Regulatory programs, and environmental, health, and safety regulation in particular, have been based on extremely ambitious goals to prevent harm and bring under government monitoring virtually all commercial and industrial activity. These statutes promise dramatic improvement and even absolute achievement in protecting the environment and reducing health risks while providing little discussion of how the costs are to be distributed and how competing policy goals are to be achieved. Regulatory power that was in the past usually limited to identifying prohibited practices in selected industries has mushroomed to include planning and directing industrial and commercial behavior and practices. In virtually every case the scope of agency responsibility and authority greatly exceeds the resources provided. Congress regularly only provides a fraction of the resources required to accomplish the regulatory tasks delegated to regulatory agencies. As a result, administrative agencies are given little guidance in their enabling statutes concerning how they should shape their regulatory agenda, set priorities and allocate scarce resources, and distribute the costs and benefits involved in the rules and regulations they issue.

Some discretion is, of course, inevitable as laws cannot possibly anticipate the myriad of situations and circumstances that agencies confront. Bureaucratic discretion is viewed as appropriate and even essential in assuring that policies be developed by experts and that scientific expertise and technical

1

calculations determine environmental, health, and safety regulations. Bureaucratic discretion, however, threatens the idea of political accountability, that important policy choices be made by elected officials, and that government ultimately be responsible to the people. It endangers the idea of the rule of law, that governmental actions be clear and specific, and applied by officials in a nondiscretionary manner so that the coercive powers of government not be exercised arbitrarily. It calls into question the structure of the separation of powers, checks and balances, and other elements of constitutional democracy that rely on formal institutions and processes. It threatens the development of clear public choices, inhibits public debate and education concerning public policies, and contributes to perceptions of "capture" of agencies by the interests that fall under their jurisdiction.

While administrative discretion is common to all bureaucracies, the problems it raises are particularly pronounced in regulatory agencies. The way in which regulatory agencies have exercised the discretion given them has evoked widespread criticism by those who champion more regulatory protection and by those who oppose government interventions. In theory, the broad discretionary power of agencies frees them to rely on scientific and technical criteria and considerations in pursuing the policies given them. The scientific basis of many regulatory initiatives, especially those involving environmental, health, and safety policy, however, has been widely criticized as being confused with and inseparable from political choices,[1] manipulated by interests for ideological purposes,[2] ignored by agency decision makers,[3] used to justify decisions made on other grounds,[4] threatened by judicial review and the role of the courts in determining regulatory policies,[5] and employed to slow down or block agency initiatives through time-consuming procedures.[6]

While there is no clear consensus concerning the problems of regulation, much activity has been directed toward ways of limiting the discretion of regulatory agencies. A number of important devices have been developed in response to these and other criticisms of regulatory agencies, ranging from changes in standard operating procedures within agencies to increased external scrutiny of administrative decision making. For some agencies, such as the Environmental Protection Agency, Congress has written increasingly detailed statutes that order certain rules to be issued, include timetables for the issuance of certain rules and sometimes even supercede agency rule making by writing regulations directly into the statutes. For most regulatory agencies, statutory language continues to be broad and general. For all agencies, however, the major focus of attention has been on limiting discretion through procedural mechanisms and devices. Although couched in politically neutral terms of due process, policy analysis, and oversight, these procedures have important political implications for the actual decisions made: They determine which interests, assumptions and values will have influence in administrative deliberations.

Three kinds of procedural approaches have become particularly important in addressing the problems of bureaucratic discretion and the power of agencies to use legally binding rules and regulations. First, legal procedures outlined in the Administrative Procedure Act and in specific enabling legislation serve as a primary constraint on administrative discretion and have become part of an elaborate and complex system of administrative law that seeks to assure that agency actions are bound by legal, procedural requirements. Second, scientific and economic decision rules and analyses have been emphasized as a way to give shape to agency decision making, and to provide limits on administrative activity. Third, oversight efforts by Congress and presidents and their staffs have sought to ensure that bureaucracies be accountable to political and electoral forces.

How well have these procedural innovations responded to the problems of bureaucratic discretion? How well have they accomplished their purposes? What has been their effect on the ability of administrative agencies to achieve their statutory purposes and missions? These procedural reforms have served to reduce some kinds of bureaucratic discretion, but in ways that have made the administrative process more confused and less effective, and have reduced the ability of administrative agencies to function. Despite the attention given to discretion, agencies have been left with little guidance for most of the difficult choices they must make. The broad scope of administrative power has invited political intervention in administrative proceedings and has produced an enormous superstructure of procedural mechanisms designed to create the illusion of legitimacy for administrative government, which fails to limit and direct administrative power and threatens the ability of agencies to accomplish their statutory mandates.

A clear understanding of the nature of administrative discretion, the challenges it poses for our expectations concerning the exercise of governmental power, and the costs and benefits as well as consequences of efforts to reduce it are central to our ability to pursue the public policies we have decided to undertake. As discretion is better understood, more appropriate responses can be fashioned that limit and direct it in ways that increase the capacity of administrative agencies to accomplish public purposes and assure that the exercise of governmental power is accountable to law and, ultimately, to the people.

THE THEORY OF
BUREAUCRATIC DISCRETION

Not only is bureaucratic discretion an inevitable, inescapable characteristic of government, but it has often been championed as a positive, desirable precondition for effective governance. For John Locke, executive discretion was necessary, given the nature of the legislative process:

This Power to act according to discretion, for the publick good, without the prescription of the Law, and sometimes even against it, is that which is called Prerogative. For since in some Governments the Lawmaking Power is not always in being, and is usually too numerous, and so too slow, for the dispatch requisite to Execution; and because also it is impossible to foresee, and so by laws to provide for, all Accidents and Necessities, that may concern the publick; or to make such Laws, as will do no harm, if they are Executed with an inflexible rigour, on all occasions, and upon all Persons, that may come in their way, therefore there is a latitude left to the Executive power, to do many things of choice, which the Laws do not prescribe.[7]

Alexander Hamilton championed an energetic and powerful executive whose authority and power assumed the legitimacy of administrative discretion[8]:

The difficulty of a complete and perfect specification of all cases of Executive authority would naturally dictate the use of general terms—and would render it improbable that a specification of certain particulars was designed as a substitute for those terms, when antecedently used. The different mode of expression employed in the constitution in regard to the two powers the Legislative and the Executive serves to confirm this inference. In the article which grants the legislative powers of the Governt. the expressions are—*"All Legislative powers herein granted shall be vested in a Congress of the UStates;"* in that which grants the Executive Power the expressions are, . . . "The Executive Po[wer] shall be vested in a President of the United States of America."

The enumeration ought rather therefore to be considered as intended by way of greater caution, to specify and regulate the principal articles implied in the definition of Executive Power; leaving the rest to flow from the general grant of that power, interpreted in conformity to other parts [of] the constitution and to the principles of free government.[9]

Presidents have also vigorously defended administrative discretion. Theodore Roosevelt argued that "every executive officer, and above all every executive in high position, was a steward of the people bound actively and affirmatively to do all he could for the people . . . I declined to adopt the view that what was imperatively necessary for the nation could not be done by the President unless he could find some specific authorization to do it."[10] Woodrow Wilson, writing almost 30 years before he was elected president, defended administrative discretion in two senses: broad discretionary authority was to be granted to the executive branch so that it can pursue its tasks in an efficient and effective manner, and, within agencies, officials were to have some discretion in pursuing their individual tasks and responsibilities. In a broad sense, politics and administration are to be separated, so that administrative officials can accomplish the tasks of government through the most efficient and effective means possible. Expansive grants of discretionary authority assure that expertise and professionalism can be harnessed in the pursuit of public purposes. For Wilson, discretion did not threaten democratic values but contributed to the idea of accountability of administrative actions: "large powers and unhampered discretion seem to me the indispensable conditions of responsibility. . . . There is no danger in power, if only it be not irresponsible."[11]

From a different perspective, bureaucratic discretion is defended as a means of diffusing conflict, reducing the coercive nature of government, permitting Congress to take on an increasingly larger policy agenda, and providing a process of decision making that champions bargaining and negotiation in administration rather than defining substantive policies and forcing compliance with them. According to this latter view, public policies are "merely the identification of the problems toward which government ought to be aimed." There are no "formal specifications of means or of ends," but, rather, an emphasis on process, where "few standards of implementation, if any, accompany delegations of power" and where the primary requirement and concern is participation by interested groups in the policy-making process within administrative agencies. Bureaucratic discretion is a central element of the kind of government envisioned by this form of pluralistic democracy.[12]

The idea of bureaucratic discretion provides the justification and basis for a number of important structural and procedural features of public administration, as well as for the broader theoretical concerns described above. The civil service system, with its emphasis on merit appointments, expertise and professionalism, rests on the idea of discretion: the idea that administrative officials should be free to employ their expertise and training in the pursuit of the policy responsibilities delegated to them. Policy analysis, planning, management strategies, and budget processes are all part of the ideal of independent, efficient, and effective administration. A powerful chief executive to "coordinate and energize the other parts of the system" is also a central feature of discretionary administration.[13]

Bureaucratic discretion is also defended as a practical response to the inability of traditionally separated governmental powers to deal effectively with the policy challenges confronting them. James Landis defended the broad grants of discretionary authority to administrative agencies not as "simply an extension of executive power" but a "full audit of authority necessary for [them] in order to plan, to promote, and to police," thus representing "an assemblage of rights normally exercisable by government as a whole." "The administrative process," he argued, is an "answer to the inadequacy of the judicial and the legislative processes."[14]

Discretion is especially important in regulatory agencies, as it permits administrative officials to be flexible and adaptable in tailoring their efforts to specific situations. Laws cannot be written to anticipate and address all of the possible situations within an agency's jurisdiction. They must permit a consideration of economic, regional, cultural, personal and other differences among those who fall within the agency's regulatory reach. Discretion permits the regulators to tailor their efforts to particular circumstances and concerns, produce regulatory actions that are reasonable and fair, and effectively accomplish their policy objectives.[15]

Discretion is a fundamental element of modern administrative theory and is consistent with important norms of pluralism and democracy. It is also consistent with political incentives and serves as an attractive way for legislators to delegate responsibility for difficult decisions to bureaucrats. Credit can be claimed for legislative action, blame can be deflected when specific efforts clash with politically powerful interests, and constituents can be cultivated by intervening in unpopular agency actions.

Kinds of Administrative Discretion

Administrative discretion takes a variety of forms, ranging from subtle and complex assessments of human characteristics to high volume, routine judgments; from decisions to initiate (or not initiate) specific actions to development of basic policy purposes and priorities.[16] Different kinds of agency activities involve different kinds and levels of discretion. A general distinction can be made, however, between two basic kinds of discretionary authority given to administrative agencies: (1) authority to make legislative-like policy decisions, and (2) authority to decide how general policies apply to specific cases. This distinction is a widely recognized one as it mirrors the familiar legislative–executive functional dichotomy, although the line separating the two kinds of authority is not always easily discernible.

The enforcement decisions of administrative agencies have been the source of some of the most widely discussed concerns with administrative discretion.[17] Virtually all agencies exercise discretion in allocating and directing resources for enforcement activities, since the number of regulated entities and actions within agency jurisdictions exceeds the available resources. Agency officials are often granted the power to waive compliance requirements or grant exceptions to administrative rules or policies. The exercise of such powers is, by nature, discretionary, since the concern is usually one of flexibility or adaptability to situations that were not or could not be foreseen or that should be treated individually. Benefits and grants are often clearly outlined in enabling statutes and may involve very little discretion. The bureaucratic task might be only that of making sure that benefit checks reach the recipients designated by law in the most efficient manner possible. But, for some policies, administrative officials may have major responsibilities and discretionary authority for determining eligibility. They may have to make complex assessments of human characteristics, or set priorities among kinds of recipients when potential beneficiaries exceed available resources. They may impose restrictions on recipient behavior by conditioning the distribution of benefits on compliance with administrative expectations and standards.[18]

For some agencies, operating under clear and specific statutes, legislative-like discretion is quite limited: the task of the agency is simply to "fill in the details" of the law. These laws spell out program objectives in great detail, specific actions to be taken by administrative officials, and the affected population. Laws that provide for grants and benefits such as public works, Social Security, and defense procurement are representative of this kind of statutory language. Most regulatory laws, however, give little guidance to agencies for the substance of their regulations and for the way in which the burdens they impose are to be distributed. The responsibilities that have been delegated to them often greatly exceed the provided resources, thus necessitating important administrative choices and setting of priorities. Some laws provide competing objectives that give administrators broad latitude. Under the Emergency Petroleum Allocation Act, for example, regulations were to be issued for the allocation of petroleum products that "protected the public health, maintained public services and agricultural operations, preserved a sound and competitive petroleum industry, allocated crude oil to refiners to permit them to operate at full capacity, resulted in an equitable distribution of supplies to all parts of the country, promoted economic efficiency, and minimized economic distortion.[19]

Agencies may also be confronted with a number of statutes that each address fragments of the agency's overall jurisdiction, rather than providing a comprehensive policy. Legislatures may identify some areas of administrative responsibility as being so technical in nature that the delegation of policy-making power is the only logical response. Even where statutes are quite specific and detailed, however, the administrative processes they engender usually evolve into discretionary activity where interaction of interest groups, congressional committee staffs, other agencies, and reviewing courts come together to produce decisions.

There are, then, important differences in the kinds of discretion exercised by administrative officials, and distinctions should be made concerning the different kinds of discretion, different ways of reducing or shaping that discretion, and the advantages and disadvantages of these efforts.[20] Some kinds of discretionary activity pose more of a threat to the legitimacy of the administrative state than other kinds. Some kinds of discretion might be desirable in some contexts but not in others. Granting discretion to regulatory inspectors, for example, in political cultures where government officials are respected and trusted, might give them flexibility that would more likely lead to the achievement of regulatory goals than would a nondiscretionary arrangement.[21] Broad rule-making power might be delegated to agencies posing fewer threats to democratic government where there is a clear consensus over values, priorities, and the direction in which agency decision making is to take place.[22] Administrative discretion can facilitate the bringing together of

interests affected by and concerned with administrative initiatives in developing mutually acceptable policies.[23]

Administrative Discretion and the Rule of Law

The theories and theorists that have encouraged and defended bureaucratic discretion have been challenged from a number of perspectives and for
a number of reasons. The most compelling theoretical criticism comes from
the idea of the rule of law. The rule of law represents the expectation that the
exercise of the coercive powers of government be limited by laws that are
clear and specific, prospective (and not retroactive), applicable to all persons
who fall within the categories specified, and enforced in a nondiscretionary
manner, thus producing a government of "laws" and not of "men." The
rule of law plays an essential role in fostering individual freedom, since it permits citizens to know what actions are prohibited so they are then free to plan
their own lives accordingly. It serves to assure that administrative agencies
are limited to powers that are expressly delegated to them by law, and provides a check against arbitrary power.[24]

The rule of law emphasizes the development of clear policy goals so that
government efforts can be evaluated and the most efficient and effective
kinds of policies identified. It serves to prevent the "capture" of administrative agencies by the interests they are supposed to be regulating, and avoids
the "privilege and tight access" that accompany discretionary bureaucracy.
It recognizes the importance of the integrity of law and the importance of
formal institutions, roles, and processes in a constitutional democracy.[25] It
contributes to democratic accountability. Clear and specific statutes contribute to the expectation that officials who are accountable to the electorate
make the basic policy decisions that bureaucracies implement. Presidents
contribute to the rule of law as they discharge their constitutional duty to
"take care that the laws be faithfully executed."

The most important political and practical manifestation of the rule of law
is the expectation that elected officials direct bureaucratic decision making
and hold administrative officials accountable for actions taken. Elected officials have great incentives to assume this role as political entrepreneurs who
capture a part of the administrative process for political purposes—to make
sure public policies of interest to them are accomplished and to shape the
implementation of policies in a way that produces political benefits. While
such efforts may ostensibly be justified as a way to render bureaucratic discretion accountable to law, it may serve to do little more than to harness it for
narrow political purposes. Much of the effort to limit bureaucratic discretion
is motivated by these kinds of practical, political concerns while couched in
the rhetoric of political accountability and rule of law.

DISCRETION AND ADMINISTRATIVE RULE MAKING

The theory and practice of administrative government must satisfy the competing expectations of discretion, on the one hand, and political accountability and the rule of law on the other. The legislative-like discretion given to agencies to issue rules, regulations, and standards deserves particular attention, since it is through such efforts that administrative agencies make important policy decisions and judgments, determine how scarce agency resources will be allocated, set priorities, and then make these decisions legally binding on those within their jurisdictions.

Agency promulgation of rules and standards has been championed as a way of limiting administrative discretion; however, the exercise of this kind of power raises significant concerns about the policy-making powers of bureaucratic officials. It has been heralded as a solution to many of the problems surrounding the administrative process and is central to a theory of administration that brings together the expectations of discretion and rule of law. For the Federal Trade Commission, rule making was viewed as a crucial innovation in achieving commission objectives more efficiently. As one scholar has argued:

> The root of the Federal Trade Commission's problem was substantially the same as the government's under the Sherman Act over half a century earlier. It was a procedural difficulty as much as anything else. The commission was attempting to regulate cigarette advertising on a case-by-case basis. Each time the commission ruled a particular advertisement deceptive, the industry came up with a variation that could squeak by under the rule of the previous case. This was proving to be an endless and fruitless process. The commission needed to write general regulations for the whole industry; the case method, whether employed by an agency or by the courts, was proving to be too cumbersome a method of developing regulatory policy.[26]

From another perspective, rule making was viewed as basic to the acceptability and viability of the administrative state. K. C. Davis, in his conclusion to *Discretionary Justice,* argued that:

> Administrative rule-making is the key to a large portion of all that needs to be done. To whatever extent is practical and consistent with the need for individualized justice, the discretion of officers in handling individual cases should be guided by administrative rules adopted through procedures like that prescribed by the Administrative Procedure Act. Agencies through rule-making can often move from more vague or absent statutory standards, and then, as experience and understanding develop, to guiding principles, and finally, when the subject matter permits, to precise and detailed rules. The constant objective, when discretionary power is excessive, should be for earlier and more elaborate administrative rules.[27]

Theodore Lowi, in his critique of administrative discretion, concluded that administrative rule making was the key to formalizing administrative decision making and rendering administration more consistent with the idea of the rule of law:

> Administrative formality would simply be a requirement for early and frequent administrative rule making. . . . A rule can be general and yet gain clarity and practicality through the specific cases to which it is applied. It was precisely this ability to perceive the public policy implications in complex phenomena that explains our reliance on expert agencies in the first place. The rule in combination with the cases to which it applies can become a known factor in the everyday life of each client. . . .
> Most importantly for all—for administrators and for clients and citizens— early rule making would improve the administrative process by making administrative power more responsible as well as more efficient. Early rule making forces reflection upon the implications of the original legislation and of the place of the agency in the society. . . . Bargaining on the rule would tend to push the focus of the political process upward toward the highest levels of responsibility rather than downward away from responsibility and away from public scrutiny.[28]

Administrative rule making has been viewed as a means of reducing administrative discretion; however, it represents the kind of administrative action that is most in need of external checks and constraints, because of its legislative nature. It has become a focal point for criticisms of government regulation and the broad discretionary powers enjoyed by administrative bodies.

The number of rules and regulations issued by agencies has reached, in recent years, as high as 7,000 annually,[29] while Congress itself regularly enacts only about 300 public laws each year.[30] Regulations issued by agencies cover a wide spectrum of concerns. Safety standards for power mowers, baby cribs, matchbooks and fireworks are formulated and enforced by the Consumer Product Safety Commission. The Food and Drug Administration establishes standards for the content of mayonnaise, ketchup, and ice cream as well as guidelines for the use of food additives in food products. Standards for the components and operation of nuclear reactors are set by the Nuclear Regulatory Commission. National Highway Traffic Safety Administration regulations mandate standards for automobile fuel economy, resistance of bumpers to collision damage, brakes and anti-theft devices. The Environmental Protection Agency issues rules governing manufacturing activity that reach nearly every industrial sector of the economy, regulating sources of air, water and noise pollution, radiation, hazardous wastes and toxic chemicals.

The Rise of Administrative Rule Making

Congress delegated legislative-type powers to the president as early as 1790, when the president was empowered to prescribe rules and regulations for traders with the Indians, and to other officials in the executive branch as early as 1813, when the secretary of the treasury was given authority to establish regulations for effectuating the Internal Revenue Administrative Act.[31] In subsequent delegations to the executive branch, authority was often granted to the president or another executive official "to make all necessary orders and regulations to carry this law into effect" or to adopt "such rules and regulations as he may deem necessary."[32] Still other delegations conferred broad authority to deal with emergency situations and crises, especially in areas of foreign affairs. For more than a century Congress granted rule-making power to the executive branch without providing any procedural standards to be followed. In a few cases, administrative officials were required to submit regulations to the president or another high-ranking official before they could go into effect; in other cases, rules were required to be submitted to Congress when issued, merely to inform Congress and not for its approval.[33]

Federal regulatory powers were generally of limited jurisdiction and of limited consequence for the conduct of private affairs until the end of the nineteenth century. As legislation began to affect more and more individuals, interests organized and became involved in the administrative process through consultation. Legislation, as well as agency initiatives, permitted "experts" and interested parties to help formulate standards for food products, banking practices and other regulatory functions.[34] Congress first began requiring public hearings and other procedural requirements for the rule-making activities of the Interstate Commerce Commission in 1903 and included related provisions in subsequent legislation.[35] Hearings were eventually imposed on some agencies and voluntarily instituted by others.

By 1903, the Supreme Court, faced with evaluating delegations that clearly went beyond routine administrative discretion, created the doctrine that it has since relied on to uphold delegation of power. It upheld a delegation of power to the secretary of the treasury because Congress had provided "standards" for limiting agency discretion.[36] Similarly, in 1928, the Court ruled that if Congress provided an "intelligible principle to guide administrative officials, the delegation would be acceptable."[37]

The great burst of regulatory activity during the New Deal relied on broadly defined delegations of power to administrative agencies. Opposition in response to these agencies, claiming the unconstitutional delegation of power, quickly developed, and the Supreme Court in 1935 struck down, in two different cases, sections of one of the broadest delegations, the National Industrial Recovery Act. In the first case, the Court found that the president had been given "unlimited authority to determine the policy" of prohibiting the shipping of petroleum products in excess of states' authority, and that "Congress ha[d] declared no policy, ha[d] established no standards, ha[d] laid down no rule."[38]

Five months later the president's power to approve trade associations' codes of fair competition was also invalidated for lack of sufficient substantive statutory standards or procedural restraints. The Court, in striking down the delegation to the president to approve trade association's codes of fair competition, again found insufficient statutory standards to guide the president. However, the Court distinguished this case from others where it had upheld broad delegations of power, such as the Federal Trade Commission's power to prevent "unfair methods of competition." In the case of the FTC, the Court argued, "Congress set up a special procedure. A commission, a quasi-judicial body, was created. Provision was made for formal complaint, for notice and hearing, for appropriate findings of fact supported by adequate evidence, and for judicial review to give assurance that the action of the Commission is taken within its statutory authority." But in providing for these Codes, the court argued, "the NIRA dispenses with this administrative procedure and with any administrative procedure of an analogous nature."[39]

Eight years later, in *Yakus v. U.S.,* the Court upheld a delegation of power to the Office of Price Administration for three reasons. First, Congress enacted the Emergency Price Control Act in pursuance of a defined policy and required that the prices fixed by the administration "should further that policy and conform to standards prescribed by the Act." Second, the Emergency Price Control Act was unlike the statutes rejected in the 1930s where "the function of formulating the Codes was delegated, not to a public official responsible to Congress or the executive, but to private individuals engaged in the industries to be regulated." Third, "the only concern of courts is to ascertain whether the will of Congress has been obeyed. This depends not upon the breadth of the definition of the facts or conditions which the administrative officer is to find but upon the determination whether the definition sufficiently marks the field within which the administrator is to act so that it may be known whether he has kept within it in compliance with the legislative will."[40]

In its most recent delegation case, *National Cable Television Association v. U.S.,* the Supreme Court found that the Federal Communication Commission's assessment on cable TV systems could be viewed as either a "fee" or a "tax": If viewed as a fee, designed to recover administrative expenses, the assessing power would be valid; if seen as a tax, implying the delegation of taxing power, the Court, in upholding the delegation, would have to make a "sharp break with our traditions to conclude that Congress had bestowed on a federal agency the taxing power." The Court, "to avoid constitutional problems," found the assessment to be a fee.[41]

Although the Supreme Court has not struck down a statute as violative of the delegation doctrine since the 1930s, the decisions issued in those New Deal cases as well as in the subsequent cases where the delegations were upheld, indicate that there are two general principles to guide delegations of power. Congress must provide substantive criteria or standards to serve as guides to administrative decision makers, or provide procedural requirements to assure that those affected have an opportunity to take part in the decision-making process. Second, some categories of delegation of powers are prohibited, such as those involving taxation, civil liberties, and powers granted to nongovernmental entities, while delegations in the area of foreign policy and during wartime and other emergencies are generally to be upheld.[42]

The Theory of Regulatory Rule Making

During the decade between the mid-1960s and the mid-1970s, the federal government produced the greatest burst of regulatory legislation since the early years of the New Deal. During the 1930s, for example, 42 major regulatory agencies and programs were created by Congress. In the 1960s, 53 new regulatory programs and agencies were formed. Between 1970 and 1980, 130 major regulatory laws were enacted,[43] although there were a number of deregulatory efforts enacted by Congress in the late 1970s in the area of transportation and other sectors of the economy.[44]

These new regulatory efforts shared several important characteristics: They were based on broadly defined objectives; they extended well beyond specific industries, unlike most of the earlier regulatory programs; they generally required that specific policy decisions be made through administrative rule making; they assumed that expertise and analysis would provide the basis for agency decisions; they provided elaborate procedural provisions to constrain administrative power; they emphasized the importance of political review of regulatory initiatives; and they relied on broad delegation of powers to administrative agencies, since agency jurisdiction and responsibility greatly exceeded the resources provided.

Congress has continued to delegate broad grants of authority to administrative agencies. It does not have the resources or the inclination to deal with complex, detailed regulations and is thus obliged to depend on experts to make policy choices. Administrators are seen as more likely than legislators to be able to monitor social and economic activity and develop flexible and rapid responses to changing conditions. Even when Congress has enacted specific, detailed legislation, administrative agencies must make basic decisions concerning the setting of priorities, the balancing of conflicting goals, and the regulation of complex and poorly understood problems.

Once Congress decides to enact a statute with broad and vaguely defined substantive requirements, it has a wide variety of additional alternatives to choose from in seeking to balance the competing expectations of discretion, political accountability and the rule of law. As indicated above, three primary means have generally been used that have become basic elements of the administrative process (Table 1.1 provides an overview of these provisions). First, Congress has imposed internal procedural restraints on agency decision

Table 1.1. Statutory Constraints on Administrative Rule Making

Kind of Constraint	Some Examples
Administrative Law	
publication of proposed and final rules	notice of proposed rule making published in *Federal Register*
public comment period	comments received for 30 days
oral hearings	cross-examination permitted
citizen petitions	petitions to force agencies to take particular regulatory actions
Federal Courts	judicial review of agency regulation and procedures followed
Scientific and Economic Analysis	
economic decision rules	benefits to exceed costs
scientific decision rules	no risk to human health permitted
advisory councils	Science Advisory Board to review technical basis for proposed regulation
Political Oversight	
Congress	legislative veto,* appropriations, oversight hearings
President	OMB review of proposed and final regulations

*The Supreme Court declared various forms of the legislative veto to be unconstitutional in June of 1983. A number of alternatives for permitting Congress to monitor rule-making activity have been proposed (see chapter 4).

making. Rule-making procedures, under the Administrative Procedure Act, have required, at minimum, advanced notice of proposed actions and an opportunity for interested persons to respond. In addition, some statutes require additional procedures such as cross-examination and oral hearings, while other statutes require formal trial-type proceedings. Congress has experimented with a variety of procedural devices, described by one legal scholar as "unbelievably chaotic" and prompting another to find that "one would almost think there had been a conscious effort never to use the same phraseology twice."[45]

The second means employed by Congress and presidents to delimit the administrative process has been to establish generic standards or decision rules and other provisions for agency rule making to assure that agencies base regulations on economic and scientific criteria. Cost-benefit analysis, risk assessment and other analytic tools are then employed by agencies in evaluating alternative courses of action. Scientific advisory and review committees are expected to contribute to the technical expertise that is to serve as the basis for administrative action.

The third means of giving direction to the administrative process has been through external political controls. Congress has given to the president oversight and control powers, including authority to reorganize the executive branch and to review agency budgetary requests and paperwork burdens through the Office of Management and Budget (OMB). Recent presidents have themselves taken the initiative, issuing executive orders that strengthen the role of the OMB and impose cost-benefit and other economic-based requirements on agency decision making and relying on informal pressure and direction aimed at administrative officials. Congress has created for itself an elaborate and complex set of procedures for overseeing the administrative process including appropriations, authorizations and budgetary reviews, investigations and reports, and the legislative veto of agency rules. Structural decisions made by Congress such as whether agencies are to be placed within the executive branch or created as independent commissions also affect the kind of political control to which the agency will be subjected.

In creating and organizing the administrative process, Congress has focused very narrowly on limiting administrative discretion at the expense of broader considerations of how agencies are expected and able to function. While procedural constraints, generic standards, and external oversight are couched in nonpolitical terms of constitutional principles, economic or scientific analysis and expertise, and efficiency, they are used for political purposes and used to pursue substantive ends. Although these devices may be proposed or defended as being neutral, they have a great effect on specific substantive decisions since they are so sensitive to the assumptions and values of those who employ them. In the aggregate, they have made it increasingly difficult for agencies to accomplish the policy tasks and responsibilities delegated to them.   —

Procedural provisions are sometimes designed to slow down or make it more difficult to accomplish the substantive objectives to which statutes are directed. Procedural barriers and hurdles may represent political compromises struck by those who have insufficient power to defeat initiatives but sufficient strength to slow down implementation. If certain procedural arrangements seem to stymie effective bureaucratic action, they may simply be accomplishing their intended purposes.

These efforts to limit discretion have been imposed independently and are, to some extent, contradictory in their underlying purposes and assumptions. The proponents of these reforms have failed to consider how these conflicting concerns might be more carefully balanced. Legal procedures that place primary emphasis on public participation in administrative decision making, for example, do not recognize the importance of, and may even conflict with, the accountability of administrative activity to elected officials. Oversight provides opportunities for individuals and interests subject to administrative authority to try and escape compliance with agency decisions. The integrity of economic and scientific analysis may be sacrificed if they run counter to political priorities and concerns.

Although the reforms have clearly reduced administrative discretion, they have done so in ways that do little to satisfy the problem of broad delegations of power. Legal procedures have infused administration with adversarial hearings that translate considerations of public purposes into discussions of private rights. The establishment of agency priorities and policies becomes a function of adversarial hearings and judicial review, rather than of political choices and values. Government actions become less predictable, less consistent, less uniform in application. Oversight of agency decisions is often in response to narrow interests and concerns, and results in vetoing specific agency decisions rather than giving more direction to agency officials. Given the broad range of possible actions agencies can pursue, there is a great need to give some direction and guidance to agencies as they set priorities and make choices, to give them positive direction rather than to simply identify specific decisions that should not have been made.

It has been a characteristically American response to political disputes that controversy can be avoided by providing a procedural response rather than a substantive solution. In noting that scarcely an issue escaped eventual action by the courts, de Tocqueville recognized the impulse of government to escape politics through the legal process. Opponents of legislative proposals can be placated through procedural conditions which weaken agency powers or assure that those interests that did not prevail in the legislative battle have another opportunity to shape policy in the administrative arena. As a result, basic policy-making decisions are often made without clearly defined standards and guidelines from Congress. Agency procedures are slow and cumbersome. Agencies are accused of being both independent of political direction and dominated by the interests they are supposed to be regulating.[46] Agency actions are criticized as being arbitrary, irresponsible and inefficient, or piecemeal and fragmented, with little effort to coordinate regulatory activity across agencies or with other public policies.[47]

These problems are particularly evident as an emphasis on fairness and private rights conflicts with the requirements of efficient and effective administration, or when the decisions of experts and scientists conflict with the demands of political groups, interests, and actors. Increasing public participation in the formulation of administrative policies, through agency hearings, necessarily diverts attention from a strict implementation of legislative intent to a consideration of issues and pressures raised in this participation. Presidential review of regulations through the Office of Management and Budget or the use of the legislative veto in overturning rules may negate the compromises made by agency officials and interested groups. Decisions that are based on cost-benefit analysis and other criteria that are expected to be politically neutral are subject to reversal in response to political pressures. Concerns with the procedural rights of those affected by regulatory action give little attention to the bureaucratic and organizational imperatives of implementation.

Emphasis on administrative procedures permits an indirect discussion of agency powers and programs and avoids direct confrontation of politically controversial issues. As one observer has noted, "one of the very reasons that procedural encumbrances is such a useful legislative bargaining chip is that its proposed effect can be so well disguised—from the Congressman who deals in it and (just as important) from the public at large."[48] Procedural devices are convenient and politically popular ways of effecting a substantive change without directly doing so.

THE REST OF THE BOOK

The chapters to follow examine in detail the way in which administrative procedures, decision rules, and oversight have been pursued as a way to limit bureaucratic discretion. Chapters 2, 3, and 4 outline the theories and ideas that underlie these efforts to limit bureaucratic discretion, and the strengths and weaknesses of each approach. A central theme here is that administrative procedures, decision rules, and oversight reflect in themselves alternative theories of how administrative power is to be exercised. The problem here is not a lack of theory of bureaucratic government, but competition among theories and a lack of consensus over how these different expectations can be integrated.

Many of the examples of administrative procedures used here are drawn from agencies responsible for the development and implementation of environmental, health, and safety policies, since these policy areas pose some of the most difficult challenges for the integration of law, science, and politics. Chapters 5 through 8 present case studies of rule making in four federal regulatory agencies—the Environmental Protection Agency, the Food and Drug Administration, the Occupational Safety and Health Administration, and the Consumer Product Safety Commission—and compare how rule making differs for these different agencies. The case studies represent a variety of policy concerns and histories and range from independent regulatory commissions to cabinet-based agencies. Yet there are some common threads— their high political visibility, their reliance on sophisticated technical analysis, and their broad statutory authority. The chapters emphasize that despite the great attention directed toward administrative discretion, these agencies are still left with little direction for making the complex decisions required of them.

The final chapter provides a summary of the four case studies, and offers some broader generalizations concerning the consequences of procedural provisions on the ability of agencies to achieve their missions, and discusses possible remedies and reforms for administrative rule making. As the strengths and limitations of the administrative process are identified and understood, the decisions concerning the substantive tasks to be assumed by government can include a consideration of the nature of the processes by which those decisions will be implemented. This requires an effort to separate substantive and procedural considerations as well as a recognition of their interdependence. Administrative agencies cannot escape the conflicting and contradictory expectations held for them, but the administrative process can reflect a more careful attempt to live with these inconsistencies.

Chapter 2 ADMINISTRATIVE LAW
AND ADMINISTRATIVE
PROCEDURES

Administrative law rests on the theory that administrative power can be limited and constrained by legal procedures. Frank Goodnow, one of the earliest and most important proponents of administrative law, argued that the primary values to be pursued in administrative agencies were, in order of importance, efficiency in government, protection of individual rights, and pursuit of general goals.[1] Others, such as John Dickinson, argued that protecting individual rights and interests was the first priority of administrative law.[2] The tension between these notions of administrative law has been central to its development and evolution, and will be briefly examined below. The chapter also compares the roles of Congress in imposing procedural restraints, through the Administrative Procedure Act and subsequent legislation, and the federal courts in interpreting these laws, and provides a brief outline of the current status of administrative law for rule making. The chapter concludes with a discussion of the effects of administrative law on bureaucratic discretion and on the administrative process as a whole.

THE EVOLUTION OF
ADMINISTRATIVE PROCEDURES

Congress first began considering proposals to improve and standardize administrative procedures in 1929 when a bill was introduced that would have created a special administrative court to review the decisions of administrative agencies.[3] In 1940 Congress passed an "Act to Provide for the Expeditious Settlement of Disputes Within the United States and for Other Purposes," popularly known as the Walter–Logan Act, which required:

1. A trial-type hearing for adjudicatory proceedings before a single hearing examiner or a three-member hearing board; any person "aggrieved" by any decision of any agency could ask for such a hearing;
2. All rules "affecting the rights of persons or property" could be issued only after proper notice and a public hearing; all rules were to be issued within one year of the passage of statutes, and rules that had been in effect

for less than three years were to be reviewed within one year of the enactment of Walter–Logan, should anyone with a substantial interest in the
effects of the rule request such a review; and
3. Any person "substantially interested in the effects of any administrative
   rule" could seek review in the Court of Appeals for the District of Columbia; the reviewing court would determine the rule's constitutionality as
   well as whether it was within the agency's statutory mandate.[4]

These provisions prompted one observer to retitle the proposal "A Bill to
Remove the Seat of Government to the Court of Appeals for the District of
Columbia."[5]

Walter–Logan was immediately attacked by President Roosevelt and others as being too rigid and crippling of the administrative process. The president vetoed the bill, calling it an attempt by opponents of regulatory
programs to defeat by procedures what they could not defeat in substantive
debate. In his veto message, he argued that

> a large part of the legal profession has never reconciled itself to the existence
> of the administrative tribunal. Many of them prefer the stately ritual of the
> courts, in which lawyers play the speaking parts, to the simple procedure of
> administrative hearings which a client can understand and even participate
> in. . . . In addition, . . . there are powerful interests which are opposed to
> reforms that can be made only effective through the use of an administrative
> tribunal. . . . Great interests . . . which desire to escape regulation rightly see
> that if they can strike at the heart of modern reform by sterilizing the adminis-
> trative tribunal which administers them, they will have effectively destroyed the
> reform itself.[6]

Others echoed Roosevelt's charge that "opponents of administrative power
are not concerned at bottom by the methods and procedures of administrative agencies but are in fact hostile to the policies which they have been
appointed to further."[7]

The war interrupted the debate over limiting bureaucratic discretion. In
1946 Congress returned to the issue and enacted in that year the Administrative Procedure Act, which has become a kind of "constitution" for the
administrative process.

The Administrative Procedure Act

There are a number of important elements of the Administrative Procedure Act.[8] First, Congress explicitly provided that the regulatory commissions be independent entities in the executive branch. Despite criticisms that
agencies were a "headless fourth branch of government," that "Congress
[had] found no effective way of supervising them" and that "they [were]
answerable to the courts only in respect to the legality of their actions,"[9] Congress was unwilling to change the structure of the executive branch. Independent agencies were to continue to be subject to congressional oversight and,
in particular, to judicial review.

The second provision of the APA granted the right to seek judicial review to "any person suffering legal wrong because of agency action, or adversely affected or aggrieved by agency action within the meaning of the relevant statute." The scope of review differs according to different kinds of agency actions: Any agency action covered by the APA can be set aside by the reviewing court if it is found to be "arbitrary, capricious, an abuse of discretion, or otherwise not in accordance with the law; . . . unconstitutional . . . ; in excess of statutory jurisdiction, authority or limitations, or short of statutory right." This standard is generally applied to informal proceedings; a more stringent test is required of formal hearings, where the court may hold unlawful any action "unsupported by substantial evidence" in the record compiled by the agency.[10]

The standard of review is important, since agency actions which are required to satisfy the "arbitrary and capricious" standard are easier to justify: Agencies need only to show that decisions are based on some plausible assumptions. Decisions requiring "substantial support" in the decision-making record place a greater burden on the agencies to defend their actions. A major concern of administrative law has been the development of legal principles for determining which standard of judicial review is to apply to particular administrative decisions.

The third element of the APA is the division of administrative proceedings into two categories, rule making and adjudication. A rule was defined as "the whole or a part of an agency statement of general or particular applicability and future effect designed to implement, interpret, or prescribe law or policy." Rule making was simply defined as the process of formulating rules. In contrast, adjudication was defined as the "agency process for the formulation of an order," an order being the "whole or part of a final disposition, whether affirmative, negative, injunctive or declaratory in form of an agency in a matter other than rule making but including licensing."[11] Again, since the act requires different procedures for rule making than for adjudication, the distinction here has been an important one.

Procedures for informal rule making required a minimum standard of notice of intended rule making, and an opportunity for interested parties to submit written opinions and data. Agencies were to be free to provide additional opportunities such as hearings for participation by interested parties. Formal proceedings for rule making would be triggered by specific statutory provisions which require that rules be "made on the record after opportunity for an agency hearing." The hearing provided for required that a hearing examiner (later retitled an administrative law judge) preside over the proceeding, make decisions concerning evidence and testimony, and issue a decision based on the record produced, much like a judge in the common-law tradition. Parties were to enjoy the right to give oral testimony and cross-examine witnesses, and were given other trial-type opportunities to participate. This same kind of formal proceeding was also required of adjudications "required by statute to be determined on the record after opportunity for an agency hearing." No procedural provisions were outlined for informal adjudications.[12]

Other important provisions of the APA required publication of rules in the *Federal Register,* mandated a strict separation of adjudicative and prosecutorial personnel, and prohibited off-the-record communication between hearing examiners and other agency personnel and outside persons in formal proceedings.

The Evolution of the Administrative Procedure Act

Although the APA was hailed as a solution to the problem of bureaucratic discretion, a number of criticisms were soon directed at it. Some found that the APA, in providing no guidelines for informal adjudication, ignored the vast majority of administrative actions. K. C. Davis, for example, has argued that over 90 percent of administrative functions are informal in nature, not subject to constraints that would limit administrative discretion.[13] Critics have argued that neither the APA nor, perhaps, any such statute, can really control decision-making processes which have developed out of political and organizational realities.[14] Others complained that there were a number of agency actions exempted from even the minimum standards established by the APA, such as decisions relating to contracts, grants, benefits, military and foreign affairs; agency rules of practice and personnel actions; interpretative rules; general statements of policy; and any other action where officials find APA-based procedures to be impracticable, unnecessary or contrary to the public interest.

A third complaint found the distinction between rules and adjudications to be an inadequate guide for determining which kind of proceeding—informal rule making or formal hearing—should apply. This is the basic distinction upon which specific procedural provisions are determined, yet the distinction is not a clear one. Orders are defined as all final actions which are not rules; rules can be statements of either "general or particular applicability." Since there may not be a great difference between an order and a rule of particular applicability, the major difference appears to be that rules have "future effect." Yet adjudications often result in decisions which have future effect as well. The choice between adjudication and rule making determines the kind of participation offered to those who are affected by agency actions and has been the basis of numerous challenges by those who are dissatisfied with either the procedural or substantive aspects of the agency's decisions. While the Supreme Court has issued opinions on several cases arising from this ambiguity, the distinction has not been made significantly clearer.[15]

A fourth criticism leveled at the APA was that it was too rigid and inflexible. Agencies assumed a variety of functions, objectives, and political relationships which prohibited generalizations and standardized procedural requirements. Rather than approaching the administrative process from one direction, critics argue that each agency and program should be structured individually.[16] Buried in the legislative history of the APA itself was a cryptic comment from the House Judiciary Committee staff, warning that where statutes were so "broadly drawn that agencies have large discretion; the situation cannot be remedied by an administrative procedure act, but must be treated by the revision of statutes conferring administrative powers."[17]

Finally, judicial review of administrative decisions has been criticized as arbitrary and capricious itself, unable to develop a clear standard of review. One legal scholar began an article on judicial review of federal regulatory agencies by sardonically noting that

> As any practicing lawyer knows, file cabinets contain two form briefs for cases involving judicial review of administrative action affecting technologies. One, for the losers below, bristles with irate talk about administrative caprice, urges exacting scrutiny, and cites *Overton Park*. The other, for the winners below, speaks dispassionately of administrative expertise, counsels deference, and cites *Vermont Yankee*. Often a party is both winner and loser below, and this calls for deft departmentalization in the brief, simultaneously urging rigorous oversight on one issue while discouraging judicial overreaching on another.[18]

Despite these criticisms, the APA provided the framework for the administrative process for more than three decades. As long as administrative agencies relied primarily on a case-by-case regulatory effort, an adversarial process relying on adjudicatory-type procedures was widely viewed as sufficient to structure agency decision making. By the mid- to late 1960s and throughout the 1970s, however, criticism was directed to the inadequacy of the APA's procedural provisions for the agencies and programs created by more recent legislative activity which had been based on extremely broad grants of power and ambitious objectives. Case-by-case regulatory efforts have been rejected for many of these programs as inefficient, as agencies were given the greater responsibility of making basic policy decisions and establishing priorities and tradeoffs among competing interests.

Legislation enacted during the early to mid-1970s began requiring administrative rule making in place of the case-by-case approach. Statutes empowered agencies to identify through rule-making proceedings the most salient problems and develop appropriate policy responses. The rule-making process became, in many areas of regulation, the primary instrument for formulating basic policy. This reliance on rule making posed a fundamental challenge to the APA. Rule making under such a broad statutory scheme takes on many of the attributes of the legislative process itself; however, because it takes place in administrative agencies, it is expected to be more restrained and limited.

The focus of congressional concern in the late 1970s and 1980s for the administrative process has been over how to regulate regulatory rule making—how to modify the old framework of the APA to meet the new demands of citizen participation, scientific and economic analyses, and coordination of policies. The great burst of regulatory activity beginning in the late 1960s brought virtually every sector of the economy and society under the jurisdiction of federal administrative agencies. Increased opposition to such an expansion of federal regulatory power was inevitable as agency jurisdictions were extended and new regulations imposed. Powerful public interest groups pressured agencies to vigorously pursue regulatory objectives, and provided political support to protect agencies from the demands of the regulated. As a result, regulatory efforts were more widespread, more likely to impinge significantly upon powerful interests, and more likely to generate opposition. As Congress delegated policy-making powers to these agencies, the political forces and pressures that had been aimed at Congress and the legislative process were redirected toward agency officials in rule-making proceedings. Because of the primary role played by the courts in monitoring the administrative process under the APA, the courts were forced to be the first to respond to the basic changes in the administrative process beginning in the late 1960s.

The Courts and Administrative Rule Making

The Supreme Court had itself contributed to the growth of administrative rule making through several decisions that permitted agencies to establish general policy through rule-making proceedings even though they had only been given adjudicatory powers, and which encouraged agencies to use informal rule-making procedures unless clearly required by statute to act otherwise.[19] But it was federal judges, charged by Congress with supervising the administrative process, who found themselves in the position of having to respond to the creation of new agencies and programs and the resultant criticism of administrative procedures. The responses of the courts were twofold. In a number of decisions in the late 1960s and early 1970s, the federal courts, led by the Court of Appeals for the District of Columbia, found that some agency procedures were inadequate, that there was insufficient attention given to the rights of those affected to participate or that all relevant interests and factors were not being considered by agencies. One legal scholar described the result of this as the transformation of administrative law into a "surrogate political process," which widened the representation of affected interests in administrative decision making. The purpose of judicial review was no longer "the prevention of unauthorized intrusion on private autonomy, but the assurance of the fair representation for all affected interests in the exercise of the legislative power delegated to agencies."[20]

The courts began requiring that agencies conduct oral hearings and permit cross-examination of agency officials and others so that those affected by agency actions would have greater input into the decision-making process.[21] Even more important was the expansion by courts of standing to such judicial review of agency action. In response to concerns that agencies were dominated by a narrow range of interests, the courts began loosening restrictions on the requirements to be met by those seeking standing.[22] As early as 1966, the Court of Appeals for the District of Columbia indicated its readiness to lay down procedural requirements deemed inherent in the very concept of fair hearing for certain classes of cases, even though no such requirements had been specified by Congress.[23]

The APA provides for judicial review for any person "suffering legal wrong because of agency action, or adversely affected or aggrieved by agency action within the meaning of a relevant statute.[24] In 1972 the Supreme Court, in *Sierra Club v. Morton,* interpreted that provision to provide a right of standing only to those who could show that the challenged action had caused them "injury in fact," and that the alleged injury was to an interest arguably within the zone of interests to be protected or regulated by the statutes that the agencies were claimed to have violated.[25] One year later the Court ruled that a group entitled "Students Challenging Regulatory Agency Procedures" (SCRAP) had standing to restrain enforcement of an ICC-granted increase in freight rates which would have increased the costs of shipping recyclable goods, thus increasing the depletion of resources and increasing refuse in recreational areas. The Court distinguished this case from *Sierra Club* by agreeing with SCRAP's argument that it suffered a "specific and perceptible harm," thus qualifying it for standing to sue.[26]

A number of additional cases have attempted to define when and to whom courts are to grant standing to seek judicial review of agency actions. No clear pattern of decisions has evolved, in part because the federal courts, and especially the Supreme Court, have relied on the organic statutes of the various agencies involved in determining congressional intent for review of agency action, and in part because decisions based on standing are sometimes difficult to separate from decisions based on the substantive claims made. While the courts have been hesitant to expand class action suits as a way to increase public participation in the administrative process, they have generally granted standing to almost any interest which the administrative agency is required (whether expressed or implied) to consider in rule-making actions.[27]

The second approach taken by the courts was to expand their role in reviewing the substance of regulations and other administrative actions. Courts began to go beyond the arbitrary and capricious standard to provide a more rigorous examination of administrative decision making. One judge of the Court of Appeals for the District of Columbia found the arbitrary and capricious standard of review to be a "highly deferential one", which presumes the validity of agency action and

forbids the court's substituting its judgment for that of the agency and requires affirmance if a rational basis exists for the agency's decision. This is not to say, however, that we must rubberstamp the agency decision as correct. To do so would render the appellate process a superfluous (although time-consuming) ritual. Rather, the reviewing court must assure itself that the agency decision was "based on a consideration of the relevant factors. . . . " Moreover, it must engage in a "substantial inquiry" into the facts, one that is "searching and careful."[28]

While the case to which this opinion was directed involved the substantial evidence test, courts have accepted its definition of the proper role of judicial review of administrative decisions for cases of informal rule making and arbitrary and capricious standard as well. Thus, the courts are expected to take a "hard look" at agency decisions to assure that agencies have "genuinely engaged in reasoned decision-making."[29] The Supreme Court eventually ratified this view, in ruling that courts give a searching and careful review while refraining from substituting the judgment of the court for that of the administrator.[30]

Since judicial review was to be based on the record developed by the agency in promulgating its rules, the courts naturally turned their attention to the adequacy of the record itself and found that under the APA's informal rule-making procedures, the rule-making record required was generally inadequate for meaningful judicial review. The courts began imposing additional requirements of a more formalized and complete record to more fully explain and justify agency decisions and facilitate judicial review.[31] This has reinforced the courts' requirement that agencies engage in a synoptic approach to decision making—that they identify all relevant regulatory alternatives, compare the advantages and disadvantages of each, and select the optimal alternative—and that this analysis be included in the rule-making record for public and judicial scrutiny. While the courts employed the language of procedural review, their interest was directed toward a substantive analysis, and an interest in moving agencies away from an incremental and piecemeal regulatory approach to a more comprehensive one.[32]

Finally, the courts sought to interpret the statutory criteria for agency rule making. Terms such as "to the extent feasible" and "best available technology" have been given some content by the reviewing courts. Court decisions here have had a significant effect on how agencies have interpreted these often vaguely worded standards.[33] Federal courts have begun to give increased attention to statutory language. The "hard look" courts give to agency decisions has been directed toward congressional purposes; thus, that the thrust of judicial review has been to assure that agencies take the actions they are required to under law and provide the benefits that are mandated, rather than to protect regulated interests.[34] While the shift for the courts was from essentially a negative posture to an affirmative one, the emphasis remains on effectuating the private rights affected by regulatory actions.

The Supreme Court has sought to put a damper on the procedural-based activism of the federal courts. In 1978 it ruled that "absent constitutional constraints or extremely compelling circumstances the administrative agencies should be free to fashion their own rules of procedure and to pursue methods of inquiry capable of permitting them to discharge their multitudinous duties."[35] Despite the chastisement, federal courts continue to assume an important role in interpreting and applying the APA to administrative proceedings and overseeing administrative actions in general.

Congress and the Reform of Administrative Rule Making

Congress joined the federal courts in imposing procedural provisions on administrative rule making that went beyond the provisions of the APA. In creating a number of regulatory agencies and programs of the 1970s, Congress was unable or unwilling to provide sufficient constraints through specific substantive provisions, and turned to procedural devices to assure that agency powers were restrained.

The burst of congressional activity in creating procedural constraints for broad delegations of rule-making power began in 1969 with the enactment of the National Environmental Protection Act, and the requirement of environmental impact statements for federally financed projects expected to have a significant impact on the environment. In 1970, Congress created the Occupational Safety and Health Administration (OSHA). Under its enabling statute, OSHA was empowered to formulate, issue, and enforce safety and health standards, applicable to most businesses, which would attain the "highest degree of health and safety protection for the employees."[36] In creating OSHA, one observer argued, Congress "never looked at the causes of workplace injuries or asked whether direct regulation was likely to work. Nor did it consider compliance costs, assuming that these could easily be paid by business or passed on to consumers. Debate centered on a symbolic issue: whether rule-making and adjudication powers should be separated from a Labor Department that was also charged with enforcement."[37]

Concerns about procedural provisions dominated the legislative history of subsequent regulatory legislation. The Consumer Product Safety Commission, created in 1972, was required to invite individuals or groups to offer an existing product safety standard or offer to develop such a standard before the agency itself could proceed with the rule making. Hearings were then to be held in which "any interested person" could participate and respond to the proposed rules. Standards were to be based "only on substantial evidence of record" generated by these hearings and were to be accompanied by "detailed finding of fact on which the order is based."[38]

Amendments to the Federal Trade Commission's organic act similarly focused on the procedural requirements to be imposed on the FTC's rule making. The elaborate structure required included an advance notice of proposed rule making, accompanied by a statement of the reasons for the intended action; an informal oral hearing; cross-examination for "disputed issues of material fact"; rebuttal of oral and written testimony; a final rule, accompanied by a statement on the expected economic effect of the rule and its expected effect on consumers and small businesses; and a requirement that the rule be "supported by substantial evidence in the rule making record."[39]

In a number of other statutes concerning environmental regulation, energy regulation, and financial regulation, Congress continued to experiment with procedural devices to constrain agency rule making, going beyond the minimum requirement of notice and comment under the APA.[40] While there were significant deregulatory initiatives in the late 1970s, congressional interest in deregulation has been generally limited to areas of economic regulation,[41] where agencies and programs were originally instituted to promote developing industries and protect them from excessive competition. Economists have been able to convince members of Congress that deregulation of these sectors of the economy is likely to increase competition and reduce costs to the public. Consumer groups are also supportive of these deregulatory efforts and, despite the opposition in some cases of the regulated industries, deregulatory statutes have been enacted.[42]

In the areas of health and safety regulation, however, and in economic sectors where deregulation is likely to increase consumer costs (such as energy deregulation), efforts have been more controversial. Particularly in the areas of health and safety regulation, the debate has been framed by those who want less regulation and those who favor more or at least present levels of regulation. Representatives of both sides of this debate, as well as those not allied with one side or the other but who have other bases for their interest in administrative regulation, agree that the regulatory process should be reformed. During the 1980s congressional debate over these areas of regulation has for the most part focused on procedural reforms, rather than directly attacking the substantive goals and objectives of these agencies and programs.[43]

In the early 1980s, Congress came close to passing legislation that focused on three kinds of reforms for administrative rule making. One set of proposals would have generally codified the kinds of change the federal courts have already tried to impose on administrative rule-making procedures, and would transform informal rule making to more of an adversarial process (involving oral hearings, cross-examination and rebuttal and other requirements) and would expand the reviewing power of federal courts over administrative rules. The second set of reforms provides generic economic and scientific standards for the formulation of agency rules. A number of legislative proposals, for example, would require cost-benefit analyses for all regulations (see chapter 3). A third group of reforms focuses on increasing external political control of agency decision making (see chapter 4).

Two distinct approaches for procedural reform of rule making have coalesced in Congress. Business groups have supported reforms that required cost-benefit analyses, regulatory budgets, regulatory impact analyses, expanded judicial review and the legislative veto, while consumer and labor groups have favored more independence from White House influence for agencies, more participation in agency proceedings, public funding of attorney fees, more disclosure of lobbying and stricter enforcement of regulations.[44] The majority of members of Congress during the past several sessions have supported some kind of regulatory reform.[45] There has been little controversy over the rule-making procedures themselves; the differences have primarily been over the nature of congressional, judicial, and White House review of regulations. The Senate passed a comprehensive regulatory reform bill in 1982 that included a two-house legislative veto, a judicial review proviso (referred to as the Bumpers amendment, after Senator Dale Bumpers) which would have eliminated the general presumption of validity of agency decisions in judicial review and require that the courts "give the agency interpretation such weight as it warrants, and provisions for Office of Management and Budget review of regulations."[46] The bill was opposed and eventually killed by key committee chairmen in the House who wanted to protect agency independence and ability to initiate regulatory activity.

Current Rule Making Procedures

As a result of specific provisions of statutes, the decisions of reviewing courts, and individual agency initiatives, the rule-making process includes more steps than those outlined in the APA. While there is considerable variation across agencies, agency rule making often follows these formal steps:

1. Publication of Advanced Notice of Proposed Rule Making in the *Federal Register,* indicating an agency decision to *consider* formulating a proposed rule;
2. Maintaining a rule-making docket, to include agency-planning documents, agency studies, contractor reports, legal memoranda, advisory committee reports, public comments, transcripts or summaries of hearings and meetings with the public, summaries of telephone conversations with outside parties, comments from other agencies, economic and scientific analyses, the proposed and final rules themselves, and other relevant materials that become available after the final rule is promulgated;
3. Publication of Notice of Proposed Rule Making in the *Federal Register,* indicating agency plans to issue a rule and information on public hearings and comment period;
4. Public hearings, presided over by a hearing officer or administrative law judge, that give interested persons the opportunity to present arguments

and concerns and to cross-examine agency officials involved in the formulation of the rule;

5. Public comment period for submission of data, studies and other materials by interested persons; and

6. Publication of the final rule in the *Federal Register,* to include agency responses to all of the major issues raised during the public participation phase of the process.

Rule making also involves a number of managerial review steps to ensure that top agency officials monitor the development of agency actions and informal discussions with external contractors and consultants, interest groups, and other federal agencies. Outside groups can request—under provisions of the Freedom of Information Act—agency materials, records, and other data, to assist them in responding to or anticipating agency initiatives. Exempt from release are materials that are classified or related solely to agency "personnel rules and practices"; privileged or confidential "trade secrets and commercial or financial information"; inter- and intra-agency communications; personnel and medical files; "investigatory records compiled for law enforcement purposes," information used in the "regulation or supervision of financial institutions"; and "geological and geophysical information and data."[47]

As a result, rule-making proceedings in the United States often take three to four years, not including external reviews by Congress and federal courts. One study of the Environmental Protection Agency found that rule making under the Clean Air Act originally involved 13 procedural steps for the issuance of National Ambient Air Quality Standards, but that by 1983 that number had grown to 53 separate steps.[48]

EVALUATING ADMINISTRATIVE LAW AND ADMINISTRATIVE PROCEDURES

Sponsors of the 1946 Administrative Procedure Act argued that it was "designed to provide guarantees of due process in administrative procedures" in providing an "outline of minimum basic essentials."[49] The APA, according to Carl McFarland, who chaired the Committee of Administrative Law of the American Bar Association (ABA) from 1941 to 1946, was designed to set up a general system of administration rather than specify detailed agency workings, resolve confusion in the administrative process, and assure that those affected by administrative actions had sufficient information about how they would be affected.[50]

The APA is based upon and represents a number of important assumptions. It assumes that the administrative process is a system of administrative justice, designed to protect the rights of individuals affected by administrative actions and to assure that administrative discretion is limited. The courts were to provide the primary check on administrative power, through litigation brought in response to agency actions. It was generally assumed that the most important administrative actions be pursued on a case-by-case basis, relying on formal proceedings. This assured that those who were to be the subject of administrative proceedings would be treated fairly and provided with an opportunity to influence the decisions that were to affect them.[51]

Congressional oversight was implicit in this framework. Agencies were to be closely supervised by congressional committees. Agency rule making rested on a "transmission belt" theory of legislative intent, where rules promulgated by agencies were expected to be essentially what Congress would have done if it had the time, interest, and expertise to write the rules itself. Consistent with this emphasis on congressional oversight, the APA did not provide for any role for the president in the administrative process.

Most importantly, administrative law serves to legitimize administrative discretionary and regulatory power. To paraphrase Thurmond Arnold's description of law in general, the function of administrative law "is not so much to guide society as to comfort it."[52] Administrative law gives comfort and assuages the expectation that administrative power is constrained and checked. It provides the constitutional due process prerequisite for the administrative taking of liberty and property. It justifies the fusion of legislative, executive, and judicial powers in administrative agencies since those powers are constrained by legal procedures and are ultimately reviewed by federal courts.

Limiting Bureaucratic Discretion Through Law

In enacting the APA and subsequent legislation, Congress had a variety of concerns to address, from questions of administrative efficiency to concerns for administrative justice. A number of studies championed different approaches to be used in dealing with administrative agencies. Congress could have empowered the president to put all agencies within his span of control; the executive could have given the power to replace agency officials who disagreed with his policies; independent commissions could have been abolished, and all agencies placed within a tightly organized hierarchical executive branch; or Congress could have written laws that granted broad discretion and autonomy to agencies.

The primary concern of Congress, however, has been to provide some kind of check on administrative discretion. The solution it has chosen for the problem of administrative discretion is attractive for a number of reasons. In giving primary responsibility to the federal courts to review the actions of administrative agencies, Congress is able to provide constraints on administrative discretion without granting broad powers to the president. In limiting presidential initiatives, members of Congress are able to maintain their power over agencies for their own personal and political objectives. Administrative procedures contributed much to the creation and maintenance of "subsystems" of government—subcommittees, agencies, and interest groups—which provide a major source of political strength for their members.[53] By creating agencies with broadly defined objectives, Congress can avoid making politically unpopular decisions by claiming to address a problem, creating an agency or program, and then delegating any blame likely to be generated to the agency as well. Members of Congress can then intervene on behalf of constituents affected by agency action, and gain committed constituents as bureaucratic problems are unraveled through congressional mediation.[54] Relying on judicial review permits members of Congress to escape ultimate responsibility and blame, as adverse decisions can be charged to the courts. And the process also provides for a number of opportunities for those affected by agency action to challenge the agency's decision, thus channelling opposition away from Congress and toward the agency.

Moreover, procedural tools provide an effective and often camouflaged opportunity to alter the substantive powers of agencies. Sponsors of procedural provisions may weaken agency effectiveness by permitting numerous delays and challenges, all the while claiming that actions are intended to assure fairness and protection of due process rights. Little attention is usually given to procedural provisions, often perceived as technical, detailed, and nonpolitical, yet able to effect basic changes in the substantive actions of agencies.

A second reason for congressional willingness to embrace the adversary process as the primary construct for the administrative process is that it is consistent with political theories of pluralism. Delegations of power to agencies that function within the constraints of the adversary process minimized the coercive nature of statutes. Individuals and groups affected by administrative actions could take part in the decision-making process. The imposition of unpopular decisions by unilateral government action was replaced by a structure of bargaining between governmental bodies and the groups that were to be affected. Much like the equilibrium generated by the free market in economic activity, the adversary process permitted private initiative to shape the governmental decisions, thus minimizing coercion and benefitting from the economic efficiency of market-like mechanisms.[55]

Pluralistic procedures were defended by critics of administrative power who saw in them a means of avoiding the "capture" of agencies by the interests they were to regulate. For others, pluralistic procedures reflected the belief that the public interest could not be objectively refined by bureaucrats, but would result from an open, democratic, bureaucratic process that championed the anticipation of all interests and responded to their concerns.[56]

A third feature of the judicialization of the administrative process is that it was consistent with the idea of the role of the common law in limiting governmental power. Discretion was minimized as decisions were reviewed to assure their consistency with previous actions as well as with constitutional and statutory standards. Judicial principles and standards would provide a check on administrative decision. Most important, the rights and interests of individuals would be protected. Congress could freely delegate to the agencies, secure in the knowledge that the courts would supervise agency actions and protect individual rights.[57]

Members of Congress naturally share this confidence in the adversary process, given the legal background of many senators and representatives. The adversary process enjoys an even broader constituency, as the public in general has great faith in adversarial proceedings as the primary mechanism for protecting individuals against arbitrary government action, as well as for the resolution of disputes and the discovery of facts. The constitutional standard of due process is viewed by lawyers and others as requiring an adversary hearing as the essence of fairness and justice. And for many it represents a way to escape "politics" and assure that decisions be made on a more "rational" basis.[58]

It is clear from the lobbying by the ABA, as well as the actual provisions of the APA, however, that the original concern was the protection of those interests subject to economic regulation. The APA exempted from coverage matters related to loans, grants, and benefits, thus permitting agencies to issue rules in these areas without any procedural checks. Such programs were seen not as involving any constitutional or legal rights, but as grants to individuals that could be withheld at will.[59] While the focus of administrative law has been considerably broadened, it still reflects this underlying concern. A final explanation for the attractiveness of administrative law is that it provided a clear theory of governmental decision making and the control of discretion. Public administration theory based on a dichotomous relationship between politics and administration has been rejected, by most theorists and practitioners, as unrealistic and unable to provide a response to the problem of discretion. Since Congress often gives agencies broad delegations of power, administration cannot be viewed as nonpolitical and routine application of politically defined objectives, as administrators are constantly making political decisions. Public administration theorists have also championed the need for administrative discretion, arguing against the kind of constraints Congress seems most interested in establishing, and gives little or no attention to the role of Congress in the administrative process except to seek to minimize it in favor of a more active, involved presidential presence.[60] As a result, Congress has had little incentive to accept the tenets of public administration theory as the basis for the administrative process.

The Promise and Performance of Administrative Procedures

Administrative law is based upon the assumption that administrative discretion should be constrained primarily to protect the private rights of those subject to administrative power. While such a concern is an important and essential one, it does not adequately provide for other important values such as political accountability and administrative efficiency. Such an emphasis conflicts, for example, with the expectation that those who exercise administrative power should be accountable to the president and to Congress—that unelected bureaucrats be responsible to elected officials. As administrative proceedings become embodied in legal proceedings, where compromises are fashioned among those affected by proposed actions, less attention is often given to legislative intent. Scientific and technical criteria upon which agency decisions are based are likely to conflict with the demands generated in legal proceedings. Resources expended in providing for extensive legal proceedings are obviously not available for other agency purposes and activities. The decentralized process of formulating regulations originally envisioned by the APA is at odds with efforts to aggregate regulatory decisions, coordinate the rule making activities of different agencies, and balance regulatory policies with competing policy concerns.

Law and administration have contradictory purposes and different underlying values. Administrative law focuses upon legal, judicial, court enforcement of the rights of individuals to limit governmental action affecting them. Administration, in contrast, focuses on efficiently and effectively achieving governmental objectives. Public policies are generally perceived as being best pursued through broad discretionary authority to implement policies in the most efficient and effective manner possible. Such a perception is especially associated with policy tasks that involve scientific or technical issues, where professional expertise is an essential element of the decision-making and implementation process. Experts are expected to be given unfettered authority to take the actions required to achieve the policy goals given them.[61]

Since much administrative decision making is informal in nature, there are significant limits to the ability of legal, procedural devices imposed from outside the agency to check administrative discretion. As mentioned above, resources devoted to legal proceedings, priorities based on anticipated rulings of reviewing courts, and the dominance of legal considerations can be a significant drain on agency activities. The interaction of internal procedural constraints with external political review mechanisms, for example, can serve to make administrative action inefficient, slow, and imprecise, and can muddle accountability for actions taken.

Administrative Procedures and the Adversary Process

Administrative rule making generally involves the formulation of policy rather than the establishment of rights. Unlike the trial-type model of adjudication, however, where rights are defined and pursued within a framework of established standards or general principles, rule making seeks to create standards that are then applied to individual action. Administrative rule making is usually further complicated by the fact that each possible solution to an issue at hand has consequences for a number of interests. These interests are not all likely to be involved in the litigation; however, as solutions are developed, any resultant tensions and repercussions are distributed across these interests.

As Lon Fuller has argued, the distinguishing characteristic of adjudication lies in the fact that it confers on the affected party a peculiar form of participation in the decision, that of presenting proofs and reasoned arguments for a decision in his favor. Adjudication is, then, a device which gives formal and institutional expression to the influence of reasoned argument in human affairs.[61] In describing the emphasis of the adversary process on rationality, Fuller argued that "this higher responsibility toward rationality is at once the strength and the weakness of adjudication as a form of social ordering," and that one weakness or limitation of an adversary proceeding is that it "tends to be converted into a claim of right or an accusation of fault or guilt." Thus, "the instinct for giving the affected citizen his day in court pulls powerfully toward casting exercises of governmental power in the mold of adjudication, however inappropriate that mold may turn out to be."[63]

There is an inescapable conflict in the adversary process between the search for truth and the representation of the parties involved. Many conflicts are based upon policy objectives where there is little consensus over scientific or technical facts: thus the search for truth, or even agreement over the basis upon which policies are to be constructed, is difficult. Yet, legal scholars and texts emphasize that, in the words of Justice White, "as part of our modified adversary system we countenance or require conduct which in many instances has little, if any, relation to the search for truth."[64] Participants in adversary proceedings have great incentives to emphasize the differences between the parties involved, conceal information damaging to their positions even though it would help resolve the dispute or improve the eventual decision, and use delaying tactics to slow down administrative action. Lawyers often either boast or express serious concerns that a good lawyer can make a scientist appear inept and confused. Cross-examination is often viewed as successful only if the witness' contribution is destroyed rather than if the testimony contributes to the information available to decision makers.[65]

The adversary process does not address the need to develop political compromises to difficult policy dilemmas. It discourages the development of consensus among those who are to be affected by administrative regulations, thus decreasing subsequent public support for effective implementation of the standards. Industry groups as well as opposing interests such as consumer advocates often take extreme positions as they seek to delay actions or force lawsuits, and agencies are caught in the middle. As one former agency official has argued, "Regulatory agencies, often ignorant of the real positions of contending parties, are forced to guess at the true priorities of each group. Thus the regulatory process encourages conflict rather than reconciliation of opposing groups. Reliance on public and highly formal proceedings makes the development of a consensus difficult, if not impossible."[66]

Reliance on adversary proceedings also directs attention away from legislative intent, as the process tends to be directed by the participation of those involved in the process rather than by congressional will. In some areas this is a natural development, since statutes often make legislative intent a nebulous consideration. A surrogate political process is the result, where interested groups compete and cajole for influence over the agency decision makers, and the idea of the rule of law—that statutory provisions should guide administrative action—is often lost.[67] While recent cases give evidence of increased judicial attention to legislative intent, the primary concern has been to assure that agencies have considered the relevant issues raised during the rule-making period and have fashioned a rule that is grounded in a comprehensive analysis. The critical test is the ability of agencies to provide a rule-making record that satisfies the reviewing court that all relevant considerations have been explored and that the decision made finds justification in the record.

A further consequence of the adversary process is that it gives a primary role to intermediaries, rather than directly bringing together government regulators and those whom they seek to regulate. Information is controlled by lawyers and other intermediaries, who represent the affected parties, organize political coalitions to support or oppose regulatory programs, direct lobbying efforts aimed at Congress, sponsor public opinion polls, and use advertising and other promotional efforts to further their cause. Once actions are initiated by agencies, these intermediaries often continue to promote their concerns through political activities, while representing the affected groups in the adversary proceedings sponsored by the agency. Their focus is on procedural concerns rather than substantive ones. They view the administrative process as a checklist to be reviewed every time a case is brought to them; each item is examined to see if there is some way the agency can be tripped up and blocked for failing to follow all the procedures required. These intermediaries eschew substantive expertise, since that might limit them to particular areas of practice. Procedural expertise and ability make them a valuable commodity throughout the range of regulatory activities.

Techniques that are often used include manipulating adversary proceedings, filing endless procedural motions, requesting injunctions, inundating decision makers with information, and seeking delays. The process emphasizes negative, reactive approaches and responses. Information is often withheld. Claims may be exaggerated and problems overstated to maximize attention to the threats of the other side or virtues of one's own side. And once the agency makes a decision, the whole process is repeated anew in the reviewing courts.

Evidence of the increased role of these intermediaries is demonstrated by the almost spectacular growth in their numbers in recent years. The number of lawyers involved in regulatory litigation and lobbying increased by about 20 percent in the late 1970s and early 1980s. According to a recent study, these intermediaries have included: 12,000 Washington-based lawyers in law firms representing businesses before agencies and courts; 9,000 lobbyists in firms specializing in lobbying; 42,000 lobbyists and other employees of trade associations; 9,300 public affairs and public relations specialists who advise businesses of regulatory issues; 1,200 specialized journalists employed by regulatory-related publications; 3,500 consultants who advise regulatory agencies; and 15,500 lawyers, lobbyists and public affairs specialists within agencies and large corporations involved in regulatory activities.[68] These intermediaries share an interest in maintaining regulatory conflict. They often move back and forth, from working in an agency to a trade association or lobbying firm to consulting for an agency, which reinforces the incentives for delay.

The emphasis on adjudicatory procedures has also contributed to the fragmentation and lack of coordination of the overall administrative process. The interests of the groups affected by agency actions are given primary concern, without considering the effect of those actions on other government programs. A compromise reached by environmental and business groups and the EPA may conflict with governmental policies on employment, inflation, or other issues. Congress may include, in statutes, provisions that agencies take other governmental objectives into consideration, but the adversary process is an inefficient and ineffective way to make such decisions. While agency actions often involve broad political concerns and tradeoffs, agencies are pressured into refereeing between the two sides pressing for action or inaction. Political accountability is muddled, as it becomes increasingly difficult to determine who is actually making the decisions.[69]

The adversary process provides a structure and a set of procedures which confine and limit administrative discretion, but at great financial and political costs. Participation is limited to those who can afford to hire counsel, yet the entire process is justified by providing a forum for all interests to be heard. Involvement by groups other than those being regulated is widely viewed as the best protection against the capture of regulators by the regulated, assuring that industry influence is countered by those representing consumers and other groups. The Senate study of the regulatory process found that

> organized public interest representation accounts for a very small percentage of participation before Federal regulatory agencies. In more than half of the formal proceedings, there appears to be no such participation whatsoever, and virtually none at informal agency proceedings. In those proceedings where participation by public groups does take place, typically it is a small fraction of the participation by the regulated industry. One-tenth is not uncommon; sometimes it is even less than that. The pattern prevails in both rule-making proceedings and adjudicatory proceedings.[70]

The primary reason for this low level of participation is cost. The Senate report found that the "single greatest obstacle to active public participation in regulatory proceedings is the lack of financial resources by potential participants to meet the great costs of formal participation. . . . In some instances, industry committed as much as 50 to 100 times the resources budgeted by the public interest participants."[71] Several agencies have, in the past, created funding programs to assist groups that might not otherwise be able to afford the costs of participating in agency proceedings: four agencies have specified statutory mandates for such programs, while others assumed the power to institute such programs from vague language. Industry groups claimed that the programs were a waste of money and expressed concern that the relatively small amount of money authorized could later mushroom. One official of the National Association of Manufacturers attacked the program in arguing that "the amount of money is small, but the principle is great. The purpose of the government is to represent the public interest. It's not the job of self-appointed consumer advocates to represent it." Supporters of the program counter with arguments that such an effort is "the only way we can begin to balance [industry] forces. . . . In order to make a good decision, bureaucrats have to hear all sides. . . . All this does is bring in a few more voices."[72] In 1981 a U.S. Court of Appeals ruled that agencies cannot provide for the expenses of participants in rule-making proceedings unless explicitly authorized by Congress, and under the Reagan administration nearly all compensation programs—even those provided for by statute—have been discontinued.[73]

Finally, the adversary process relies on the courts for the ultimate resolution of controversies. It is an attractive solution because courts are generally forced to make a decision, thus providing a final resolution of the controversy. The courts become the final expositor of national law. They are expected to develop a consistent set of policies, fill in the legislative gaps, reconcile differing statutory and administrative views, integrate narrow policy concerns with other related ones, and resolve the specific dispute at hand. In areas where the statutory law is unclear, the courts usually rely on a balancing of the competing demands brought before them, thus shaping their decisions according to the merits of the case at hand. The courts are caught in a contradictory position in trying to achieve all of these objectives.

Adversary procedures grant, to the interests involved, rights to the status quo which are enforced in the courts. By design, such rights make change increasingly difficult. Procedural delays are not necessarily in the interest of industry alone; they can be used by groups that seek to block any actions to which they are opposed. The consequences of procedural devices favor those who wish to slow down governmental action rather than favoring one ideological position or another.[74] Moreover, as one observer has argued, "the recent encumberment of rule making will produce a renaissance of the previously favored mode of making law and policy—a movement back to basics, to adjudication,"[75] which would make it even more difficult for those who are affected by regulations to predict what policies the agencies are pursuing and to plan accordingly. Agencies have been less able to plan and execute their agendas, as they too suffer from the uncertainty of protracted litigation. Rule-making procedures encourage agencies to focus on procedural questions even more and make rule-making proceedings even more protracted, cumbersome and accessible only to well-financed groups that can afford to take part in extensive litigation.[76]

Judicial review has posed equally difficult problems for the functioning of these agencies as a whole. Courts do not take an overall, comprehensive look at agency activities, but focus on specific issues. These agencies have largely had their rule-making agendas determined by court orders, thus prohibiting them from developing their own priorities. Much of the EPA's rule-making effort for reducing water pollution, for example, has resulted from consent decrees involving the Environmental Defense Fund, the National Resources Defense Council, and Citizens for a Better Environment. Individual regulations are shaped by decision makers who are isolated from the environment in which the decisions are implemented, and who have few resources to monitor the effect of their decisions.

As Martin Shapiro has argued, there is a great paradox in administrative law, as it seeks to accommodate the rationalist expectations of "legally objective principles, rights and duties and single, correct solutions to problems of the governance" that the legal profession ascribes to trials with the pluralist model that relies on group competition and bargaining to produce appropriate policies. In an attempt to satisfy both pluralist and rationalist expectations, federal courts have begun to require that agencies respond to every concern, every fact, every alternative raised by interested parties, and agencies have reacted by enveloping rules in massive technical reports and analyses. As a result, courts are overwhelmed and unable to provide independent, common-sense review of agency actions, which is the kind of contribution expected of judicial review.[77]

Reliance on judicial proceedings gives a much too narrow definition to the idea of fairness and due process. It sacrifices broader concerns in emphasizing a particular "form of participation" in governmental decisions.[78] Justice Felix Frankfurter warned against a dependence upon a narrowly defined formula for fairness:

> Expressing as it does in its ultimate analysis respect enforced by law for that feeling of just treatment which has been evolved through centuries of Anglo-American constitutional history and civilization, "due process" cannot be imprisoned within the treacherous limits of any formula. Representing a profound attitude of fairness between man and man, and more particularly between individual and government, "due process" is compounded of history, reason, the past course of decisions, and stout confidence in the strength of the democratic faith which we profess. Due process is not a mechanical instrument. It is not a yardstick. It is a process. It is a delicate process of adjustment inescapably involving the exercise of judgment by those whom the Constitution entrusted with the unfolding of the process.[79]

Chapter 3　SCIENTIFIC AND ECONOMIC ANALYSIS IN ADMINISTRATIVE RULE MAKING

Scientific and economic analyses assume a primary role in regulatory decision making, especially for environmental and health regulations. The decisions and actions of regulatory agencies are expected to be based on technical expertise that produces objective, politically neutral analyses of risks, costs, and benefits. One of the great paradoxes of the regulatory process is that scientific and economic analyses are championed as both a means of limiting and directing administrative discretion and as a means of insulating administrative decision making from external pressures. Congress has sought to limit administrative discretion through the imposition of decision rules, scientific review procedures, and technical analyses. The emphasis on administrative expertise, however, has also contributed to the expectation that agency officials enjoy considerable autonomy and independence. This chapter describes these approaches to limit and shape administrative discretion, reviews the assumptions and objectives underlying these efforts, and considers their effect on agency discretion and on the ability of agencies to accomplish their statutory objectives.

The ideal of expertise is pursued through a variety of elements of the rule-making process. Congress relies, to some extent, on the directives to agencies in their enabling legislation that provide general rules or guidelines for regulatory decision making. Some statutes mandate the prevention of environmental or health hazards as the primary concern, outweighing costs of compliance; other laws require that agencies impose the "best available" or "best practicable technology" for pollution sources, or that agencies balance the benefits of regulatory initiatives with the costs imposed. The underlying interest of Congress here has been the limiting of administrative discretion by requiring that technical analyses serve as the basis of administrative decisions. The Reagan administration's 1981 executive order sought to direct administrative rule making by requiring agencies to demonstrate that the benefits of the rules they propose exceed the costs to be imposed, unless such a standard is contrary to the agency's enabling laws. Some agencies have attempted to develop broad guidelines for the assessment and management of environmental and health risks, to guide agency officials and help outside parties anticipate agency initiatives.

A second means of limiting administrative discretion and choice is through requirements that science advisory bodies review agency decisions or that officials consult established groups and organizations before issuing regulations. Agencies may contract with external institutions and individuals to conduct specific research or assessment of the environmental and health risks associated with particular chemicals or industrial processes. Agencies also rely on scientific journals and publications to identify suspect substances for agency consideration.

The actual decisions of agencies to take (or not to take) regulatory action involve a combination of scientific analysis and policy choice. In theory, regulatory agencies might separate the assessment of risks (the existence of a health or environmental hazard, evidence that exposure to the hazard results in an identifiable harm, and information on the level and breadth of exposure) from the management of risk (the decision concerning the kind of regulatory action to take). In practice, the line is blurred between risk assessment and management, as agency decisions rely on a combination of facts supported by data, areas of general scientific consensus, assumptions concerning the relationship between exposure to health or environmental hazards and their adverse effects, and policy choices.

DECISION MAKING RULES AND SCIENTIFIC ANALYSIS

Every major environmental and health statute in the United States includes some standard or decision rule to guide administrative decision making. There is great variation in these rules, however, that reflects changes in accepted scientific thinking and represents an important means by which Congress seeks to direct and shape administrative discretion. Although they do not fall neatly on a continuum, these decision-making criteria roughly range between a mandate to ignore economic costs of compliance to a requirement that agencies give careful attention to costs. Some statutes oblige agencies to take whatever action is necessary to protect human health, irrespective of associated costs. The Delaney clause of the Food, Drug, and Cosmetic Act requires that any food additive shown to cause cancer in humans or animals be banned, giving the FDA no discretion once it identifies a substance as carcinogenic.[1] Other standards are also cost-oblivious: Under the Clean Air Act, EPA standards for stationary sources of pollution are to assure "an ample margin of safety to protect public health"; for mobile sources, standards are to reflect the "greatest degree of emission reduction achievable through . . . technology . . . available."[2] OSHA standards are also expected to reflect a consideration of available technology in assuring "to the extent feasible that no employee will suffer material impairment of health or functional capacity."[3] Requiring the "best available technology" (or, under other statutes, the "best practicable technology") can itself be considered a decision rule that, in theory, limits administrative discretion to simply ordering installation of the state-of-the-art equipment. There is rarely, of course, a "best" technology; expensive equipment can usually be added to industrial processes, but the marginal benefits may be minimal.[4]

A third decision rule requires a balancing of risks and benefits: The EPA, under hazardous waste legislation, must take whatever actions are "necessary to protect human health and the environment."[5] The Food and Drug Administration, in regulating food contaminants, has a similar mandate to take action "necessary for the protection of public health."[6] The FDA, for example, has balanced the risk to consumers of sodium nitrite (a substance added to meat products to help prevent botulism but considered by some scientists to be a carcinogen) with the benefit of the protection it offers against botulism.[7] This kind of decision rule is quite general and permits broad discretionary decision making on the part of administrators, although it precludes consideration of costs of compliance and requires that agency deliberations focus on protecting human health.

A fourth decision-making criterion requires that costs of compliance be considered and that the most cost-effective regulatory alternative be selected. Under the Toxic Substances Control Act, the EPA is to establish standards for the production of dangerous chemicals in order to "protect adequately against . . . risk using the least burdensome requirement."[8] The Reagan Administration has imposed a similar requirement on all executive branch agencies:[9] "to the extent permitted by law . . . among alternative approaches to any given regulatory objective, the alternative involving the least net cost to society shall be chosen." Agencies are also to select regulatory alternatives that "maximize the net benefits to society."[10]

A fifth criterion is a cost-sensitive standard that obligates agencies to consider costs and benefits of regulatory initiatives. The Safe Drinking Water Act, for example, provides that EPA regulations protect health "to the extent feasible . . . (taking costs into consideration)."[11] In regulating pesticides, the EPA is to pursue regulatory actions that prevent "unreasonable risk to man or the environment taking into account the economic, social and environmental costs and benefits."[12] The Consumer Product Safety Commission's mandate includes the requirement that the standards it issues "be reasonably necessary to prevent or reduce an unreasonable risk of injury"; the benefits expected from the standard are to "bear a reasonable relationship to its costs."[13]

The final decision-making rule obliges agencies to engage in formal cost-benefit analysis, although none of the environmental, safety, and health agencies function under such a statutory mandate. The only legal basis for such a standard is a Reagan executive order which, in addition to the criteria indicated above, requires that "regulatory action shall not be undertaken unless the potential benefits to society from the regulation outweigh the potential costs to society."[14] Since this decision rule applies only to the "extent permitted by law," there is some question of whether it could be binding on agencies that operate under different mandates. The Office of Management and Budget, under that executive order, is empowered to review the regulatory impact analysis that agencies must prepare for all major regulations they propose. This document contains the cost-benefit analysis prepared for both proposed and final versions of rules: Any analysis that fails to satisfy OMB officials is returned to the agency along with the rule itself. This review process, as well as the power of the president to appoint senior agency officials, has resulted in general compliance with the cost-benefit requirement even as the legality of this provision remains unclear.[15]

Table 3.1 outlines and compares the kinds of decision-making criteria provided by Congress for the four agencies primarily involved in environmental, health, and safety regulations. Rather than reflecting a comprehensive scheme of regulation, the criteria provided by statute vary according to the political pressures surrounding each program area and current scientific concerns. These criteria appear to be a somewhat haphazard and inconsistent collection, but they reflect efforts by members of Congress to protect certain groups or to redistribute benefits and costs associated with environmental and health hazards. Taken as a whole, however, the various criteria produce some confusion and uncertainty as agencies are required to develop different regulatory responses to substances posing similar kinds of health hazards and may not be able to develop a comprehensive approach to reducing health hazards within their jurisdiction.

As indicated in Table 3.1, the statutory language is at times specific and at other times vague. Provisions such as the Delaney clause, for example, which was the result of overwhelming political pressure on Congress to take strong action and to delegate significant powers to agencies, provide a clear standard for agency officials. Political pressures at other times press for broad delegations that are less clearly defined, because the issues involved are more complex (or perceived as so) or opponents are able to force compromises through vague language. In his dissent in OSHA's benzene case, for example, Justice Rehnquist discussed the legislative history of the development of OSHA's rule-making criteria. The standard evolved from one which "most adequately assures worker protection" to some which "adequately assures to the extent feasible" the protection of workers. Rehnquist characterized that standard as a "legislative mirage, appearing to some members but not to others, and assuming any form desired by the beholder." "It is difficult to imagine," Rehnquist wrote, "a more obvious example of Congress simply avoiding a choice which was both fundamental for purposes of the statute and yet politically so divisive that the necessary decision or compromise was difficult, if not impossible, to hammer out in the legislative forge."[16]

Table 3.1. Decision-Making Criteria for Health and Safety Agencies

Agency/Program			Criteria for Regulatory Actions
EPA	Clean Air:	stationary sources	Avoid risk: provide "an ample margin of safety to protect public health."
		mobile sources	Balance risk with available technology: standards to reflect the greatest degree of emission reduction achievable through . . . technology . . . available."
	Clean Water:	toxic pollutants	Balance risk with available technology: "provide an ample margin of safety," based on best available technology economically achievable.
		safe drinking water	General balancing: protect health "to the extent feasible . . . (taking costs into consideration) . . . "
	Hazardous Wastes		Avoid risk: take action "necessary to protect human health and the environment . . . "
	Toxic Substances		General balancing: "protect adequately against such risk using the least burdensome requirement."
	Pesticides		General balancing: Avoid "unreasonable adverse effects" meaning "unreasonable risk to man or the environment taking into account the economic, social and environmental costs and benefits."
CPSC			General balancing: standards to "be reasonably necessary to prevent or reduce an unreasonable risk of injury," benefits expected from the rule (to) "bear a reasonable relationship to its costs."
OSHA			Balance risk with available technology: standards to "adequately assur(e) to the extent feasible that no employee will suffer material impairment of health or functional capacity."
FDA	Food:	additives	Avoid risk: ban if substance shown to be carcinogenic.
		contaminants	General balancing: take action "necessary for the protection of public health."
	Drugs		General balancing

Decision Rules in the Regulatory Process

The importance of these differences in statutory language should not be overstated, however. Agency officials function in an uncertain, highly political environment, where they are susceptible to a variety of political pressures and there is often little consensus over scientific and economic information.

BD-C

As a result, agency officials sometimes move toward similar approaches and decision rules as they seek to balance political, economic, and technical considerations.

Agencies have also sought, more formally, to develop general decision rules, approaches, and guidelines for risk assessment. One of the earliest such efforts was in 1979, when the Interagency Regulatory Liaison Group, comprised of the Environmental Protection Agency, the Consumer Product Safety Commission, the Food and Drug Administration, and the Occupational Safety and Health Administration, issued guidelines for the identification of potential carcinogens and the estimation of health risks (see Table 3.2).[17] The guidelines sought to provide a common basis for "making a qualitative evaluation of whether a particular substance presents a carcinogenic hazard" and the methods to be used in "making quantitative estimates of the carcinogenic risk posed by the substance." They represented the "best judgment" of agency scientists concerning the principles to guide the identification and evaluation of potentially harmful substances. These guidelines also outlined the types of evidence to be considered (epidemiological, experimental or animal bioassay, and chemical structure) and emphasized the importance of animal bioassays as the primary source of information for the carcinogenicity of substances.

The Reagan administration abolished the Interagency Regulatory Liaison Group, concluding that the IRLG had actually served to promote regulatory activity, and gave to the Office of Science and Technology Policy the responsibility to develop guidelines for risk assessment. The OSTP, under direct White House control unlike the regulatory agencies, issued proposed guidelines that were widely criticized by scientists and others, both within the federal agencies and outside of government, for their lack of scientific rigor and clear anti-regulation bias. They were ultimately withdrawn due to the political opposition, and new guidelines were issued in 1984.[18]

The new guidelines focused on the problem of inconsistent laws regulating environmental and health hazards, and attributed the differences to shifts in the accepted scientific wisdom. The guidelines embraced some important principles, including the judgment that substances shown to cause cancer in animals should be considered suspect human carcinogens. Considerable attention was given as well to the need to differentiate between facts that were supported by data, areas of general consensus in the scientific community, assumptions underlying computer models and statistical formulas that were used to estimate exposure and risk levels, and the final policy decisions and choices. These guidelines, while providing general principles for assessing existing scientific research and estimating exposure-response relationships, emphasized that the various kinds of data and factors must be weighed on a case-by-case basis.

Table 3.2. Generic Guidelines for Scientific and Economic Analysis:
The Federal Government's Experience

Title/Date Issued	Issuing Body	Comments
Executive Order 11821 (1974)	President	Every major rule to include an inflation impact statement.
Executive Order 12044 (1978)	President	Regulatory analysis for major rules to discuss economic consequences of regulatory alternatives.
Executive Order 12291 (1981)	President	Regulatory analysis for major rules to demonstrate that benefits exceeded costs and that least costly alternative was selected.
Scientific Bases for Identification of Potential Carcinogens and Estimation of Risks (Proposed, 1979)	Interagency Regulatory Liaison Group	Product of Environmental Protection Agency, Food and Drug Administration, Occupational Safety and Health Administration, USDA Food Safety, and Quality Service Scientists.
Identification, Classification and Regulation of Potential Occupational Carcinogens (1980)	Occupational Safety and Health Administration	Reevaluated and altered as a result of litigation.
Chemical Carcinogens: Review of the Science and Its Associated Principles (1986)	Office of Science and Technology Policy	Earlier draft withdrawn after adverse publicity. Produced with FDA, CPSC, EPA, USDA Food Safety and Inspection Service and National Institute of Health.
Proposed Guidelines for Carcinogen Risk Assessment (1986)	Environmental Protection Agency	Revision of 1976 Interim Procedures and Guidelines for Health Risk Assessments of Suspected Carcinogens.

These guidelines were much more favorably received by government, industry, and public interest group scientists. The Environmental Protection Agency used the OSTP document as the basis for its own Proposed Guidelines for Carcinogenic Risk Assessment issued in late 1984.[19] The document sought to promote quality and consistency within the agency and inform outsiders of EPA practices and procedures by outlining the steps to be taken in identifying environmental hazards, determining the relationship between exposure and adverse response, identifying levels of exposure, and characterizing the nature of the risk.

The OMB and Economic Analysis

While agency attention has been directed toward the development of standardized approaches to the assessment of risks, the Office of Management and Budget has assumed primary responsibility for defining the way in which the costs and benefits of regulatory initiatives are to be estimated.

Under Executive Order 12291, issued in 1981, executive branch agencies must prepare a regulatory impact analysis to accompany regulations demonstrating that:

1. "the potential benefits to society from the regulations outweigh the potential costs";
2. "regulatory objectives shall be chosen to maximize the net benefits to society";
3. "among alternative approaches to any given regulatory objective, the alternative involving the least net cost to society shall be chosen"; and
4. agencies are to maximize the "aggregate net benefits to society, taking into account the conditions of the particular industries affected by regulations, the condition of the national economy, and other regulatory actions contemplated for the future."[20]

The agency's description of the expected benefits of the proposed rule is to include "any beneficial effects that cannot be quantified in monetary terms, and the identification of those likely to receive the benefits." The costs of the initiative are to include "any adverse effects that cannot be quantified in monetary terms, and the identification of those likely to bear the cost." The analysis must also describe the costs and benefits of alternative approaches that could "substantially achieve the same regulatory goal at lower cost" and indicate the legal reasons why such an alternative could not be pursued.[21] While the OMB review process is legally binding only on executive agencies, most of the independent regulatory commissions have also followed these guidelines.

Judicial Review of Agency Analyses

The executive branch, through OMB oversight and through joint agency actions, has attempted to standardize the assessment of risks, costs, and benefits, and members of Congress have introduced legislation to impose a standardized approach to risk assessment.[22] Yet the differences in statutory language remain, reflecting a decentralized legislative process, small group dynamics in committees and conferences, differences in congressional interests in the allocation of risk and responsibilities, and alternative assumptions and attitudes regarding risks.[23] While there has been an administrative attempt to mute these differences, judicial review of agency actions has focused attention on them, as they often become the basis for court challenges by groups opposed to agency decisions. The task of determining exactly what criteria agency actions are to be based upon is given to federal judges, who may seek to discover in legislative intent a resolution of the problem created by legislators who at times have consciously sought to make their intent vague.

Court decisions have been inconsistent and confusing for a number of reasons. Litigants naturally push for interpretations of statutory-based decision rules or criteria that further their interests rather than contributing to the development of a consistent, standardized approach. Policy proclivities and interests of different judges produce differing interpretations of similar statutory provisions. Courts have also fashioned their own decision rules to help evaluate agency actions, and judges have differed over the expectations agency decisions must satisfy. In reviewing decisions concerning occupational and consumer health, for example, one federal court upheld agency action that was based on incomplete scientific evidence as long as the agency avoided "arbitrariness or irrationality" in the promulgation of rules, while another court rejected an agency rule for failing to provide "substantial evidence" that the rule was appropriate. The Supreme Court, in yet a different case, decided that scientific hypotheses were an insufficient basis for regulatory decision making and that agencies must provide the "best available evidence" to justify the regulations it issues.[24]

In reviewing EPA decisions, courts have emphasized the "reasonableness" of the agency's action. The agency must show a "significant risk of harm," but it can emphasize precaution and preventative actions and need only show that its decisions rest on rational judgment.[25] Judicial deference to agency decisions appears to be a function of the quality of the risk assessment presented to the court, the relevant statutory language, the level of public opinion and general consensus concerning the risk, the personal policy views of the judges, and judicial attempts to develop a consistent body of decisions for similar regulatory efforts. As a result, the fragmented legislative scheme is reinforced by the lack of universal decision rules evaluating risks, costs, and benefits.

Regulatory Agencies and Advisory Bodies and Groups

A number of regulatory statutes provide for science advisory bodies to advise agencies and review proposed actions. The Consumer Product Safety Commission, for example, may not issue an advanced notice for proposed rule making for any product that is suspected of causing cancer, birth defects, or genetic mutations until the scientific evidence upon which the commission relies has been reviewed by a Chronic Hazard Advisory Panel, appointed for each proposed rule by the commission from a list of scientists nominated by the president of the National Academy of Sciences. The findings of the panel, however, are not binding upon the CPSC.[26] The EPA has made broad use of science advisory committees that function in each of the agency's areas of regulatory responsibility and are supervised by the Science Advisory Board. The board's primary purpose is to "provide advice to EPA's administrator on the scientific and technical aspects of environmental problems and issues," as well as "reviewing and advising on the adequacy and scientific basis" of agency testing, methodological approaches, and regulatory proposals.[27]

Individual statutes also provide for scientific review committees: under the Clean Air Act, such a committee is to be appointed by the agency head to review ambient air quality standards issued, to recommend new standards or revisions of existing ones, and to advise the agency of "any adverse public health, welfare, social, economic, or energy effects which may result from various strategies for attainment and maintenance of . . . ambient air quality standards."[28] While the agency is not bound by the recommendations of its Science Advisory Board, it is usually careful to satisfy the board's concerns and gain its stamp of approval. This adds significant delays to the rule-making process and permits the board to go beyond a purely advisory role in shaping agency actions.[29] Figure 3.1 outlines the interaction of agency personnel and outside experts in the promulgation of air quality regulations.

The primary sources of scientific expertise for agencies are external. Agencies rely heavily on the research conducted by academic, foundation, and industry scientists and reported in professional journals. Agencies also contract with institutions and scientists to conduct specific investigations. A variety of government and private institutions serve informally, and, in some cases, more formally, to supply agencies with analyses of environmental and health risks. Within the federal government, the Office of Science and Technology Policy, whose role in the development of general principles for the regulation of carcinogens was discussed above, serves as a general advisory body. The National Institute of Occupational Safety and Health provides technical assistance and conducts research that underlies OSHA regulations. The National Institutes of Health, including the National Cancer Institute and the National Institute of Environmental Health Sciences, conduct research themselves as well as fund external efforts that seek to expand scientific knowledge concerning cancer and other environmental and health hazards. The National Center for Toxicological Research in the Food and Drug Administration also conducts research on toxic chemicals and particularly on the health effects of "long-term, low-level exposure to chemical toxicants" and the "extrapolation of toxicological data from laboratory animals to man" in its national toxicology program.[30] The National Science Foundation supports a variety of scientific research, through grants and contracts, concerning the assessment of environmental and health risks. In the legislative branch, the Office of Technology Assessment and the Congressional Research Service have prepared studies and reports on risk assessment technologies and methodologies. Table 3.3 outlines the variety of governmental institutions that are involved in environmental and health risk assessment.

Private institutions provide parallel efforts to identify hazards and estimate effects. The National Academy of Science's National Research Coun-

Figure 3.1. The Environmental Protection Agency's Process for Establishing and Revising National Ambient Air Quality Standards

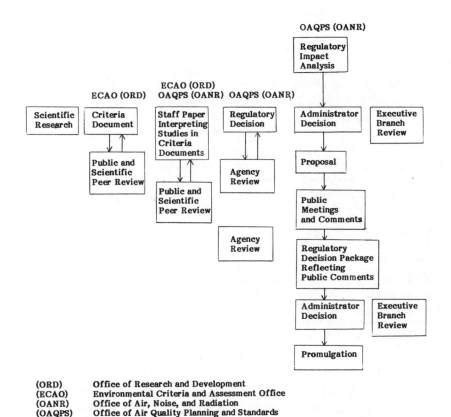

(ORD)   Office of Research and Development
(ECAO)   Environmental Criteria and Assessment Office
(OANR)   Office of Air, Noise, and Radiation
(OAQPS)   Office of Air Quality Planning and Standards

Source: Joseph Padgett and Harvey Richmond, "The Process of Establishing and Revising National Ambient Air Quality Standards," Journal of Air Pollution Control Association, Vol. 33 (1983), p. 14.

cil, a private, nonprofit corporation, seeks to provide information to government on technical and scientific issues through its Committee on the Institutional Means for Assessment of Risks to Public Health.[31] The Food Safety Council, the Conservation Foundation, the Brookings Institution, and a variety of other industry, research, academic, and public interest organizations conduct research and issue reports directed, at least in part, toward agency officials.[32]

Scientific and Economic Analyses in Agency Proceedings

Figure 3.2 outlines the process generally followed by agencies as they bring together the decision rules under which they operate and scientific and eco-

Table 3.3. Governmental Agencies Involved in Environmental and Health Risk Assessment

Department-Based Agencies
Department of Health and Human Services
    Public Health Service
        Centers for Disease Control
            Center for Environmental Health
            National Institute for Occupational Safety and Health
        Agency for Toxic Substances and Disease Registry
        Food and Drug Administration
            National Center for Toxicological Research
        National Institutes of Health
            National Cancer Institute
            National Institute of Environmental Health Sciences
Department of Labor
    Occupational Safety and Health Administration
Department of Agriculture
    Food Safety and Inspection Service

Independent Agencies/Commissions
Environmental Protection Agency
Consumer Product Safety Commission

Executive Office of the President
Office of Science and Technology Policy
Council on Environmental Quality
Office of Management and Budget
    Office of Information and Regulatory Affairs

Legislative Branch
Office of Technology Assessment
Congressional Research Service
General Accounting Office

*Source: *The United States Government Manual* (1984–85)

nomic analysis in regulating environmental and health risks. While the process varies somewhat across different agencies, they face similar problems and concerns. Agencies rely on reviews of current scientific literature, studies of other government agencies and private institutions and organizations, and, occasionally, research conducted by agency personnel themselves. As agency officials review existing research and access risks, they are confronted with a vast array of choices. In regulating toxic chemicals, for example, agencies confront some five million chemical substances that have been identified. One estimate concluded that some 66,000 chemicals are used in food additives, pesticides, drugs, and cosmetics alone.[33]

In assessing the relationship between exposure and adverse effects (the dose-response assessment), agency decision makers must sort out a variety of human, animal, and chemical tests. Table 3.4 outlines the kinds of data sources that officials might have to choose from in assessing risks. Epidemiological data can provide the most direct evidence of health risks, but such data are either often not available, given the long latency period of cancer, or uncertain, given the lack of scientific controls and the difficulty of demon-

Figure 3.2. Risk Management and Assessment in Federal Agencies

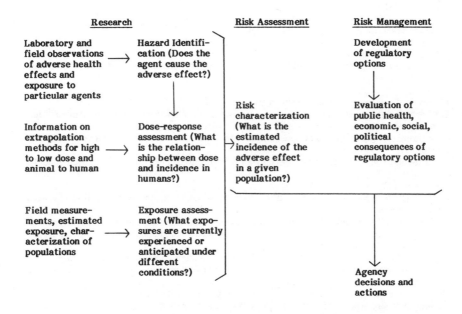

Source: National Research Council, Risk Assessment in the Federal Government: Managing the Process (Washington DC: National Academy Press, 1983), p. 21.

strating causality. As a result, animal tests have become the most widely used means of assessing carcinogenicity despite great uncertainty over the extrapolation to high test doses to lower actual exposure levels, and from animals to humans. There are a variety of models that enjoy general acceptance yet produce diverging results.[34]

In calculating the costs associated with regulatory initiatives, agencies may include a variety of costs including capital expenditures (installation of pollution control equipment), operating and maintenance expenditures, increased cost of goods and materials used in manufacturing, and administrative and paperwork compliance costs. Costs of industry instability, unemployment, and decreased ability to compete with foreign firms, social costs such as opportunity costs, increased prices to consumers, increased demand for social and other local government services and other consequences of unemployment and higher costs could be considered.[35] Agencies must also select a discount rate (10 percent is often used) that discounts future income or expenditures (in assuming that current activity is more valuable than future occurrences) so that alternative approaches can be compared in equivalent terms.[36]

BD-C*

Table 3.4. Kinds of Data Used in Risk Assessment

HUMAN DATA

Clinical Studies (for example, for sulfur dioxide)
A planned research experiment is conducted, with controlled exposure levels.
Ethical considerations and legal restrictions limit the use of this approach.
The data are generally for a pollutant's impact on an index of organ function rather than for disease (and clearly not death).

Cohort Studies (prospective or retrospective)
Groups with different exposures to a suspect substance are followed over time to determine differences in response.
Large samples, long follow-up periods, and statistical analysis to account for other influences are required.
It is difficult to detect rare effects, especially for retrospective studies with poor exposure records.

Case Control Studies
A group with a disease is compared to a control group without it to see if exposure differs between the two groups.
Studies may be macroepidemiological in which aggregate mortality and morbidity rates are related to characteristics of relevant population groups or microepidemiological in which analyses are based on data for particular individuals.
They can adjust for other influences such as sex, race, smoking, income, diet, and exercise.
Sample sizes can be smaller than for cohort studies, but finding a suitable control group may be difficult.
Data usually do not consider lag between exposure and adverse health effect.
Current exposure typically is assumed to be the same as past exposure for cumulative health effects.
Results can be biased by population migration or mitigating actions that make actual exposure differ from apparent exposure.
Results from occupation-related studies may not be applicable to the much lower doses expected in the environment, especially for people with varying sensitivities compared with workers.

Episodic Studies (for example, methylmercury poisoning from contaminated grain in Iraq)
These studies depend on accidents, so investigators are unprepared, control groups may not exist, and therapy takes precedence over research.

ANIMAL DATA

Animal (in vivo) Experiments
Controlled laboratory setting permits isolation of effects from a specific substance.
The full effects of the substance can be examined because animals can be permitted to get a disease and die.
Response identification often is not clear-cut.
Shorter life spans for animals yield results faster than for cohort studies of humans.
Uncertainties arise in predicting response at much lower environmental exposures, based on high test doses.
Uncertainties arise with respect to translating animal response into predictions of human response for equivalent exposures.
A controlled experiment may show no response to the isolated substance, whereas a realistic setting may involve synergism with other substances.

Short-term (in vitro) Tests
Bacteria, mammalian cell cultures, or small organisms are observed (after exposure) for a few days to a few weeks.

(continued)

Table 3.4. Kinds of Data Used in Risk Assessment *(continued)*

Tests are far less costly than lifetime animal experiments.
Tests have been developed for relatively few endpoints.
Concordance between the results of short-term tests and lifetime animal studies is imperfect for the (relatively few) substances that have been compared.

STRUCTURE ACTIVITY ANALYSIS

Molecular structures of suspect substances are compared with substances whose toxicity and metabolic pathways are well known.
The data base is weak for some classes of chemicals in this relatively new field.

Source: Ann Fisher, "An Overview and Evaluation of EPA's Guidelines for Conducting Regulatory Impact Analyses," in *Environmental Policy Under Reagan's Executive Order: The Role of Benefit-Cost Analysis,* V. Kerry Smith, ed. (Chapel Hill: The University of North Carolina Press, 1984), pp. 104–5.

Agency estimates of benefits associated with proposed regulations may include broad goals, such as increased life expectancy or decreased incidence of disease, or may focus on intermediate measures, such as the amount of pollutants emitted. Benefits may be immediate, or may be long-term and take decades or more before they are realized. They may be direct benefits, such as improved worker health, or more indirect, such as reduced health insurance costs.[37]

The analysis of costs and benefits requires three kinds of choices: what factors to include in the analysis, what dollar values (or other quantitative values) to be attributed to each factor, and what formula for relating the various factors is to determine the final calculation.[38] This becomes most controversial when agencies assign a dollar value to human life as part of the comparison of costs and benefits. The EPA, for example, has used a figure of from $1 to $2 million for each human life; OSHA's figures range from $2 to $5 million. The Federal Aviation Administration is more precise in its assumption that a human life is worth $650,083. The median OSHA program was found, in one study, to be some 400 times more expensive per life-year saved than was the median for the National Highway Traffic Safety Administration's regulatory programs.[39]

THE ASSUMPTIONS UNDERLYING SCIENTIFIC AND ECONOMIC ANALYSIS

The expectation of expertise and autonomy surrounding bureaucracy rests primarily on the idea of professional norms and political neutrality. Scientific and economic analyses are expected to legitimize the exercise of governmental power because they are "objective" and independent of partisan considerations. As agency experts are given the primary responsibility for decision making, the decision-making process is made consonant with other political values precisely because it is, in theory, nonpolitical, interested only in the rational pursuit of scientific truth. Professional norms and peer review serve as additional checks on discretion, which, in turn, reinforces the acceptability of expertise as a basis for decision making.

There appears to be a general desire that the assessment and management of risks be separated, that the determination of risks and benefits and costs be independent of decisions concerning the actual regulatory actions to be taken.[40] In theory, such a separation is perhaps possible. Risk assessment is expected to precede policy decisions and not to be used to provide some justification for decisions made on other grounds. Risk assessment can be conducted without consideration of the policy decisions that might be based on it. This is not to argue that risk assessment is "objective" or "neutral." It involves a number of choices, and thus reflects biases and assumptions— such as whether estimates should be conservative and cautionary and focus on worst-case scenarios, should focus on the most susceptible populations, or should assume no threshold exposure for cancer-causing agents. These assumptions can be clearly specified, however, so that the resultant conclusions can be better understood. Risk management can also be viewed as an exercise in political choice, based on a combination of facts, unproven but generally accepted ideas, assumptions, and policy decisions. Neither risk assessment nor risk management is objective or neutral, yet there are important differences between the two processes.[41]

The assumptions and values underlying the assessment of risks, benefits, and costs vary considerably. To some extent, cost-benefit analysis for environmental and health policy may be biased towards costs, since benefits are often more difficult to quantify and are thus softer and likely to be overcome by cost estimates that are more solid. In the Reagan administration, cost-benefit analysis has been intertwined with the goal of reducing regulatory burdens and granting regulatory relief to industry. Cost-benefit analysis is expected to make it more difficult for agencies to impose regulatory burdens. Similarly, risk assessment is expected to assure that only clearly demonstrable risks will be addressed through regulatory initiatives, that hypothetical risks lacking clear evidence of actual harm will not serve as the basis for new regulations.

George Keyworth, the first director of the Office of Science and Technology Policy in the Reagan administration, argued that the administration's intent was to "reduce the excessive burden of federal regulations by improving the rational basis on which regulations are made." This belief that a more rational regulatory process will result in less regulatory costs is an important expectation for the Reagan administration, but it is not at all clear why increased rationality would reduce regulatory activity. In contrast, cost-benefit analysis in the Carter administration was expected to show that the benefits of proposed regulations were worth the costs involved. Risk assessment was expected to identify potential harms so that hazards could be prevented and the public be protected from uncertain threats.[42]

Cost-benefit analysis is often assumed to champion considerations of economic efficiency. Utilitarian calculations of costs and benefits are expected to assure optimal efficiency in the use of resources and the satisfaction of individual wants, thereby rendering agency decisions optimal and rational. Economic efficiency, however, need not be the only objective motivating regulatory action. Efficiency competes with other values, such as protection of worker health, reduced incidence of cancer, clearer vistas in national parks or other goals. The analysis of costs and benefits may focus on the extent to which these objectives are achieved, independent of (or at least not primarily determined by) considerations of economic efficiency. In practice, however, cost-benefit analysis has been dominated by the expectation of economic efficiency, as it has usually been part of budgetary considerations and has been dominated by the Office of Management and Budget (and its predecessor, the Bureau of the Budget).[43]

The reliance on expertise and on scientific and economic standards conflicts with the other expectations of how administrative agencies are to operate. Agencies with jurisdictions involving complex scientific and technical analyses must give significant discretion to their scientific staffs; at the same time they may impose managerial constraints that conflict with the pursuit of scientific knowledge. The primary value underlying the idea of policy analysis is that of discretion and autonomy, free from the vagaries, pressures, compromises and uncertainties of political life. It rests upon Max Weber's model of bureaucracy, emphasizing "fixed and official jurisdictional areas," "hierarchy and levels of graded authority," "written documents," "expert training," "general rules," and the "tenure for life" of officials.[44] Professional norms, peer review, and standard analytic techniques, rather than legal procedures or political oversight, are expected to check administrative discretion and to render administrative government acceptable and legitimate, as scientific and technical calculations serve as the basic mechanism for administrative decision making. Administrative activity is viewed primarily as a neutral, nonpolitical calculation of the costs and benefits of alternatives, where economic and technical formulas and norms are sufficient guides for governmental action. Herbert Kaufman has characterized this as the "quest for neutral competence," where the objective was to "do the work of government expertly, and to do it according to explicit objective standards rather than to personal or party or other obligations."[45]

EVALUATING ECONOMIC AND SCIENTIFIC ANALYSIS

It is uncertain to what extent economic and scientific analyses significantly constrain administrative discretion. The identification and evaluation of risks and the calculation of costs and benefits are extremely sensitive to assumptions about how to quantify variables. Cost-benefit analysis has been defended by OMB and other officials as a necessary response to the scarcity of resources that are available for regulatory purposes and the tradeoffs that must be made between regulatory and other objectives such as reducing inflation. Cost-benefit analysis is viewed as essential in identifying regulations which generate the most benefits and require the least costs.[46] It does not, however, enjoy universal support and approbation: Three criticisms of its current use in federal agencies are particularly important. Some have argued that cost-benefit analysis is ethically suspect, that its utilitarian roots raise traditional questions of the desirability of attempting to impute rationality to moral issues, or that there are certain public virtues to be pursued irrespective of their costs.[47] Other criticisms charge that cost-benefit analysis, in practice, is used to justify predetermined policy positions or to defend decisions made on more subjective grounds. For these critics, economic analysis is a mirage, unable to provide an objective basis for administrative rules.[48] As one observer noted:

> A cost-benefit analyst has tremendous discretion in resolving [issues], and honest disagreements can easily result . . . More significantly, because the choices made in framing the cost-benefit analysis can easily influence whether total benefits end up exceeding total costs or vice versa, it becomes possible to choose a desired result and then construct the analysis in a manner that supports it. Seen in this light, cost-benefit analysis is anything but an objective procedure yielding a mathematically precise answer. Yet the fact that the analysis results in a number gives exactly that false sense of precision.[49]

Cost-benefit analysis is also criticized because of its methodology. The problems encountered in actually trying to do the analysis are numerous and present significant limitations for its use in administrative rule making. Some of the data upon which cost-benefit analysis is to be based are difficult to quantify. It may involve placing values on human life, environmental quality, or other factors not easily reducible to numerical figures. While there is some general agreement over the kinds of factors that *might* be included in estimating risks, costs, and benefits of proposed regulations, there is little agreement over what factors *should* be included in specific regulatory analyses. Agencies must choose from among competing computer models, sets of assumptions, and chains of causal events and consequences. One study of the experience of ten agencies with regulatory analyses found that "because every proposed regulation is so different, not only across agencies but even within agencies, it is impossible to reach any consensus as to what costs are appropriate for including in a [regulatory analysis]."[50] Other studies indicate that risk assessment is more the exception than the general rule in agency decision making, and that cost-benefit analysis is distrusted because of its frequent use to justify decisions already made.[51]

There are often significant differences among expert opinions over the basis for cost and benefit calculations. Much of the information to be used comes from industry or other sources that have some interest in administrative decision making, or have incentives to overestimate costs. Cost-benefit analysis requires a great deal of information that often is simply not available.[52] Causal links are also imprecise and can be expansively or narrowly defined. Compliance costs, for example, might be limited to the actual expense of pollution control devices, or might extend to increases in the costs of social services for workers who lose jobs through industry closings or layoffs resulting from regulations.

Some studies have argued that cost-benefit analysis is "most helpful in assessing well-defined projects" facilitative of choices among alternatives when intended objectives are clearly defined, while of limited value in deciding whether or not to pursue an effort itself. Cost-benefit analysis has thus been defined as an "approach to decision making," "no more than a tool" which "forces the judgments out into the open," rather than a complete decision-making mechanism.[53] The use of cost-benefit analysis in rule-making proceedings for health and environmental regulation is especially problematic. Balancing of costs and benefits to workers or to the public is inevitably a political decision, where scientific or medical evidence cannot provide the basis for making these kinds of choices.[54]

There is little information available concerning the health effects of most chemicals and little understanding of the relationship between exposure and contraction of disease. Figure 3.3 gives some idea of the amount of information available concerning the health risks associated with different chemicals. There are significant differences in sensitivity to chemicals and pollutants among different groups in the population, and little is known about the synergistic or interactive effect of exposure to a variety of potentially harmful substances. Epidemiological data on which regulatory initiatives might be based are often incomplete or inconclusive, because of conditions in the environment in which the exposure takes place. Most of the information concerning environmental and health hazards comes from laboratory tests with animals that produce, at best, only tentative knowledge, since it is not clear to what extent results can be extrapolated from animals to humans and from high experimental doses to low actual exposure levels.

There is also considerable confusion concerning the decision rules or criteria to be used in determining whether or not to initiate regulatory activity and in the methodology to be employed in the formulation of regulations. Agen-

Figure 3.3. Availability of Information Concerning the Health Effects of Selected Chemicals

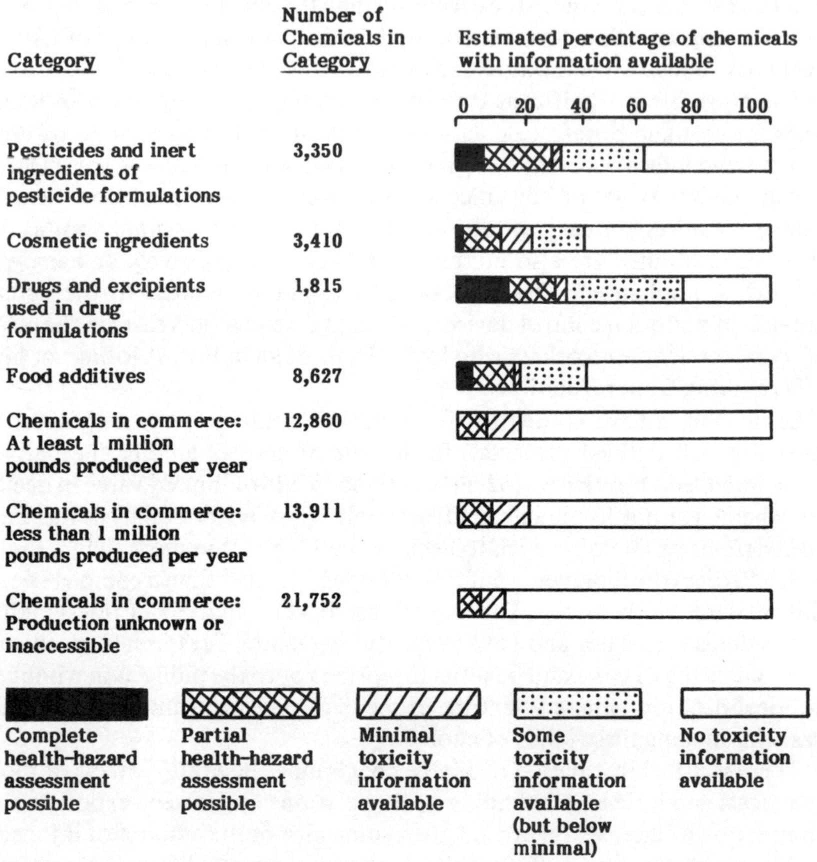

Category	Number of Chemicals in Category	Estimated percentage of chemicals with information available
		0 20 40 60 80 100
Pesticides and inert ingredients of pesticide formulations	3,350	
Cosmetic ingredients	3,410	
Drugs and excipients used in drug formulations	1,815	
Food additives	8,627	
Chemicals in commerce: At least 1 million pounds produced per year	12,860	
Chemicals in commerce: less than 1 million pounds produced per year	13.911	
Chemicals in commerce: Production unknown or inaccessible	21,752	

Complete health–hazard assessment possible	Partial health–hazard assessment possible	Minimal toxicity information available	Some toxicity information available (but below minimal)	No toxicity information available

Source: "Toxicity Testing: Strategies to Determine Needs and Priorities", National Academy Press, 1984; reprinted in Conservation Foundation, *State of the Environment: An Assessment at Mid-Decade* (Washington DC: Conservation Foundation, 1984), p. 64. Reproduced with permission of the National Academy Press, Washington, D.C.

cies operate under a variety of statutes that range from requiring agencies to ignore the costs imposed by regulatory initiatives to requiring that agencies balance the benefits of the proposed regulation with the anticipated costs of compliance. There are a variety of models that can be used to project the health effects from exposure to dangerous substances. One study of the relationship between saccharin consumption and bladder cancer, for example, projected that the number of cancer cases resulting from saccharin consumption could range from 0.22 to 1,144,000, depending on the model used and the assumptions made.[55]

Agency procedures such as provisions for public participation, opportunities for submission of comments concerning the regulatory analysis on which proposed actions rest, and the examination of agency initiatives by scientific review panels do not resolve the problems that result from the blurring of the lines that separate scientific facts and political judgments. There is considerable tension between the internal decision-making process of agencies and the political review of decisions that is often initiated by parties seeking to escape from compliance with agency directives. The Office of Management and Budget and congressional subcommittees compete for influence over regulatory decision making and agencies have often been caught in an uncertain middle ground.

Even where there exists a significant amount of scientific research in the area of a proposed agency action, there may not be much consensus among scientists. The adversary process in which agency decisions take place usually serves to line up experts on either side to be cross-examined by lawyers, without aiding conflict resolution. If there is reasonable agreement over the risks involved, the calculation of costs can be done in many different ways, from the narrow counting of the direct costs of compliance to a comprehensive consideration of nonquantifiable values and secondary and associated costs. Thus it is no surprise that the regulations issued by these agencies are more dependent upon external political considerations than on careful internal analyses. This has also been encouraged in judicial review of agency decisions, as courts increasingly have demanded that regulations respond to all relevant issues. As a result, policy analysis is designed to give the appearance of rationality and synoptic decision making and to protect the agency against possible reversal, thus creating the illusion that policies are a result of objective, nonpolitical considerations.

Criticisms of the role of science in regulatory decision making also address broader problems. Some argue that scientific analysis is used by scientists and others in and outside of regulatory agencies to pursue nonscientific goals, such as criticisms of large corporations and big business or the redistribution of economic and social power. Science, it is argued, is used to legitimize decisions that, in reality, are not based on neutral analysis but are highly ideological.[56] Others argue that science is used to insulate decision making from public scrutiny, that democratic participation in decisions affecting public health and resources is unfairly limited in deference to claims of scientific expertise.[57] Some criticize risk assessment as incapable of evaluating the possibilities and consequences of harms that result from technological innovations and accidents.[58] Still others charge that science is "too competitive, too big, too entrepreneurial and too bent on winning" and that fraud and misconduct threaten the integrity of scientific research.[59]

The institutional affiliation of scientists also appears to have some relationship to their views on the assessment of environmental and health risks. One survey, for example, asked scientists whether findings that a substance induces cancer in animals should be interpreted to mean that it also causes cancer in humans. Some 69 percent of government scientists responded in the affirmative, while only 52 percent of academic scientists and 27 percent of industry scientists agreed. Similarly, 80 percent of industry scientists believed that there was a threshold exposure to carcinogens below which there was no danger of exposure, while 60 percent of academic scientists and 37 percent of government scientists believe that no such threshold of safe exposure exists.[60]

The precarious foundation of economic and scientific analyses upon which regulatory initiatives rest is further weakened by the political pressures that surround important agency actions. The void created by scientific uncertainty is often quickly filled with public concerns and fears, with public demands for action which may produce, instead, appropriate regulatory responses. Figure 3.4 depicts the gaps between public perceptions and realities of health hazards. Public demands may reflect an attempt to find a "simple and plausible explanation for dreaded diseases" or to exonerate victims of health problems from responsibility for "their personal life-style decisions contributing to the outcome" or to "provide an outlet for a variety of anti-business attitudes, particularly . . . strong resentment of the power and perceived indifference of large corporations."[61]

Public perceptions that can determine policy responses in highly visible cases are usually a result of cultural factors more than scientific information.[62] "The focus on pollutants," one critic has argued,

> provides a simple and plausible explanation for dreaded diseases such as cancer and birth defects. It provides a ready answer—other than pure chance—for their occurrence. Moreover, this explanation exonerates the victims from responsibility for their personal life-style decisions contributing to the outcome, such as the foods they eat, the amount of alcohol they drink, and the extent to which they smoke. The link to pollutants frees individuals from blame by reducing the multiple factors involved in contracting these diseases to a single, unavoidable event.[63]

Environmental and health dangers are "exaggerated or minimized according to the social acceptability of the underlying activities."[64] That tendency, combined with the technical ability to detect contaminants at the level of one part per billion or trillion and the frequent inability among scientists to produce a consensus over the risk involved in exposure to dangerous chemicals, further complicates the search for rational regulatory rule making.

The marriage of science and politics in the regulatory process is a fragile one. One study of five agencies in the area of health and safety concluded that

Figure 3.4. Public Perception of U.S. Annual Death Rates from Selected Causes

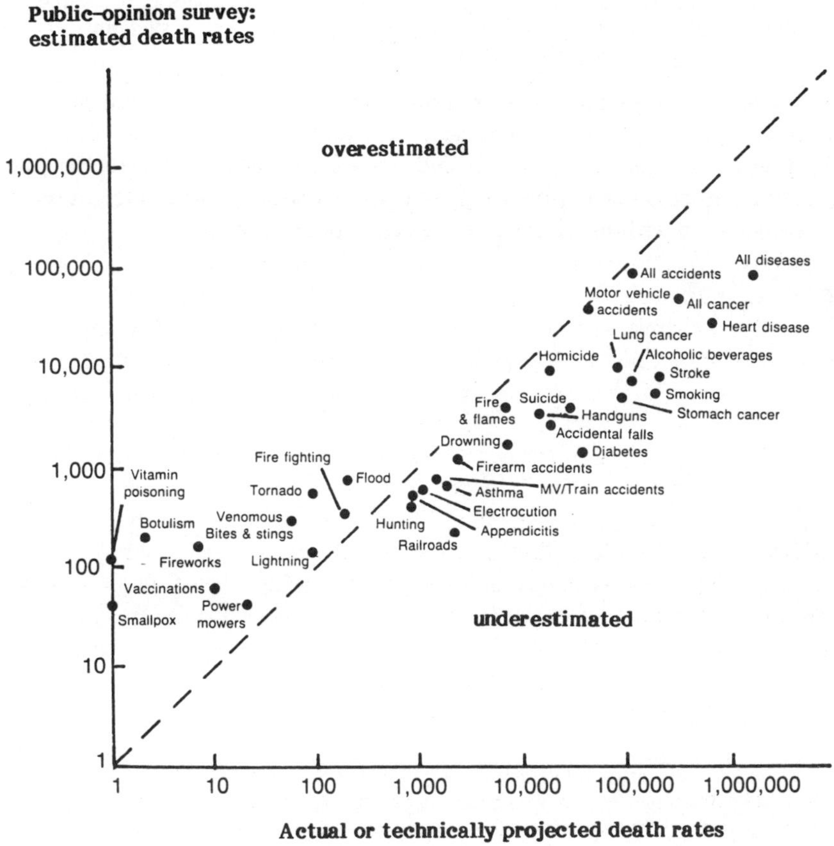

Public–opinion survey: estimated death rates

overestimated

1,000,000

100,000

All diseases

All accidents

Motor vehicle accidents · All cancer

10,000

Heart disease

Lung cancer · Alcoholic beverages

Homicide · Stroke

Fire & flames · Suicide · Smoking

Handguns · Stomach cancer

Accidental falls

Drowning · Diabetes

1,000

Fire fighting

Vitamin poisoning · Flood · Firearm accidents

Tornado · Asthma · MV/Train accidents

Venomous Bites & stings · Electrocution

Botulism · Hunting · Appendicitis

Railroads

100

Fireworks · Lightning

Vaccinations

Power mowers · underestimated

Smallpox

10

1

1   10   100   1,000   10,000   100,000 1,000,000

Actual or technically projected death rates

Source: Conservation Foundation, State of the Environment: An Assessment at Mid–Decade (Washington DC: Conservation Foundation, 1984), p. 275; reprinted by permission of Paul Slovic, Decision Research, Eugene, Oregon.

"scientific evidence was not the determining factor in the regulatory action, and in only one instance . . . were scientists able to estimate risks with reasonable confidence." Scientific information was only one source of information for decision makers. The ultimate decisions made were "dominated by political judgments" because

. . . regulators do not seek scientific contributions in a way that is likely to elicit the most helpful analysis and are not able to use the material they do

receive. Both problems stem partly from an inability of agency heads to understand the limitations of science and to interpret inconclusive information. The
problems are exacerbated by scientists' alienation from the chaotic, pressured
world of the regulator, with its need for timely answers, even if such answers
require making arbitrary decisions.[65]

The paradox of scientific and economic analysis is striking. Analysis contributes to agency autonomy and discretion, yet the incompleteness of scientific knowledge and the inconclusiveness of risk assessment render the
regulatory process susceptible to a variety of pressures and reduce bureaucratic discretion without giving agencies clear policy direction.

Chapter 4 POLITICAL OVERSIGHT OF ADMINISTRATIVE RULE MAKING

Presidents, staff members of the White House and others in the Executive Office of the President; members of Congress, their staffs, and congressional support agencies; and federal courts—all have assumed increasingly important roles in assuring that administrative agencies are subject to political oversight. The appointments of agency officials, changes in the enabling statutes of agencies, the budget process, oversight hearings and investigations, intervention in agency proceedings in response to constituent complaints, and monitoring of agency rule making have all been part of these legislative and executive efforts to monitor agency activity. Judicial review of administrative actions, a central element of administrative law, is, at least in part, designed to assure that agencies act in a manner consistent with statutory intent and thus contributes to the idea of political accountability. This chapter compares the efforts by presidents and members of Congress to oversee regulatory decision making and discusses the advantages and disadvantages of these efforts.

PRESIDENTIAL REVIEW OF ADMINISTRATIVE ACTIVITY

Presidents have become increasingly burdened with the expectation that they are responsible for the operation of the federal government in general, and thus accountable for the actions of individual administrative agencies.[1] There are important electoral incentives for presidents to be able to gain control over bureaucratic activity to assure that presidential programs and priorities are pursued: Important political constituents demand (or are anxious to reward) presidential intervention in administrative decisions on their behalf. White House involvement also responds to concerns that there be some attempts to coordinate an increasingly fragmented regulatory agenda and that there be a mechanism to resolve conflicts between agencies. The president's constitutional mandate to assure that the laws are faithfully executed naturally places upon him some responsibility for administrative conduct.[2]

65

Presidential efforts to direct administrative decision making rest upon a number of tasks: appointing senior agency personnel; establishing guidelines for agency enforcement activities; reorganizing and restructuring agencies and administrative jurisdictions; reviewing and altering agency budgets, including changes in personnel and priorities for use of agency resources; direction of agency activity through personal suasion, occasional personal intervention in policy disputes, publicizing presidential response to agency actions and other informal means; proposing changes in the statutory authority of agencies; and monitoring the rule-making activities of agencies.

Presidents have generally had little continued interest in the appointment of individuals to regulatory agencies. The selection process has often been relegated to middle-level status in the White House; criteria, either for a specific position or even of a general nature, are rarely enunciated; and Presidents have frequently not insisted upon the most able appointees. According to a major congressional review of the appointments process in regulatory agencies, one major disability is the disinterest at the very highest levels of government in first-rate regulatory appointments.[3]

The Reagan administration, however, has taken great interest in its power to appoint senior administrative officials. Ideological compatibility with the President's political views and willingness to pursue presidential policies have been the primary criteria for appointments. Consistent with Reagan's promise to "get government off the backs of business" and to provide "regulatory relief," appointees have been selected who have been openly in disagreement with or even hostile to past administrative decisions and priorities. This has been particularly true of appointments to agencies responsible for environmental, natural resources, and safety regulation.

President Reagan has been quite explicit and open in his determination to gain control of administrative activity through his appointive power. In a speech in September 1980 he indicated that: "Crucial to my strategy of spending control will be the appointment to top government positions of men and women who share my economic philosophy. We will have an administration in which the word from the top isn't lost or hidden in the bureaucracy."[4] Observers were quick to note once Reagan took office that the "role of cabinet officers and senior appointed officials [was] to function as loyal lieutenants dedicated to the pursuit of presidential objectives."[5] The Reagan administration has effectively exploited the reform of the civil service system which had occurred in 1978, under President Carter, that gave the president power to create a new set of senior civil servants who could be placed in strategic places throughout the bureaucracy to pursue his policy agenda.

In part, reliance on appointments rather than statutory changes has permitted the Reagan administration to concentrate its legislative efforts on taxing and spending initiatives. And, in part, this concern with appointments was in response to a belief that past regulatory reform efforts, especially those in the Carter administration, demonstrated that administrative reforms must precede statutory changes.[6] Nor did the administration find much support for a basic rewriting of environmental, health, and safety laws.

The political backlash resulting from the performance of many Reagan appointees, especially those in the Environmental Protection Agency, has blocked some of the changes that the administration has sought. Inexperienced appointees, unwilling to trust career officials to help them with complicated procedural requirements and conflict-of-interest and other restrictions, have had their actions reversed by reviewing courts and Congress; or else, they have generated enough political controversy and opposition to force them to resign, and thus have defeated the purposes for which they were appointed. Nevertheless, the appointments to regulatory agencies have played an important role in shaping the rule-making process and the rules that have been produced. There have been few disagreements between agency heads and officials of the regulatory review bureau in the Office of Management and Budget; the few times that the head of OSHA or EPA have tangled with OMB reviewers are rare, attention to ideology in appointments having assured general agreement in executive agencies over policy concerns and priorities.[7] Such an ideological commitment on the part of Reagan appointees led some forty senators, in response to the nomination of William P. Clark to replace James Watt as Secretary of the Interior, to cosponsor a resolution calling on the new secretary to follow the "expressed will of Congress" in department decisions.[8]

The second kind of opportunity for presidential control over administrative decision making is that of reorganizing or altering the structure of the executive branch and the way in which policy responsibility is distributed across agencies, as well as making changes within agencies to assure political control. Reorganization efforts that cross existing agency lines may seek to "shake up" existing patterns of influence, control, and standard operating procedures; increase administrative susceptibility to presidential direction; simplify or "streamline" existing organizations and encourage efficiency; promote increased effectiveness by reducing overlapping or duplicative jurisdictions, facilitating economies of scale and integrating policy efforts; and provide symbolic support for a policy area or concern.[9]

The Nixon administration sought a major reorganization of executive agencies into four "superagencies" in order to consolidate and increase presidential influence over administrative activity, but the reform efforts collapsed in the wake of Watergate.[10] President Carter's reorganization initiatives were of two kinds: The creation of the Department of Education, for example, was in response to campaign promises to give more visibility and attention to education by creating a separate cabinet department for it, while the creation of the Energy Department was designed to integrate the various entities responsible for energy policy in assuring that the Carter energy plan would be effectively pursued. In reality, these reorganizations probably had some symbolic impact, but they did not alter significantly the functions of the various agencies that were brought under the umbrella of a cabinet department, since lines of jurisdiction and responsibility were not redrawn.

The Reagan administration has not given major attention to reorganizational reforms, at this broad level, relying instead on other alternatives. It borrowed, during its first term, from the Nixon plan in creating five cabinet councils to serve—along with the National Security Council, which is mandated by law—to centralize and coordinate policy decisions. There were some 150 meetings of the councils during the administration's first year; the president himself attended about one-third of them.[11] While some critics have argued that the councils play, at best, a minor role in policy development, it appears that such a scheme, along with the personnel selection policies described above, has served to increase the ability of the White House to monitor the rule-making and other activities of agencies. More importantly, the Reagan administration has restructured agencies internally, increasing agency directors' control of agency enforcement activities.

Delegation of responsibility to state and local governments is a related kind of reform, which has roots in the Nixon administration and has been championed by Ronald Reagan. Many regulatory statutes, such as the Clean Air Act and the Occupational Safety and Health Act, divide responsibility for implementation of these programs between federal and local agencies; general guidelines or minimum standards are set at the national level, and actual monitoring and enforcement activities take place in local agencies. Under the Reagan administration, other programs that are not thus divided by statutory demands have been restructured through administrative changes.[12]

Critics have leveled two criticisms at these initiatives. First, financially strapped state and local governments may not be able or willing to pick up the cost of administering programs delegated to them. As a result, enforcement activity declines, as does, eventually, voluntary compliance. States have few incentives to aggressively enforce regulations that may discourage industries from locating or maintaining facilities within state borders, although some state officials face, elsewhere, strong lobbying for effective enforcement of laws and regulations and public pressure resulting from major, visible environmental and health hazards.

A second fear, that this delegation of responsibility to states will produce different sets of standards, thus making compliance even more expensive and complicated than before, has prompted representatives of some industries to lobby for maintenance of federal regulatory responsibility. The evidence that is available indicates that states have generally followed the lead of other states or relied on guidelines from federal agencies, and that regulations do not vary widely across the nation.[13] There are, however, still some policy areas where state boundaries do not match the parameters of regulated activity. For example, pollution that is produced in one state yet travels and comes to rest in another requires agreement and coordination between the states involved, so that industries in the receiving states are not penalized by the fruits of less stringent standards in adjoining states.

The enforcement decisions of administrative agencies are especially discretionary, yet there are a number of ways political appointees can influence and direct enforcement activity. Funds can be cut for enforcement personnel and activities. Criteria established by agency heads that are used to trigger enforcement proceedings or otherwise guide agency officials can be weakened (or strengthened). Formal and informal agency reward and promotion systems can be shaped to encourage particular enforcement priorities. Data on the enforcement of civil rights, environmental, safety, and health regulations indicate that the Reagan administration has significantly departed from the enforcement practices of the previous administration. Inspections, citations, the dollar value of assessed penalties, and other measures of enforcement activity show dramatic decreases from earlier efforts.[14] One recent study by Environmental Safety, an environmental organization headed by William Drayton, who served as an EPA assistant administrator in the Carter administration, charged that noncompliance with environmental regulations has reached 80 percent throughout the nation. William Ruckelshaus, EPA administrator at the time the study was released, disputed the 80 percent figure for sources of air and water pollution, but conceded that noncompliance with hazardous waste regulations might be that high.[15]

Cuts in agency budgets have been a parallel means of imposing some control over agency decision making. Cuts range from reductions in research funds, which means agency officials have a smaller base for generating regulatory initiatives, to reductions in staff members and agency functions. Such cuts, of course, can only be used to impose reductions on agency activity and are an extremely important means of imposing control over administrative activity. Defenders of the Reagan initiatives, such as former EPA head Anne Burford, have argued that such cuts only eliminate agency "fat" and that effective agency activity has actually been enhanced; however, the experience of the EPA is clear evidence that efficiency and effectiveness have not been cultivated. A much more accurate characterization of the administration's position appears to be that since agencies should be doing much less, budget cuts are appropriate. Such cuts obviously place significant constraints on rule-making efforts themselves, as well as on agency research and investigation that identifies areas for possible rule making.

Seeking statutory reforms is not usually viewed as a direct means of developing presidential control over administrative agencies, although it can serve to make permanent changes made initially through administrative means.

The Carter administration's deregulatory initiatives were originally administrative innovations that were subsequently enacted into law. The Reagan administration has sought to follow this pattern, yet most of its administrative reforms are not built upon the careful economic and technical analyses provided by officials of the Civil Aeronautics Board and other agencies in the late 1970s. Nor has the Reagan administration cultivated the broad political support for reforms that Carter initiatives enjoyed. This is undoubtedly due to the nature of the regulatory practices subject to reform; Carter programs were able to capture the support of the business community as well as consumer advocates, while Reagan proposals have even generated some opposition among business groups, who feel that regulatory programs must be maintained or that since some firms have already absorbed the cost of compliance with regulations, their competitors should not be permitted to escape those costs. The Reagan administration has given little attention to statutory reforms for the reasons indicated above, and due to its desire to concentrate on other statutory initiatives of greater importance to it.

Presidential Review of Rule Making

Like the other oversight techniques and efforts described above, presidential intervention in the rule-making process has developed in an incremental fashion, with every president during the last 15 years building upon the experience of his predecessors and increasing presidential opportunities to intervene in agency deliberations. In the Nixon administration, concern over costs to industry of the regulatory initiatives of the Environmental Protection Agency led John Erlichman to establish the "quality of life" review process, under the direction of then Office of Management and Budget Director George Shultz. Although the primary concern was with EPA regulations, the process applied to rules issued by all agencies; each agency was required to circulate proposed regulations to other interested agencies, who reviewed the proposals and submitted recommendations. No rules could be issued until these reviews were completed.[16]

During President Ford's tenure, the cost of regulations became the primary concern, and the Council on Wage and Price Stability began issuing inflation impact statements to accompany all major rules. Agencies eventually prepared economic impact statements for each major regulation proposed. This served to produce an increased awareness of the potential costs of regulations, according to one study,[17] yielding a major White House preoccupation with regulations.

It was not until the Carter administration that there was a significant effort made to monitor administrative rule making. The emphasis continued to be upon the inflationary effects of regulations as well as, to a lesser extent, an interest in reducing overlapping agency efforts, conflicts, and lack of coordination. The Carter program included the creation of a regulatory council, composed of the heads of the major regulatory agencies and commissions, that was expected to meet, resolve interagency conflicts, and assure appropriate coordination; the preparation and publication of a regulatory calendar in the *Federal Register* which listed all major regulatory initiatives agencies anticipated taking during the following six months; and, most importantly, the formation of the Regulatory Analysis and Review Group.

The RARG was composed primarily of staff economists of the Council of Economic Advisers who prepared analyses of the costs and benefits of major regulations. The analyses were filed with the agency during the rule-making public comment period, and were open to review and rebuttal by other interested parties. Agency action was monitored by staff members from the CEA, joined by inflation fighter Alfred Kahn and his staff, who eventually provided an informal sign-off on the final issuance of the regulation. If the agency disagreed with the RARG report, senior White House staff and even the president were called upon to mediate. After a few interventions by Carter himself, which proved politically unpopular and alienated important constituents, the president pulled back and the RARG process lost some of its influence. It became, in the words of one of its members, a "kibbitzer" to encourage agencies to consider costs of proposed actions rather than a systematic White House control mechanism.[18]

The RARG process did have two important consequences, however. First, it helped produce a staff of experienced regulatory analysts that future presidents could draw upon, and, second, it provided a significant precedent for subsequent oversight efforts, including an enthusiastic enforcement of the process by the Court of Appeals for the District of Columbia, in response to a challenge to presidential and White House staff intervention in the rule-making process of the EPA.[19] The Reagan administration significantly expanded upon the Carter program through the creation of the Office of Information and Regulatory Affairs in the OMB, which was empowered to review all major regulations issued by executive branch agencies (but not independent regulatory commissions) to assure that an adequate Regulatory Impact Analysis accompanied the initiative. Under Executive Order 12291, the RIA was required to include a cost-benefit analysis of the proposed and final rules; unless specifically prohibited from doing so by law, agencies could only issue rules whose benefits exceed their costs, and whose consequences for price increases and productivity decreases were as small as possible while still achieving the objectives sought.

The second major element of the Reagan approach was the creation of the Vice President's Task Force on Regulatory Relief, formed to assure that concerns of industry and state and local governments were addressed and that regulatory burdens were reduced whenever possible. The task force solicited suggestions for regulations that should be altered or rescinded and served as a focal point for regulatory relief effort for the public as well as within the executive branch.

The Reagan administration claimed victory in its war on regulatory excess in August of 1983. It abolished the task force and gave responsibility for its activities to the OMB. George Bush, in announcing the termination of the task force, celebrated the creation and operation, by the Reagan administration, of a "credible, effective and even-handed executive oversight mechanism . . . for the review and coordination of new regulations" that was analogous to the executive budget process.[20] The task force reviewed 119 rules during its 28-month tenure.[21]

The number of new rules issued by agencies dropped by 25 percent between 1981 and 1983, according to the task force report, and the number of pages in the *Federal Register* fell by one third. During this period of time, the OMB reviewed 5,436 proposed and final agency rules; 86 percent were approved by OMB reviewers, 8 percent were approved after minor changes, 2 percent were returned for agency reconsideration (with no final action as yet), 1 percent were withdrawn by the agency, and 3 percent were found to be either exempt from the review process or improperly sent. Savings to business, consumers, universities, and state and local governments from task force and OMB review efforts were estimated by the task force to be $150 billion over the next ten years.[22]

The vice president argued that the "regulatory review process has been sufficiently institutionalized in OMB to make further Task Force monitoring unnecessary" and that "the ultimate measure of the success of the regulatory review program is that it is so well accepted that it is likely to survive a change in administration."[23] While the political fallout from the controversial actions taken in pursuit of regulatory relief apparently led to the dismantlement of the task force, with increased reliance on the less politically visible OMB office, the vice president's last statement is probably true—even a new administration, while it might differ in emphases, would likely avail itself of this kind of process to assure some role for the White House in rule making.

Despite the efforts of Executive Order 12291 and the task force, the Reagan administration concluded that it still lacked sufficient control over administrative rule making, and in January 1985 issued Executive Order, 12498, which significantly extended the reach of OMB into the executive branch bureaucracy. Agencies must now submit annually to their OMB overseers a regulatory program that outlines all rules they are likely to propose during the year, as well as all agency activity, such as research contracts and collection of information, that might lead to a "significant" regulatory action. Unlike the earlier executive order, which indicates that OMB involvement is advisory only and is limited to a review of the analysis accompanying proposed rules, OMB here is empowered to reject any part of an agency's submission to the regulatory calendar, and explicitly prohibits any significant regulatory activity not included in the calendar. A presidential memorandum accompanying the executive order makes it clear that OMB is to reject any agency initiative that is not "consistent with general administration policy". While it is too early to assess the impact of this review process, it clearly has the potential for dramatically increasing the ability of the White House to direct and shape regulatory activity.[24]

CONGRESSIONAL CONTROL OF ADMINISTRATIVE ACTIVITY

Congressional oversight has a number of purposes, ranging from preventing waste and fraud to evaluating program effectiveness to ensuring that the implementation of laws is consistent with legislative intent.[25] Oversight of administrative rule making is particularly directed toward assuring that discretionary authority is not abused, and that regulations issued by agencies do not conflict with the will of Congress and its members.

Congress has a variety of oversight tools at its disposal. The most direct method of control is through enactment of a statute which expressly reverses or alters an agency rule or regulation, its jurisdiction, or its powers. One example of such a congressional response was the reversal, by statute, of the Department of Transportation's regulation that required a safety belt ignition interlock for all new automobiles.[26] While such action by Congress is quite rare, some have argued that the threat of enactment is an important deterrent: "In a dispute over agency policy one committee recently held hearings and a mark-up on a proposed amendment to the agency's enabling act. The committee then reported the bill to the floor of the House. At that point, the agency dropped its opposition to the committee's position for fear of an embarrassing defeat."[27] An agency's jurisdiction can also be altered to prohibit certain kinds of rule-making efforts. Statutes enacted in 1976 and 1978 to deregulate the railroad and airline industries are examples of such actions,[28] as well as less extensive alterations of agency jurisdictions, such as exempting father–son and mother–daughter activities from rules promulgated under Title IX of the 1972 Education Amendments.[29] Riders to appropriations bills that prohibit the expenditure of funds for regulatory efforts in certain areas are also potent means of congressional control over administrative activity.

Authorization committees also have a number of nonstatutory means of oversight, such as hearings, investigations, and the requiring of agency and program reports. A study of committee hearings by Congress between 1947 and 1970, for example, found a dramatic increase in the number of hearings, from about 300 Senate and 600 House hearings during the 80th Congress to 700 Senate and over 800 House hearings during the 91st Congress. The number of hearings held by different committees between 1947 and 1970 ranged from less than 100 by the House Rules Committee to over 1,000 by the Senate Judiciary Committee. Significantly, the study noted whether each hearing was oriented toward broad policy issues or narrow agency oversight. Most committees were predominantly oriented toward general policy issues; only five held hearings that were classified as being primarily agency-oriented. The study concluded that hearings "give more attention to investigations of broad policy questions than to inquiries into agency implementation of programs," and that oversight of implementation is "haphazard" at best.[30]

In addition, the rise in number of subcommittees has dispersed committee power and expanded the number of agency overseers. The average number of subcommittees overseeing each agency has risen from 2.0 in the Senate and 2.5 in the House in 1947 to 3.0 in the House and 4.7 in the Senate in 1970.[31] The total number of committees (including standing committees, subcommittees of standing committees, select and special committees and their subcommittees, and joint committees and their subcommittees) reached a peak of 205 in the Senate and 204 in the House during the 94th Congress (1975–1976). Changes in committee organization in the mid-1970s significantly reduced those numbers, however, so that by the 98th Congress (1983–84) Senate and House committees numbered 137 and 172, respectively.[32] The personal staffs of members have also increased dramatically in recent years. In 1947, the personal staffs of senators totaled 590 and staffs of representatives, 1,440. By 1983, those figures had grown to 4,059 and 7,606. Staff members of standing committees also swelled from 167 in the House and 232 in the Senate in 1947 to 2,068 in the House and 1,176 in the Senate in 1983.[33]

All of this indicates that Congress, while much more able to oversee agency activities, is doing so in a much more decentralized and fragmented manner. Agencies may be able to play one set of overseers off against another, maintaining their autonomy. The potential for effective oversight is constrained by the limited power and resources of oversight committees and by the difficulty they face in challenging an agency with influential friends and supporters elsewhere in Congress. These committees must ultimately rely on the support of the authorization and appropriation committees before any real action can be taken.

There are few incentives for members of Congress to invest much time in oversight of agency rule making and other actions, except in cases where constituent support can be cultivated by responding to specified complaints about bureaucratic decisions, including proposed or final rules that constituents find particularly onerous. This kind of oversight does not provide any kind of a systematic, careful oversight of agencies; of course, that is not its purpose. But such time-consuming, uncoordinated effort provides only a very narrow kind of accountability and one that might often run contrary to the intent of law and the extent to which rules and regulations are applied fairly and consistently.[34]

Annual or periodic reauthorizations hold some promise for a structured review of agency activity, yet such reviews are rare. Members of Congress who have created programs are likely to defend them against attacks by others, authorization and appropriation subcommittees in both houses may disagree over their evaluation of agency activity, and there may be little consensus over the criteria to be used.[35] Periodic reauthorization does, however, provide an opportunity for committee members and their staff to instruct agencies on new regulatory initiatives. Advocates of more regulatory activity have increasingly used amendments in reauthorizing legislation, listing specific rules to be issued and imposing deadlines that agencies must meet.[36]

General hearings and investigations can do much to put pressure on particular administrative officials and programs, but such efforts are very irregular. Congressional pressure did much to force the ouster of Anne Burford and James Watt in 1983 and to identify problems with EPA and Interior Department rule-making and enforcement activities, yet these efforts could not be mistaken for careful examination of agency performance. Congress has had a significant influence on the ability of the Reagan administration to make appointments to administrative agencies. Between January 1981 and October 1983, for example, some 26 nominations were submitted to the Senate and then withdrawn by the president; the Senate also failed to act on 18 nominations by the end of the 97th Congress (1982) and six more names were not resubmitted after the 1983 congressional Labor Day recess.[37] While the number of rejected and withdrawn nominees is small compared to the number of appointments ratified, Congress clearly has some influence through the threat of rejection of presidential nominees.

Congressional Oversight and the Legislative Veto

Congress, then, clearly has a variety of mechanisms and means at its disposal for influencing and controlling the activities of the executive branch. It had, until recently, come to rely more and more on the threat of the legislative veto as a means of overseeing administrative rule making and other executive activity. Prior to their elimination (see below), legislative vetoes existed in various formats and purposes, ranging from committee to one-house to two-house vetoes. They had three primary purposes:

1. to facilitate the sharing of executive and congressional power in areas where decision-making responsibility under the Constitution is hard to allocate, such as foreign policy and national security questions (the provision under the War Powers Act that requires congressional review of presidential troop deployment, and arms sales legislation that requires

congressional approval of major weapons to foreign countries are examples of this);

2. to permit the president to make managerial and budgetary decisions, subject to congressional review (congressional vetoes of budget recisions and reorganization plans are relevant examples here); and

3. to allow Congress to delegate broad powers to administrative agencies and still exercise some control over agency actions (statutorily required review of administrative rules, and review of immigration decisions by the Immigration and Naturalization Service are examples of this).

The concept of the legislative veto is not a new one, although it only captured the attention of most members of Congress in recent years. As early as the 1790s in the United States, Congress empowered executive officials with legislative powers that could only be exercised after initiatives were laid before Congress for possible disapproval.[38] Its modern use dates from 1932, when Congress and the Hoover administration worked out a compromise that permitted the White House to formulate reorganization plans and Congress to review and possibly reject the proposals. Between 1932 and 1982, Congress included some 318 legislative veto provisions in 210 statutes. As of mid-1982, over 1,100 legislative veto resolutions were introduced in Congress; 230 such actions were approved. Of the 230 vetoes exercised, 111 were in response to decisions of the immigration judges concerning the deportation of aliens; 65 related to budget impoundment disputes; 24 were in response to presidential reorganization plans; and 30 were for all other purposes, including vetoing of administrative regulations.

The legislative veto was an attractive tool for members of Congress, many of whom like to delegate broad and often open-ended powers to presidents and agencies while maintaining opportunities to reverse decisions. As is true of other oversight mechanisms, it enabled Congress to delegate responsibility for making difficult policy choices and blame for politically unpopular ones, and claim credit for acting in response to political demands in reversing unpopular actions. The legislative veto allowed Congress to permit presidential judgment, discretion and initiative while safeguarding its own prerogatives and served as a practical basis for compromise over the division of authority and responsibility between the legislature and executive in areas of shared constitutional jurisdiction and political conflicts and disagreements. It often induced compromise on particularly intractable policy disputes.[39]

Congress was especially attracted to the one-house veto, since majority action in both chambers to overturn agency action is often hard to obtain. Even the two-house veto, as long as it does not include presentment to the president, was more appealing than the normal legislative process, since an extraordinary majority must be mustered to reject administrative action if an initial congressional veto is subject to a presidential one. For example, during 1973 Congress passed legislation on two occasions to end U.S. involvement in the Vietnam war, but was unable to override President Nixon's vetoes. The enactment of the War Powers Act permitted Congress, through a joint resolution, to reverse a presidential decision to commit troops to hostile areas if there is no declaration of war. The legislative veto also permitted Congress to give some flexibility to the president in budget decisions, without having to enact appropriations legislation a second time should presidential actions run contrary to congressional views. Under the 1974 Congressional Budget and Impoundment Act, either house could veto presidential requests to defer or rescind funds previously appropriated.

In 1983 the Supreme Court ruled in *Immigration and Naturalization Service v. Chadha,* that the legislative veto violated the process outlined by Article I of the Constitution for all legislative-like actions of Congress. The veto process, in many cases, failed to satisfy the bicameral requirement, and in all cases violated the presentment clauses, according to the Court, which, in effect, voided the more than 200 statutory provisions that include legislative vetos.[40] Almost immediately after the Court announced its ruling on the legislative veto, however, members of Congress began proposing alternatives for continuing its use. One proposal calls for the "use of a joint resolution of approval for major regulations combined with the use of a joint resolution of disapproval for the other regulations," which, according to Rep. Elliott Levitas, "offers the best alternative to the legislative veto."[41] Major rules (those with an expected economic impact or compliance cost of $100 million or more) would have to be approved through a traditional legislative process, including presidential signature or veto, or they would not be put into effect, while "minor" rules would take effect unless Congress and the president took action to reject them. In its first post-*Chadha* action, the reauthorization of the Consumer Product Safety Commission, Congress voted both to require that Commission rules be approved by Congress and the president before taking effect and that CPSC rules would automatically take effect unless rejected by congressional-presidential action, and left it to the conference committee to decide on one version or the other. Members of Congress have proposed variants of this approach for other agencies as well as for a generic legislative veto proviso.

The second congressional response to *Chadha* has been to push for a constitutional amendment permitting the legislative veto. One version provides that: "Executive action under legislatively delegated authority may be subject to the approval of one or both Houses of Congress, without presentment to the President, if the legislation that authorizes the executive action so provides."[42] This amendment, according to its sponsors, "would reinstate the means by which Congress can delegate broad authority to the executive branch, yet retain its constitutional mandate to check the exercise of that power."[43]

Much more important than these proposals, however, have been the arrangements that members of Congress have made formally and informally with the agencies they oversee. Formal or statutory arrangements range from requirements that agencies gain the approval of appropriations committees before expending certain amounts of money, to report-and-wait provisions where agencies must send to congressional committees all proposed regulations. Since report-and-wait provisions present the potential for significant delay in issuing regulations, they can lead to negotiations and compromise. More informal relations are often employed by committees to pressure agencies to issue regulations. Committee reports are carefully written to build a detailed legislative history that can be used to instruct agencies, and frequent meetings between agency officials and committee staff members provide opportunities for negotiations. Members of Congress clearly do not lack the means to influence agencies, but this involvement is ad hoc and decentralized, and rarely reflects broad congressional interest and agreement.[44]

ASSUMPTIONS UNDERLYING POLITICAL ACCOUNTABILITY OF RULE MAKING

Since the Constitution does not recognize and provide for a large administrative branch of government itself, its legitimacy must rely on some other basis. Congress and the president both serve to legitimize the operation of the federal bureaucracy by directing and monitoring agency actions and thereby render administrative power accountable to constitutional institutions. The Constitution provided for a complex sharing of a number of powers to assure the independence of each branch. The president's executive powers of appointment were matched by senatorial advice and consent for these appointments. The president's responsibility to assure that the laws were faithfully executed was checked by congressional control of all appropriations. The lawmaking powers of Congress were made subject to presidential review and possible veto. Presidential authority to receive reports from department officials was matched by congressional investigatory powers implicit in the legislative process. The independence of the President was eventually provided for but, as was true of other constitutional provisions, control of the administrative powers of the new republic was left for future debate and definition.

Early legislative decisions by Congress did little to clarify the ambiguity of the Constitution over political control of the federal administrative apparatus. Administrative discretion was seen as appropriate and necessary for some functions and inappropriate for others. This discretionary power, enjoyed by the executive branch, became the primary focus of concerns for the control of administrative power. Congress, the president, and the executive officials themselves all had varying responsibility for the actual execution of the laws enacted by Congress.

While the executive branch has undergone a dramatic transformation, the constitutional issues that lie at the heart of concerns over political control of the administrative process have undergone little change since the late 1700s. Both Congress and the president enjoy important political benefits in exercising control over administrative officials, and are thus jealous of each other's efforts. This tension is particularly pronounced as a result of the separation of powers, and of the evolution of Congress and of the presidency as institutions. Christopher Pyle and Richard Pious have summarized the competing views of presidents and members of Congress: "Presidents assume that any powers or responsibilities that Congress by law assigns to department officers become part of the president's authority, subsumed under his duty to execute the laws faithfully. Congress assumes, when it delegates authority by law directly to an agency official, that the president is to be excluded from the business."[45]

The constitutional charge to "take care that the laws be faithfully executed" gives to the president some power and responsibility to hold administrative officials accountable for their action. Yet the president is clearly not just an arm of Congress, expected to assure obedience to congressional intent, but is also a political leader with a constituency largely independent of Congress. As a result, the office of the presidency has developed in response to political pressures and demands that have defined the president as a political leader, equal to or perhaps greater than Congress as the source of legislative proposals and policies, and a manager of the executive branch, responsible for the efficient execution of statutes. Since the president's time and resources are limited, attention given to policy formulation and agenda setting inevitably subtracts from that given to oversight and management concerns. These two efforts are not mutually exclusive, however, especially when agencies are given discretionary authority. Managerial decisions concerning agency practices and procedures inevitably shape the policies pursued. Congress may then be hesitant to confer increased managerial powers on the president, because of the enhanced control over policy development that would inevitably result. Much attention has been given to defining the extent of presidential power to control or direct agencies whose legislative authority does not provide for such intervention.[46]

The Supreme Court, in a series of cases, has provided several interpretations of the "take care" clause. The "executive power" provided for in Article II of the Constitution gave to the president, according to the Court, the power to hire and fire agents to assist him in fulfilling his responsibility to "take care" that the laws be faithfully executed since he could not do that alone.[47] In a subsequent case, however, the Court concluded that independent regulatory commissions were given "quasi-legislative" and "quasi-judicial" powers and could not "in any proper sense be characterized as an arm or an eye of the executive," thus preventing the president from firing commissioners.[48] In *U.S. v. Nixon,* the Supreme Court found a constitutionally based presidential privilege of confidentiality that permitted the president and other executive officials to confer in private in coordinating policy. This concept of the executive privilege reinforces the constitutionality of presidential control of administrative officials.[49]

In the Steel Seizure case, Justice Jackson's concurring opinion provides a useful summary of the indefiniteness of the Constitution's provisions for the control of the administrative process. He found that the constitutional definitions of presidential power were not fixed, but that they were to "fluctuate, depending on their disjunction or conjunction with those of Congress."[50] Jackson presented a three-pronged analysis of the relationship between presidential and congressional power:

> 1. When the President acts pursuant to an express or implied authorization of Congress, his authority is at its maximum, for it includes all that he possesses in his own right plus all that Congress can delegate. . . . If his act is held unconstitutional under these circumstances, it usually means that the Federal Government as an undivided whole lacks power. . . .
> 2. When the President acts in absence of either a congressional grant or denial of authority, he can only rely upon his own independent powers, but there is a zone of twilight in which he and Congress may have concurrent authority, or in which its distribution is uncertain. Therefore, congressional inertia, indifference or acquiescence may sometimes, at least as a practical matter, enable, if not invite, measures of independent presidential responsibility. In this area, any actual test of power is likely to depend on the imperatives of events and contemporary imponderables rather than on abstract theories of law.
> 3. When the President takes measures incompatible with the expressed or implied will of Congress, his power is at its lowest ebb, for then he can rely only upon his own constitutional powers minus any constitutional powers of Congress over the matter. Courts can sustain exclusive Presidential control in such a case only by disabling the Congress from acting upon the subject. Presidential claims to a power at once so conclusive and preclusive must be scrutinized with caution.[51]

The leading case defining the extent of presidential authority in rule making is a 1981 decision of the Court of Appeals for the District of Columbia. In that case, the appeals court argued that

> The authority of the President to control and supervise executive policy making is derived from the Constitution; the desirability of such control is demonstrable from the practical realities of administrative rule making. Regulations such as those involved here demand a careful weighing of cost, environmental, and energy considerations. They also have broad implications for national eco-

nomic policy. Our form of government simply could not function effectively or rationally if key executive policymakers were isolated from each other and from the Chief Executive. Single mission agencies do not always have the answers to complex regulatory problems. An overworked administrator exposed on a 24-hour basis to a dedicated but zealous staff needs to know the arguments and ideas of policymakers in other agencies as well as the White House.[52]

The primacy of the concept of the separation of powers, and the doctrines that have evolved therefrom, provide some standards for the delegation of authority to administrative agencies by Congress and for the exercise of presidential power over administrative decision making. But the separation of powers ultimately provides little guidance in balancing presidential and congressional prerogatives for controlling the action of administrative agencies, and agencies are often caught in the middle of the political tug of war.

EVALUATING POLITICAL OVERSIGHT OF RULE MAKING

The review of administrative decision making in federal agencies may involve all or none of the following: involvement by authorization and appropriation subcommittees and committees, from both chambers of Congress; White House and OMB intervention and review; public participation through hearings, public comments and Freedom of Information Act requests; pressure from reports of agency activities leaked to the media; and review by federal courts. Almost all of this activity, however, is directed toward individual regulations: Individuals and groups affected by those actions prefer to seek to have them overturned rather than comply with them. Administrative discretion is limited, but this kind of oversight gives little direction to agency activity. Vetoes of specific decisions indicate what agencies are enjoined from doing, but do not help them set priorities, balance conflicting goals and purposes, or determine how to allocate scarce resources. Agency agendas are defined by court orders and statutory deadlines, rather than by attempts to set priorities and make judgments about what problems can and should be given greatest attention.

This kind of oversight often obscures responsibility and reduces democratic accountability. It is not clear who will ultimately be responsible for agency decisions—OMB officials, federal judges, subcommittee staff members, or agency officials. Alexander Hamilton's argument, written in defense of the proposed Constitution in 1788, that the "plurality of the executive tends to deprive the people of the two greatest securities they can have for the exercise of any delegated power" seems no less true today. For Hamilton these "securities" that were central to accountability of administrative activity were: "First, the restraints of public opinion, which lose their efficacy, as well as on account of the division of the censure attendant on bad measures among a number as on the account of the uncertainty on whom it ought to fall; and , secondly, the opportunity of discovering with facility and clearness the misconduct of the persons they trust, in order either to effect their removal from office or . . . their actual punishment in cases which admit of it."[53]

OMB Review of Regulations

A study by the General Accounting Office identified a number of problems with OMB's effort to monitor administrative rule making. The GAO found that OMB "appears to review so many rules that it cannot have a substantial impact on most of them," although the study did conclude that "for those few rules in which OMB takes a more active interest . . . it appears to affect the substance and the timing of the rule significantly."[54] OMB reviews were found to be inconsistent and incomplete in integrating economic analysis into the formulation of rules, and agency actions that did not provide "adequate support for their conclusions" were routinely approved by OMB. Regulatory impact analyses for half of the major rules reviewed in 1982 were waived, with little explanation. When reasons were given, they often conflicted with agency explanations or failed to refer to analyses already complete by the agency. This reinforces the perception that the OMB review process was more sensitized to political calculations than to neutral, analytic ones.[55]

In practice, the emphasis has been on preventing, as far as possible, the imposition of new regulatory burdens, and on the reduction of existing ones regardless of the "net benefits" involved. The Occupational Safety and Health Administration, for example, proposed significantly less stringent and expensive regulations for the labeling of toxic workplace chemicals than those proposed by the Carter administration. The OMB regulatory review office blocked the proposal. While there were disagreements over the number of cancer cases among workers that might be saved by the proposal, as the OMB found OSHA estimates "wildly optimistic," the primary concern appeared to be that this proposal represented the "first substantial new regulatory costs to be imposed by the Reagan Administration."[56] Pressure by Labor Department officials who warned the White House that the issue could be used by representatives of organized labor to attack the president, by industry leaders who feared that each state would write its own regulations in the absence of a national standard, and by Congress, who held hearings to investigate the one-year delay in the rule-making process, resulted—on the eve of the hearings—in sudden authority to go ahead with the regulation.[57]

The OMB review process is clearly concerned with the costs of regulation. The OMB evaluation worksheet has, according to one observer, no line for benefits of actions under review but only room to indicate costs.[58] While it is difficult to calculate benefits, that does not appear to be the primary interest: "You consider it, but to put it in numbers is crazy," observed Jim Tozzi, while serving as deputy director of the OMB review office. "Of course, this isn't benefit–cost [analysis] . . . we're just here to represent the President." Tozzi indicated that he could "tell in about four minutes if a rule made sense,"[59] indicating that there must be some shortcut to a review of regulations that sometimes run into the hundreds of pages.

The reversal by federal courts of a number of Reagan administration efforts to alter or rescind existing regulations also demonstrates problems with the economic analyses of OMB reviewers.[60] Efforts to reverse regulations requiring passive restraints in automobiles, weakening of EPA air and water regulations and Nuclear Regulatory Commission standards for hazardous waste disposal, and other initiatives have been rejected by reviewing courts. In the case of passive restraints, for example, the National Highway Traffic Safety Administration's proposal to rescind the regulation was hailed by the OMB as a "model of judicious decision making"[61]; yet, when NHTSA presented its "auto relief" package to Congress, it could not provide any information on the benefits of the regulations in question. The Supreme Court, in its unanimous opinion rejecting the NHTSA action, found it to be arbitrary and capricious, lacking a demonstration of "reasoned decision making."[62]

The claims of costs saved through OMB and task force efforts also demonstrate a less than analytically neutral approach to the costs of regulation by the Reagan administration. Much of the announced "savings" are more appropriately viewed as transfers of funds. The administration, for example, claimed $42 billion in savings by removing caps on interest rates for savings accounts, which, however, also led to higher interest rates to borrowers. (This action was also initiated before President Reagan took office.) Some $300 million in savings were claimed from a reduction in standards for the crashworthiness of auto bumpers, with no mention of increased insurance rates and repair bills, which arguably could exceed the $300 million figure. And the administration even claimed as its own $1.5 billion in savings because the Supreme Court did not retroactively apply its decision concerning pension plans that paid women less then men.[63] Other actions, such as EPA proposals to soften restrictions on lead content in gasoline and on pesticides such as EDB, generated such a public outcry that the proposals were shelved.[64]

The second set of criticisms of the regulatory relief effort is that it has been, in fact, a means of providing relief to business and industry groups, rather than a venture in improving the regulatory process and the regulatory analyses upon which administrative decisions are to be based. As indicated above, the emphasis on costs rather than cost–benefit analysis is evidence of the nature of the administration's program. So is the secrecy in which the OMB review process takes place. EPA regulations for dumping toxic wastes into municipal sewage treatment plants, for instance, were formulated over a four-year period and were based upon four public hearings, yet were suspended without notice or explanation three days after they were to take effect. The OMB has regularly been the target of congressional investigations and hearings that seek information concerning secret meetings with industry officials that have often taken place just before actions have been taken favoring those interests. To business groups, OMB officials welcome the opportunity to intervene in their behalf. Boyden Gray, counsel to the vice president's task force, indicated in a speech to the Chamber of Commerce: "If you go to the agency first, don't be too pessimistic if they can't solve the problems there . . . That's what the task force is for. The system does work if you use it as a sort of an appeal. You can act as a double check on the agency that you might encounter problems with."[65]

While the OMB guidelines require that all documentation sent to OMB officials be forwarded to agencies, the review process is not documented. James C. Miller III, who first headed the OMB review office, stated that "I see no problem in off-the-record contacts by us. We will not maintain a file and a record . . . [rejection of rules] will be communicated over the telephone." Or, in the words of his then deputy, "I don't leave fingerprints."[66] Congress has subpoenaed OMB records of contacts with regulated industries, charged OMB officials with providing copy of proposed regulations before they have been made public, and criticized the OMB for issuing political threats to agencies who threaten to ignore its advice. In one instance, Task Force officials, including the vice president, who have financial interests in oil and gas companies, met with industry officials and then pressured OSHA to reduce safety standards for divers on oil rigs. Earlier standards had been based on testimony of 81 witnesses, 44 days of hearings and several thousand pages of transcripts; the task force mustered one paragraph of criticism in justifying the change.[67]

Perhaps most troublesome is the effect of the OMB in muddling lines of accountability and responsibility for agency actions. As the GAO report concluded,

> OMB generally avoids putting its comments on pending rules in writing. It is therefore generally impossible to determine what role OMB plays in any given rule making. While the agency remains formally accountable for the regulatory decision, it is impossible to determine to what extent the rule making decision is made in the agency, as provided by the agency's statute, or in the OMB. It is equally difficult to determine whether OMB input is concentrating on improving the quality of the economics and the objectivity of the tool. The lack of documentation makes it impossible for others, whether interested parties or those with an interest only in cost-effective rule making, to comment on OMB's oversight performance.[68]

While OMB review may contribute rather than detract from the quality of administrative rule making, the review demonstrates a general commitment to reduce regulatory burdens and to delay or deter agencies from issuing expensive or burdensome regulations whenever possible.

The regulatory relief program of the Reagan administration has sought to reduce the costs of compliance with regulations imposed on business. It has clearly been successful in that task. But it has not been able to show that it has improved the regulatory process or enhanced the ability of agencies to issue higher-quality and more analytically sound regulations. One study of the review by the federal courts of Reagan administration deregulatory initiatives concluded that "in sharp contrast to the regulatory experience of prior decades, today the agencies are finding a substantial percentage of their deregulatory decisions overturned for failure to pass the 'arbitrary and capricious' test."[69] While a centralized review process may have some potential for improving the analytic capabilities of regulatory agencies, that has not as yet been realized. It has demonstrated that the rule-making process can be made more sensitive to political demands and pressures. The potential is there for refining and enhancing regulatory decision making through such a process, but most of the evidence indicates that this has not, as yet, happened. In reality, the review process may have set back efforts to improve regulatory decision making, by equating regulatory reform with relief for business interests.

Congress and Regulatory Oversight

The legislative veto has been championed as a means of facilitating the public's right to petition the government. Despite its rejection by the Supreme Court, the legislative veto continues to attract the interest of members of Congress. Elected officials could overturn actions of unelected bureaucrats, in response to concerns of citizens; clarify legislative intent; and provide some accountability for administrative rule making that is otherwise independent of direct monitoring. Although the OMB review process has served a similar function, it has been defended as a politically neutral, analytic review rather than a means of channeling political pressure to overturn agency action. Since the OMB review does not extend to independent regulatory commissions, the legislative veto is championed as essential to constitutional checks and balances.

Ironically, the executive branch, rather than Congress, was probably the greatest beneficiary of the legislative veto, as it permitted the president or administrative agencies to receive broader grants of authority than they would likely otherwise receive.[70] Yet every president from Herbert Hoover to Ronald Reagan attacked the legislative veto, joined by a variety of other critics. Some argued that the legislative veto encouraged sloppy legislation, permitting Congress to be careless in enacting laws on the assumption that it can subsequently review them. According to one study, legislative veto provisions "often accompany broader grants of power than Congress would have made without having the veto power as a check."[71] Indeed, the counsel for the House of Representatives, in response to the rejection of the legislative veto by the Supreme Court, recommended that all laws containing veto provisions be rewritten, since they did not reflect congressional intent absent the veto proviso.[72]

Other critics have argued that veto provisions encourage Congress to delegate broad discretionary power to agencies with less legislative guidance. Time spent on Capitol Hill reviewing agency rules could be spent writing clearer and more specific laws. Legislative vetoes are negative actions; once exercised they leave a void in the agency's agenda, rather than a clear statement of congressional intent to provide some positive guidance. Antonin Scalia argued that the "delusion that it will be able to control the agencies through the legislative veto will render Congress all the more ready to continue and expand the transfer of basic policy decisions to the agencies."[73]

The use of the legislative veto did serve to increase interaction between congressional staffs and agency officials, while the threat of the rarely used veto encouraged agency compliance with these congressional directives. As the Administrative Conference study suggested, most of the review "occurred at the committee or subcommittee [level], often focusing on the concerns of a single chairman or member. Indeed, much settlement of policy occurred in behind-the-scenes negotiations between the staffs of the committees and the agencies. . . . Congress did not form policy as a whole and in a politically accountable way" through the exercise of the legislative veto.[74] This process provided some accountability, but only in a narrow sense—oversight was motivated by an interest in responding to offended constituents, rather than to broader purposes of institutional accountability and control.

Public interest groups and other advocates of environmental, consumer, safety and health regulation are critical of the legislative veto for the same reasons they attack the Reagan administration's regulatory relief efforts. They argue that these attempts at political control are primarily used by business and industry groups, to reverse agency decisions that conflict with their interests or priorities. The recent experience with the vice president's task force, which was explicitly designed and operated to provide a forum for business interests to reduce regulations imposed upon them, and the threat or actual exercise of congressional veto of administrative regulations, lend support to such charges. These review mechanisms clearly are at odds with the rule-making process outlined in the Administrative Procedures Act, which assumes that rules will be produced through a legally prescribed process of agency deliberations and public participation.

Administrative agencies find themselves caught between a variety of overseers—congressional subcommittees, the General Accounting Office, the

Office of Management and Budget, other agencies in the Executive Office of the President, and federal courts. Such activity does place significant constraints on agencies, but the constraints are chaotic, imprecise, competitive with each other rather than carefully crafted limitations on administrative discretion. Administrative rule making rests on a foundation of conflicting and contradictory demands and expectations. Scientific rationality, political accountability, due process, and other objectives are not pursued in a vacuum, but they naturally attract political attention, because of their consequences for the policies themselves. In resolving conflicts between economic analysis and political responsiveness, for example, Robert Reich has argued that the determining variable is that of the interests involved:

> Where the benefits of the regulation are apt to be spread widely and thinly over the population while the costs initially fall on a smaller group—as with much environmental, health, and safety regulation—there will be a strong demand for economic impact analysis. This is because those who bear the costs will assume that they cannot look to the political process to guard their interests (after all, that process imposed the costs in the first place); they therefore will demand that all such regulations are at least economically unjustifiable. . . . [75]

Conversely, where the benefits of regulation are narrowly focused while the costs are spread more widely and thinly—as with price supports, marketing orders, tariffs, and licensing—the strongest demand will be for political responsiveness. Those who enjoy the benefits will know that they can rely on the political process to guard them. They, therefore, will insist on participation in the regulatory process, along with congressional oversight, to ensure continued protection of their special interests. And they will successfully avoid analysis of economic effects.

Tension between Congress and the president over control of the administrative process is likely to continue, muddling the lines of political accountability. As Morris Fiorina has argued, "Congress has the power but not the incentive for coordinated control of the bureaucracy, while the President has the incentive but not the power." [76] As a result, the administrative process is not given firm direction. Most importantly, presidential and congressional oversight takes place at the wrong end of the rule-making process. Oversight, therefore, usually accomplishes little more than enjoining agencies from actions rather than giving guidance to them in setting priorities, determining how to apply their limited resources to their expansive jurisdictions, and balancing competing policy objectives.

Part 2
Case Studies

Chapter 5 THE ENVIRONMENTAL PROTECTION AGENCY

Environmental, health, and safety regulatory programs present imposing challenges to democratic governments. The broad authority granted to agencies, as well as their power to impose significant costs on those whom they regulate, have made political control of these agencies a primary concern. Agencies rely heavily on rule making to formulate a variety of important policies; these are often only vaguely set forth in legislation, increasing the demand for accountability and responsibility to more democratic forces. These agencies are expected to base their regulatory actions on scientific and economic analyses and expertise, yet there is often little knowledge or agreement among experts concerning the technical facts and issues involved. Extremely broad responsibilities and jurisdictions are given to these agencies, accompanied by relatively limited resources, thus requiring agency officials to make important policy decisions concerning the focus and direction of agency activity and the relative importance of competing tasks.

This has been especially true of the Environmental Protection Agency, established in 1970 as an independent agency within the executive branch.[1] The EPA is charged with the authority to formulate and implement regulatory programs that range from relatively simple pollution problems to highly specialized and technologically sophisticated industrial activity and complex natural processes. The agency is an extremely visible element of the federal government and is closely monitored by Congress, the White House, the courts, and a vast array of interest groups. The experience of the EPA provides some important and useful examples of the tension between procedural constraints (and the political pressures active within those constraints), scientific analysis, and political oversight. And the EPA is especially important in terms of this study because of its central role in the development of administrative procedures. Congress, White House advisers, and federal courts have all largely developed their views concerning administrative procedures with the EPA clearly in mind.

THE EPA'S STATUTORY AUTHORITY

The EPA was established in response to concerns that the federal government's environmental protection efforts were ill-defined and diffused throughout the executive branch. Its creation brought together a number of existing federal programs in other agencies: Water quality responsibility was taken from the Department of the Interior, pesticide control from the Agriculture Department, regulation of radiation exposure from the Atomic Energy Commission, and environmental health from Health, Education and Welfare. Other responsibilities were subsequently given to the EPA through a variety of statutes enacted in the 1970s. Table 5.1 lists the major environmental laws under which the EPA functions, along with their major substantive and procedural provisions. The Clean Air Act amendments of 1970 and 1977 empowered the EPA to regulate stationary and mobile sources of pollutants in order to improve air quality in polluted areas and protect the clean air found in other areas.[2] Water pollution control laws were passed by Congress in 1972, 1974, and 1977, which provided for grants to states for water treatment facilities and created a system of pollutant discharge permits, regulations limiting the discharge of chemical and bacteriological pollutants into drinking water systems and into the ocean.[3] The EPA was given additional responsibility for the regulation of pesticides in 1972 and toxic chemicals and substances in 1976.[4] Powers to establish standards for shipping, storage, and disposal of hazardous wastes and to clean up toxic waste hazards were given to the EPA in 1976 and 1980.[5] Still other legislation directed the EPA to control noise levels from air traffic and commercial products.[6]

Table 5.1. EPA Enabling Statutes: Substantive and Procedural Provisions

Enabling Statutes	Substantive Powers	Procedural Provisions
Air Pollution		
Clean Air Act Amendments (1970, 1977)	Set standards for national ambient air quality, stationary and motor vehicle emissions, and hazardous air pollutants; states to enforce regulations	Extensive rule-making record provided for; citizen suits (to force EPA to perform nondiscretionary duties); rules to be based on available technology (except for stationary sources)
Water Pollution		
Federal Water Pollution Control Act Amendments (1972)	Grants to states for waste water treatment projects; set standards for industrial and municipal pollutant discharges	Base regulation on best available technology economically achievable
Safe Drinking Water Act (1974)	Set standards for pollutants in drinking water systems	Oral hearings; citizen suits

(continued)

Table 5.1. EPA Enabling Statutes: Substantive and Procedural Provisions *(continued)*

Clean Water Act (1977)	Set regulations for water quality, grants to states for water treatment projects	Oral hearings if requested; cross-examination; "substantial evidence" review standard
Marine Protection Research and Sanctuaries Act (1972)	Regulate dumping of waste into ocean	—
Hazardous Wastes Resource Conservation and Recovery Act (1976)	Set standards for handling and storage of hazardous wastes; grants to states for waste treatment programs	Citizen suits; rules to assure human health and environment are protected
Comprehensive Environmental Response, Compensation and Liability Act or "Superfund" (1980)	Set regulations to administer $1.6 billion clean-up fund	One house legislative veto of regulations
Hazardous Chemicals Federal Environmental Pesticide Control Act; Federal Insecticide, Fungicide and Rodenticide Act (1972)	Regulate pesticides, including their registration regulations concerning testing, and ban those found to be hazardous	Two-house legislative veto (in 1980 amendments); rules to be based on economic, social and environmental costs and benefits
Toxic Substances Control Act (1976)	Test and set standards for chemicals posing risks to human health and the environment	Oral hearings, cross-examination; publicly financed citizen participation; balance risks with costs
Other Noise Control Act (1972)	Set noise standards for commercial products	—
Aviation Safety and Noise Abatement Act (1979)	Regulate aviation noise	—
Atomic Energy Act, Uranium Mill Tailings Radiation Control Act (1978)	Regulate radiation exposure, set standards for exposure and for clean-up of uranium mill tailings	—

This accumulation of statutory responsibilities has generated extremely high expectations for the EPA. The agency's three primary areas of effort depict the broad scope of activity for which the EPA has responsibility. First, the EPA formulates and issues regulations for national air quality, pollutants emitted by stationary sources such as power and chemical plants, motor vehicle emissions, pollutants discharged into navigable water and water systems, drinking water standards, generation and transportation of hazardous wastes, pesticides, and testing and marketing chemicals considered to be toxic or hazardous to the environment.

The EPA's second responsibility, that of licensing and monitoring polluters, includes: issuing permits for the discharge of pollutants into navigable waters, oceans, and underground water supplies, as well as for the construction and operation of water and solid waste treatment, storage, and disposal facilities; maintaining inventories of hazardous waste sites; inventorying all chemical substances in commercial use; registering commercial pesticides and the facilities producing them, requiring that the manufacturers provide evidence that their products are not harmful to humans or livestock, and removing from commercial sale any pesticides posing a threat to humans, animals, or the environment; monitoring the level of radiation in the water supply and air; overseeing state efforts to administer clean air plans; and reviewing the environmental impact statements filed by other federal agencies in advance of taking actions which would have a significant impact on the environment.

Research and support activities comprise the third element of the EPA's agenda. The agency assists states in developing water quality standards and hazardous waste control programs, administers grants to states for sewage treatment plants, maintains a multi-billion-dollar "superfund" for cleaning up hazardous waste dumps when the responsible parties cannot be identified, conducts and sponsors research on pesticides and other potential sources of environmental problems, and works with other agencies in studying ways of limiting radiation exposure and water pollution.

The EPA is responsible for regulating some 60,000 points where pollutants are discharged into bodies of water, 200,000 stationary sources of air pollution, pollutants generated by 125 million automobiles, 50,000 hazardous waste dumps, 500 to 1,000 new chemicals introduced each year, and between 35,000 and 40,000 pesticide products, as well as for reviewing some 14,000 environmental impact statements submitted to the EPA each year.[7] Costs of compliance with EPA regulations were estimated at $55.9 billion in 1979; the cumulative expenditures for compliance with pollution regulations between 1979 and 1988 were estimated to reach $735 billion.[8] The EPA's expansive jurisdiction, its slice of environmental responsibility in the fragmented structure of the federal government, and its volatile political environs all come together in EPA rule-making proceedings, the most important and visible of the EPA's regulatory efforts.[9]

RULE-MAKING PROCEDURES IN THE EPA

All of the EPA's enabling statutes require that the agency promulgate regulations and standards, while state agencies are primarily responsible for enforcing them. Some of these statutes include specific regulations and detailed instructions to the EPA; the clean air laws, for example, actually set the acceptable levels for carbon monoxide, nitrogen oxide and hydrocarbons to be emitted by automobiles and list other air pollutants that are to be the subject of EPA standards. Strict deadlines for EPA actions accompany many of the responsibilities delegated to the agency.[10] The Toxic Substances Control Act prohibits the manufacturing and sale of specific chemicals and establishes detailed requirements for records and inventories to be maintained by the EPA.[11] The Clean Water Act lists 65 toxic pollutants to be regulated.[12] Other provisions of the relevant laws give the EPA broader, less specific responsibilities for protecting the quality of water supplies and monitoring dangerous waste disposal sites but impose a number of "action-forcing" requirements to assure that the EPA pursues particular policies.[13]

Environmental statutes also usually include procedural requirements that go beyond the Administrative Procedure Act's provisions for informal rule making. These restraints were added in response to demands by those subject to EPA regulations that they be assured participation in agency decision making. Agency supporters in Congress have usually acquiesced to these demands as part of the compromise necessary to gain passage of the legislation. Under the Clean Water Act, effluent standards for toxic pollutants require the publishing of a proposed standard and an initial 60-day period for the receipt of written comments; a public hearing, if any person requests one, to include oral and written presentations and cross-examination for "disputed issues of material fact"; and the publication of the final standard within 270 days of the publication of the initial standard. In reviewing standards established through this process, the courts are to reject standards that were not based on "substantial evidence" in the rule-making record.[14] (See Table 5.1 for a summary of these procedural provisions.)

The 1977 amendments to the Clean Air Act have gone even further, requiring that proposed rules be accompanied by a statement of the purpose of the rule, the data upon which the proposal was based, the methodology used in generating and analyzing the data, and the "major legal interpretation and policy considerations underlying the proposed rule"; specifying in detail the materials to be included in the rule-making docket; obliging the agency to give "interested persons an opportunity for the oral presentation of data, views or arguments" and to receive rebuttal and supplemental views for thirty days after the completion of the oral proceedings; and directing that the final rule be accompanied by an explanation of the reasons for any changes in the final rule from the proposed rule and a "response to each of the significant comments, criticisms, and new data submitted in written or oral presentations during the comment period." Rules can be overturned in court if they are found to be arbitrary and capricious, or to have been developed "without observance of procedure required by law if such failure to observe such procedure is arbitrary or capricious . . . or if the [procedural] errors were so serious and related to matters of such central relevance to the rule that there is a substantial likelihood that the rule would have been significantly changed if such errors had not been made."[15]

The Toxic Substances Control Act permits the EPA to compensate participants in rule-making proceedings who "represent an interest which would substantially contribute to a fair determination of the issues to be resolved in the proceeding", and who do not have "sufficient resources adequately to participate in the proceeding without compensation."[16] The Resources Conservation and Recovery Act compels the EPA to consider any petition from any person who seeks to have the agency promulgate, repeal, or amend a regulation and to publish a response to the petition, along with an explanation of the response, in the *Federal Register*.[17] The Federal Insecticide, Fungicide and Rodenticide Act, as amended in 1980, requires that EPA regulations be reviewed by the Department of Agriculture and then submitted to Congress, where they can be vetoed if both chambers pass a resolution of disapproval within 90 days, while the 1980 superfund legislation provides for a one-house congressional veto of any regulation implementing the law within 60 days of its final publication.[18] These provisions, however, fell victim to the Supreme Court's rejection of the legislative veto in 1983.

The federal courts have also imposed additional procedures that went beyond the statutory standards. In a series of decisions in the early and mid-1970s, reviewing courts found that EPA regulations were often carelessly prepared and lacked adequate supporting documentation. Led by the Court of Appeals for the District of Columbia, the courts began requiring that the EPA provide a fuller explanation of the grounds for rules it issued; that it formally respond to criticisms and comments received by the agency during the public comment period;[19] that it include documentary support for the rule, comments and responses, and other relevant materials in the rule-making record; that the publication of the rule include an adequate response to industry criticisms, while considering the health and other interests of the public and the good-faith efforts of manufacturers to limit emissions; and that an oral hearing be provided to assure that EPA officials responded to industry criticisms and concerns.[20]

In their review of EPA regulations, the federal courts have also expanded the social and economic considerations to be examined. They reflect an effort to counter a perceived singlemindedness on the part of the agency in pursuit of environmental goals. The courts have expanded the range of interests to be considered and have developed and imposed new procedural provisions to assure that the agency's discretion is constrained and that those affected by agency decisions have an opportunity to confront agency officials. As one scholar has argued, "court decisions that appear to reflect special judicial solicitude for environmental interests must be understood as a part of a more general judicial effort to curb perceived agency biases and ensure consideration of the full range of interests affected by agency decisions."[21] Reviewing courts have also sought to counteract the perceived capture of the agency by narrow interests, expanding the scope of factors to be considered by agencies and assuring that all relevant interests have an opportunity to participate in the agency's decisions.[22] The courts have also determined to insure that agencies produce sufficient records of informal rule-making proceedings to allow thorough court review.[23]

Congress has relied on judicial views concerning the kinds of rule-making procedures to be imposed on the EPA. In considering the Clean Air Act Amendments of 1977, for example, the House explicitly agreed with the findings of the reviewing courts discussed above, and sought, in its version of the proposed amendments, "to cure each of the problems which have been identified [by the courts] under the current act's approach to rule making . . . [and] to retain the flexibility and expedition of the informal rule making approach."[24] Relying on suggestions contained in a 1975 law review article written by an EPA attorney, the House committee included in the bill a section defining what the rule-making record was to consist of and how it was to be maintained.[25] The committee, influenced by arguments in other legal writings, also included requirements for expanded oral hearings and cross-examination. The House bill adopted the "substantial evidence" test for judicial review of agency rules, indicating that "the purpose of the committee's provision in this regard is to endorse the court's practice of engaging in searching review without substituting their judgment for that of the Administrator." The House also concluded other provisions relating to judicial review which "confirm[ed] the court's decision" in relevant cases.[26]

In the Senate, sponsors of the Clean Air Act Amendments gave little attention to procedural concerns, assuming that the Administrative Procedure Act's informal rule-making procedures and its "arbitrary and capricious" standard of judicial review would continue to apply. In the conference committee formed to resolve Senate–House differences, the debate focused on a number of controversial and substantive issues, such as the balancing of public health and economic growth and the role of state governments. Senate conferees argued that they could see "no reason why the Environmental Protection Agency should be singled out" for special treatment by imposing procedural restraints.[27] The conferees did accept the House requirements of a formal rule-making record, but rejected the House cross-examination provisions.

Perhaps the most important factor in shaping the procedural amendments to the act was that of Senator Muskie, who, in the Senate and in the conference, argued against procedural restraints on the EPA. Uninterested in the rule-making experience of other agencies, Muskie sought to protect the autonomy and flexibility of the EPA in discharging its regulatory responsibilities under the clean air statutes.

In contrast, the procedural provisions included in the Toxic Substances Control Act were taken directly from enabling legislation of the Consumer Product Safety Commission and Federal Trade Commission Act Amendments. The procedural provisions, such as oral hearings, cross-examination, public funding for participating groups, and the stricter substantial evidence test were included in response to concerns that the EPA's power to enjoin the manufacture or sales of chemicals be balanced by procedural protection for those industries being regulated. Initial bills in both chambers contained these provisions.[28]

Finally, in addition to the statutory and court-imposed requirements, EPA rule making is subject to the procedural requirements of President Reagan's 1981 Executive Order 12291,[29] which requires a regulatory analysis demonstrating that the costs to be imposed through the regulation are less than the projected benefits and that the rule represents the most cost-effective approach to achieve the intended purposes. This analysis must be reviewed and approved by the Office of Management and Budget before proposed and final rules are published.

Steps in EPA Rule Making

A typical rule-making proceeding in the EPA follows a complicated series of steps.[30] The initial element of the rule-making process is the drafting of a preliminary rule package, comprised of the objective of the proposed rule, the alternatives to be considered, plans for internal EPA coordination and external participation, and a schedule. The majority of EPA rules are initiated as a result of either explicit statutory language or court orders from suits brought by environmental groups. A small number of proposed rules are generated by new technical or scientific research, within or outside the EPA, and brought to the attention of agency officials through scientific exchanges. A "lead office," a unit of the agency specializing in a substantive area such as water or pesticides and toxic substances, prepares the preliminary draft of the rule and the developmental plan which must be cleared by the administrator before work begins. A public docket is established at this point to include "all material of general relevance" to the rule and to serve as the "public record" in the event of court review. Table 5.2 outlines this and other elements of the rule-making process to follow.

The second step involves the formation of a working group, an ad hoc committee organized around the proposed rule and chaired by a member of the lead office. Other members of the working group are likely to include representatives of the regional offices, the Office of Enforcement, the General Counsel's Office, Office of Research and Development, and other program areas. Figure 5.1 presents an organizational chart of the EPA which places these and other offices in their bureaucratic context. The working group is the central element of the EPA's rule-making process, responsible for developing the regulation itself and the accompanying analysis and providing opportunities for public participation. All of these concerns are discussed in

Table 5.2. The EPA Rule-Making Process[a]

Phase I. Start-up (one month).

Initial decision to begin a rule-making proceeding
Organization of working groups
Preparation of background and preliminary materials
Creation of public docket

Phase II. Development (six months).

Preparation and review of development plan
Consultation with EPA management and technical advisory groups
Consultation with external contractors and consultants
Consultation with interest groups, federal agencies, congressional committees
Internal management review: Steering Committee
                            red border
                            administrator
Publication of advanced notice of proposed rule making in *Federal Register*

Phase III. Preparation and review of proposed rule-making package (10 months).

Working group preparation of proposed rule and supporting materials
Internal management review: Steering Committee
                            red border
                            administrator
OMB review of paperwork requirements
OMB review of proposed rule making package and regulatory analyses
Publication of notice of proposed rule making in *Federal Register*
Public comment period

Phase IV. Preparation and review of final rule-making package (20 months).

Working group preparation of final rule and supporting materials
Internal management and OMB reviews—same as for phase 3
Publication of final rule in *Federal Register*

Legislative and judicial review.

[a]This figure is based on an EPA study which found that before the OMB review process was instituted, the total time to complete a typical rule making was 30 months. The OMB adds, at minimum, three months to the length of the process. Rules which are especially controversial and are expected to generate significant disagreement within and without the agency and affect a number of EPA programs rather than just one, or require coordination with other agencies, or raise new or unexplored scientific or technical issues are likely to take considerably longer to promulgate.

the working group's "development plan," which identifies the major issues and alternatives to be considered, indicates what agency resources are required, and provides a budget and schedule. For major rules (those with an anticipated impact on the economy of $100 million or more, likely to result in a "major increase in costs or prices for consumers," or expected to have "significant adverse effects on competition, employment, investment, productivity, or on the ability of U.S.-based enterprises to compete with foreign-based

Figure 5.1. The Environmental Protection Agency

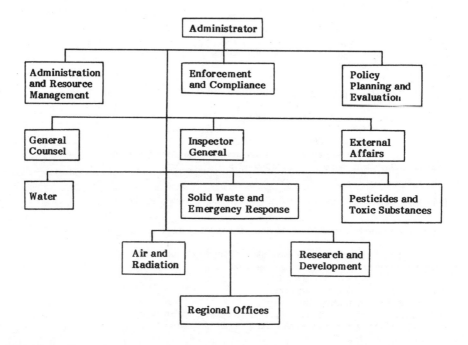

Source: Adapted from Congressional Quarterly, Federal Regulatory Directory, 5th ed., (Washington DC: Congressional Quarterly, 1986), p. 126.

enterprises in domestic or export markets''),[31] the working group prepares an array of special analyses including an operations/resources analysis, an information burden analysis, an environmental impact statement, and a regulatory flexibility analysis, which are all to be integrated within the comprehensive regulatory impact analysis. These analyses are briefly described in Table 5.3. A memorandum of law is also required, which indicates how the proposed regulation fits within the agency's authority and is consistent with congressional intent.

During this step in the process the working group may involve more than two dozen different agency resources and offices. Ten separate agency planning and management offices oversee the working group's regulatory analyses and budget, review assumptions and data upon which technical judgments are made, suggest alternative regulatory strategies, assist in developing ways of measuring the costs and benefits of alternatives and reducing the overall regulatory burden, and seek to coordinate environmental rules with energy- and civil rights–related issues. Seven agency offices provide liai-

Table 5.3. Analytic Support Documents in EPA Rule Making

Type	When Required	Description
Regulatory impact analysis	All major rules	Summarizes and integrates all supporting analysis; describes benefits and costs of rule and indicates net benefit of rule; describes any alternatives with lower costs and reasons why they aren't being used.
Regulatory flexibility analysis	All rules affecting small businesses, jurisdictions and organizations	Identifies burden on small entities; identifies costs and benefits of alternatives that could minimize regulatory burden for small utilities; indicates how the alternative recommended minimizes those burdens.
Supporting analyses[a]		
Economic analysis	All rules	Estimates the costs and benefits of each alternative; covers the *direct* economic consequences of the rule on the nation as a whole, the regulated public, and particular sectors of the environment.
Environmental impact statement	Most major rules and rules for certain sections of some statutes such as sections 109 and 111 of the Clean Air Act	Evaluates the *ecological* impact of each alternative considered on the quality of such basic environmental factors as air, water, etc., and on selected segments of the environment (e.g., wetlands, endangered species).
Information burden analysis	All rules that impose information collection requirements	Estimates the total cost to society of information collections; for each alternative, estimates the burden of reporting or recordkeeping for both the public and private sectors.
Operations/ resource analysis	All rules	Estimates the cost (in resources and dollars) of each alternative for public agencies (federal, regional, state, and local) to implement the regulatory program.
Evaluation plan	Optional for all rules	Describes the methods the agency will use to assess the progress and effectiveness of the rule after promulgation.
Technical analyses	Most rules	Vary greatly, contain scientific and technical studies which support agency proposals.

[a]Generally involve outside consultants in their preparation.

Source: EPA, "The Environmental Protection Agency's 1981 Rule Making Manual," (May 1981): 3–52.

son resources for agency rule making; these offices maintain EPA relations with Congress, foreign governments and industries for environmental issues of international scope, regional EPA offices, state and local governments, major public interest groups, and the Office of Management and Budget.

Several other offices regularly take part in the rule-making process: editing materials, coordinating the efforts of different working groups, approving consulting and contracting agreements involved in the rule-making analyses, and assisting the administrator and other senior officials who eventually review agency rules. A number of technical advisory groups review rule-making materials. The Science Advisory Board, comprised of scientists, engineers and other technical specialists from outside the agency, advises the administrator and reviews documents from all divisions of the agency, although the board's views are not binding on the agency. In addition, there are special advisory panels for specific agency programs such as drinking water, pesticides and air pollution.

Informal hearings are sometimes held to inform the public of proposed agency rules and to receive input from interested persons. Ad hoc advisory groups comprised of private citizens, representatives of public interest groups, federal, state and local officials and representatives of organizations with a significant interest in the proposed action, are often organized for the same purpose. The EPA's "outreach" program involves informal activities such as distributing publications, press releases and other materials and preparing public service advertising and education programs. More formal efforts generally rely on publications in the *Federal Register*, which usually occur during the next step of the rule-making process.

This phase of EPA rule-making procedures also includes the first level of internal management review of a proposed regulation package, a presentation by the lead office to the Steering Committee. The Steering Committee, comprised of representatives of the six assistant administrators, the general counsel and the relevant office directors, is a forum for examining the development plan, resolving conflicts and problems, and assuring that legal requirements have been complied with. The Steering Committee may require changes to be made before sending the development plan to the next level of review; it may require a second review by the committee, or it may approve the plan and forward it to the next level or "red border" review.

The "red border" review, named for the color of the border on the cover sheet of the materials, involves an individual review of the development plan by the assistant administrators, the general counsel, the principal office directors, and the ten regional administrators themselves. No joint meeting is held; officials make written responses and attempt to resolve any disagreements among the working group, the lead office, and the Steering Committee. Plans must then be approved and signed by the administrator. An advanced notice of proposed rule making (ANPRM) is then published, which provides a brief summary of the action being considered, the reasons why the action is needed, the expected effects, relevant dates for receiving comments or public hearings, and background information describing the major issues and alternatives under consideration.

Phase three of the process involves the preparation of the proposed rule-making package which includes the proposed rule; an "action memo" summarizing the proposal, the alternatives considered and the reasons for selecting the alternative chosen, and anticipated public, congressional, and

White House response; analytic support documents (the regulatory impact and other analyses); relevant scientific and technical documents; public outreach materials; and other managerial documents. The proposed rule-making package is then subjected to the same review process as the development plan, with a few exceptions.

Once "red border" review is completed, the package goes to the OMB for review as required under Executive Order 12291.[32] The OMB has 60 days to approve the proposal or indicate that it is to be amended, and may delay the proposal for additional review beyond the 60-day period. The OMB review, as indicated in chapter 4, is designed to identify conflicts, duplications and overlaps with other regulations, uncover any inconsistencies "with the policies underlying statutes governing agencies", and assure compliance with the requirements of the regulatory impact analysis. And although not formally required, proposed major rules are likely to be sent to House and Senate committees with jurisdiction over the EPA for informal review.

Rules which survive this round of review are then signed by the administrator and published in the *Federal Register* in a notice of proposed rule making. This notice includes the proposed rule as well as a preamble which presents supplementary information such as a statement of agency objectives and the alternatives considered, summaries of the required analyses, a discussion of the legal authority under which the rule is proposed, and a schedule of any hearings or public meetings.

The publication of the notice of proposed rule making initiates the public comment period which lasts from 60 to 130 days. Hearings, required for all major rules, are generally informal, permitting interested parties to submit written materials, present oral testimony, and, for rules issued under some statutes, take part in limited cross-examination. These hearings are sometimes supplemented with workshops, conferences, meetings, personal conversations and correspondence, and discussion with advisory groups. During the public comment period, transcripts or summaries of hearings, meetings, and conversations between agency officials and the public must be placed in the public record along with comments—or summaries of comments—from the OMB and other agencies.

Phase four of the rule-making process begins at the close of the public comment period where the agency begins preparing the final rule-making package. The package is comprised of the notice of final rule making as well as revisions of the "action memo," analytic support documents and the legal memorandum from the proposed rule-making package, and materials to be distributed to the public explaining the final rule. During the preparation of the final rule-making package by the working group, agency officials are prohibited from discussing it with the public, officials of other federal and state agencies, and Congress. The package undergoes the same internal review process as did the proposed rule. Once again, the package is shipped to

the OMB for a 30-day review period, and eventually signed by the administrator and published in the *Federal Register* in a notice of final rule making.

This notice includes the rule itself as well as a preamble which includes a
summary of the public comments and those of the OMB and other agencies
received, the agency's responses and how the rule was subsequently modified, a brief history of the rule and the major issues involved, an explanation
of significant differences between the proposed and final rules, a memorandum of law demonstrating the legal basis of the rule and its congressional
intent, a description of efforts to coordinate this rule with those promulgated
by other agencies and with the concerns of state and local agencies, a summary of the analytic work upon which the rule was based, and a discussion of
the reasons why the agency concluded that the factual bases for the rule have
"substantial public support" in the rule-making record. The rule-making
record is now complete and includes all the materials placed in the rule-making docket. It is this record that is submitted to reviewing courts if the rule is
challenged. Table 5.4 summarizes this material, which for many rules runs
into thousands of pages.

This tortuous process is modified somewhat for rules that are not major.
They do not require the "red border" review, do not require the regulatory

Table 5.4. The Public Docket in EPA Rule Making

Phase I. Start-up

"Start action notice"
Background information

Phase II. Development

Important legal interpretations
Development plan
"Notice of intent" or "advanced notice of proposed rule making"

Phase III. Proposed rule

"Notice of proposed rule making" and other *Federal Register* notices
Agency studies or contractor reports
Factual memoranda (technical data, reports of field studies, advisory committee minutes, etc.)
Summaries of the findings or recommendations of advisory groups such as the Science Advisory
    Board
Drafts and summaries of all supporting analyses such as the regulatory impact analysis, environ-
    mental impact statement, regulatory flexibility analysis
All public comments
Memoranda of meetings or telephone conversations with the public
Transcripts or summaries of hearings
Post-hearing comments
Copies of all materials sent to other agencies for comment, their comments, and EPA's response to
    those comments
Information collection clearance requests, including the proposed reporting or recordkeeping
    forms, and EPA's comments on these requests

(continued)

Table 5.4. The Public Docket in EPA Rule Making *(continued)*

Phase IV. Final rule

"Final rule"
Final support documents
Responsiveness summaries

Phase V. Reconsideration (if any)

Request for a court order seeking or directing reconsideration
Documents that become available after promulgation (if the administrator determines they are
   relevant)
New factual materials, correspondence, comments, memoranda of meetings or conversations, etc.,
   relevant to reconsideration
Agency decisions granting or denying reconsideration

Source: "EPA Rule Making Manual," pp. 2–69.

impact and other analyses, are subjected to much shorter review periods
within the agency and the OMB, and generally receive less scrutiny at all levels of internal review. Expedited rule-making procedures are also available
for specialized rules and for rules designed to respond to emergency situations.[33]

Finally, regulations issued by the EPA are reviewable in the federal courts
under either the "arbitrary and capricious" or the "substantial support"
standards. While EPA enabling statutes have provided for both of these
standards of review, the reviewing courts generally have not clearly deline-
ated any difference between them. Since many EPA laws grant specific rights
to seek judicial review by those who are adversely affected, as well as by any
person who seeks to compel the EPA to discharge a regulatory responsibility
that is not discretionary, and since courts have loosened standing rights, virtually all EPA rules are subject to challenge in the federal courts. Such challenges are likely to take several years before resolution, thus adding
significantly to the length of the rule-making process. And every major regulation is likely to be challenged once it is issued.

The rule-making process at EPA is a complicated and complex one. The
case study to follow provides a specific example that helps demonstrate some
of the elements of the process.

REGULATING OZONE: A CASE STUDY OF
THE RULE-MAKING PROCESS

Ozone is a major air pollutant, blamed for causing coughing and choking,
aggravating respiratory problems in humans and damaging agricultural
crops. It is an oxidant created by a chemical reaction between nitrogen oxides
and hydrocarbons, generated by automobile exhaust, petroleum refinery and
other emissions, and is the primary component of photochemical smog.[34]

(Photochemical ozone or smog should not be confused with the stratosphere's ozone layer which protects the earth from harmful ultraviolet rays and is threatened by increased use of fluorocarbons.) Under the Clean Air Act of 1970, the EPA was instructed to establish national ambient air quality standards for air pollutants, which were to serve as goals for air quality programs to be implemented by the states. State implementation plans, developed by state governments to reduce emissions from stationary and motor vehicle sources, reflect the EPA's air quality standards but are enforced by the states themselves. The more stringent these EPA-developed standards are, the greater the eventual costs of compliance with the state implementation plans.

The Clean Air Act requires that air quality standards serve to "protect the public health . . . allowing an adequate margin of safety."[35] As a result, the EPA sought to identify a threshold point which assures the protection of public health without completely banning pollutants. In 1971, the EPA issued a national ambient air quality standard for photochemical oxidants which limited discharge to 0.08 parts per million (ppm) for a one-hour average, not to be exceeded more than once a year.

In establishing this standard, the EPA relied on a study that demonstrated increased asthma attacks and eye irritation resulting from exposures to ozone at levels as low as 0.15 ppm. The study examined 157 asthma patients who recorded each asthma attack they suffered during a three-month period. This information was then correlated with the level of oxidant detected at nearby measuring stations. The study found that between 6 and 14 percent of the asthma attacks were due to changes in ozone levels, and that significant increases in asthma attacks occurred during days where the oxidant level exceeded 0.25 ppm. The study did not control for other factors, such as the level of other air pollutants and other determinants of ozone levels—such as temperature and weekday vs. weekend traffic—which some researchers believe are associated with respiratory problems.[36] The EPA then set the standard, to be "safe," at 0.08 ppm.

State implementation plans, based on this standard, were developed, but by 1976 all but one of the major metropolitan areas in the United States had failed to meet the required standards, and in some cases failed to meet them for more than 40 days each year. In 1976 the EPA began receiving petitions, from industry and from cities, asking the agency to loosen its ozone standard. The EPA had already begun to review the standard, and in June of 1978 issued a proposal for a revised standard of 0.10 ppm. It acknowledged that its 1971 standard was probably too low and that it had been unable to establish a clear threshold for ozone levels. The new standard proposed by the agency was based on evidence including several German and Japanese studies demonstrating the adverse health effects of low-level exposure to ozone, a clinical study detecting adverse effects at a 0.15 level of exposure, and other estimates that identified 0.15 ppm as a significant exposure level.[37] Most other epidemiological and laboratory studies, however, failed to find appreciable effects on health below levels of 0.25 and 0.30 ppm.[38] The agency's selection of the 0.10 ppm level was apparently based on an acceptance of the 0.15 figure, reduced by 0.05 as a margin of safety.

In compliance with the Carter administration's Executive Order 12044, requiring executive agencies to describe the costs and benefits of proposed rules and relevant alternatives, the EPA predicted that compliance costs would be $6.9 to $9.5 billion per year, in 1978, measured in 1978 dollars. However, the agency also argued that it was prohibited from considering compliance costs under the Clean Air Act.[39]

The regulatory analysis and review group (RARG) created by Executive Order 12044 to review selected regulations began examining the EPA's proposed ozone standard in 1978. In October of that year, the RARG report was given to the EPA to be included in its public record. The report criticized the EPA's methodology, its interpretation of medical studies, its lack of sensitivity to the costs of compliance and the process used by the agency in developing the proposal. The report argued that the EPA ignored the range of sensitivity of individuals to ozone and that it did not justify its choice of the level of acceptable risk. The report also attacked the agency's reliance on a clinical study which concluded that the 0.15 ppm level was necessary and its failure to consider other studies that found health effects only at levels greater than 0.25 ppm. EPA cost calculations were criticized as being significantly underestimated; RARG calculations put costs generally at twice those estimated by the EPA. The RARG report did not propose an alternative standard, but concluded that the cost of meeting a 0.16 standard was significantly less than the EPA's proposal while the increased risk to health was negligible.[40]

Industry groups joined the RARG in attacking the EPA's proposed standard during the public comment period, while environmental groups either attacked the proposal as too weak or supported the agency. The EPA, the Council of Economic Advisers, and the Council on Wage and Price Stability then began exchanging memos rebutting the RARG report and responding to EPA arguments. Presidential adviser and inflation fighter Alfred Kahn and the president's Office of Science and Technology Policy also began reviewing the medical and economic issues, as pressure was increased on the EPA to revise its proposal. The EPA held firm for several weeks, arguing that since the medical evidence was so inconclusive, the rule should be strict and that any inflationary impacts were several years away.[41]

By January of 1979, the EPA informed the White House that it would shift the standards to 0.12 ppm and a number of meetings ensued. No further compromise was made by the EPA, however, except to agree to sponsor research on the effects of ozone and to review the standard in 1984. White House officials considered appealing the issue to the president but eventually decided not to, finding that it "was simply not the right issue or the right time."[42] The EPA issued its final standard for ozone, based on the 0.12 ppm standard, in February of 1979[43] and was immediately sued by the American Petroleum Institute and the Natural Resources Defense Council.

In September of 1981, the court of appeals in Washington, D.C., upheld the EPA's ozone standard. The court rejected the claims of the NRDC that the standard was too weak as well as rejecting the arguments of the American Petroleum Institute that the standard was too stringent, that it was not based on sufficient scientific evidence, that it did not consider the costs and feasibility of complying with the rule, and that it had been set in violation of procedural rules. In defending the agency's standard, the court first found that "attainability and technological feasibility are not relevant considerations in the promulgation of national ambient air quality standards," and that the agency acted correctly in considering only standards that would provide sufficient protection to health, ignoring economic and technical feasibility. The court also argued that the "proper function of the court is not to weigh the evidence anew and make technical judgments; our role is limited to determining if the administration made a rational judgment." Finally, the court found that while EPA procedures "were not a model of regularity," this did not significantly affect the standard, since the agency had considered a variety of scientific studies and thereby satisfied procedural requirements.[44] The Petroleum Institute appealed the decision and the Supreme Court, without comment, refused to review the appeals court's ruling.[45]

The case study demonstrates the difficulties of environmental rule making, from the uncertainty of the scientific information underlying the decisions to the slowness of the political and legal review process. Despite intense political pressure, the EPA appeared to maintain its independence. One EPA staff analyst claimed that the RARG report and subsequent White House involvement had little impact on the agency's decision: "The environmentalists think we caved in to White House pressure, but the decision was our own and was based on scientific data, not the RARG report."[46]

EVALUATING EPA RULE-MAKING PROCEDURES

The EPA's rule-making process reflects a variety of purposes. The internal development and review of regulations facilitates administrative control over specific decisions, integrating the agency's efforts while permitting the necessary division of labor and specialization. Involvement in the rule-making process of a number of scientific advisory and review steps, internal research conducted and applied to the development of regulations, and consulting and contracting with outside experts all are designed to assure that agency deci-sions have adequate scientific and technical bases. The requirement that the EPA prepare a variety of economic analyses for each proposed rule was enacted to assure that compliance costs are identified, the most cost-effective alternative is selected, and the benefits of regulations exceed their costs. Citizen participation provisions provide opportunities for those affected by agency decisions to express their views and defend their interests, as well as for agencies to receive input from interested groups and thus to consider a variety of viewpoints and perspectives. Finally, the political and judicial oversight elements of the rule-making process are aimed at assuring that regulations are consistent with congressional and presidential purposes.

Evaluating the effect of the rule-making process on the ability of the EPA to achieve its statutory mandate is a difficult task, since the achievement of the agency's objectives hinges upon the adequacy of its budget, the level of commitment and expertise of agency officials, the extent of enforcement of the regulations, the appropriateness of legislative requirements, external political pressures, and the effectiveness of rule-making procedures. Environmental and consumer groups often argue that "administrative procedures and remedies now in place provide an advantage to those manufacturers that would keep their products on the market despite health and safety information that shows a clear danger to the public," while industry groups usually contend that the time-consuming procedures are necessary to protect their interests.[47] Rule-making procedures are an imperfect compromise between competing concerns and expectations of administrative discretion, expertise, political accountability, and due process.

Internal Agency Management and Review Procedures

During its early years, the EPA was widely criticized for producing ill-conceived regulations. The EPA's enabling statutes set strict deadlines for EPA actions, often causing the agency to act more rapidly than it was prepared to do. However, by the middle of the Carter administration, the EPA had become, to some observers, a model of bureaucratic efficiency, and while its rules continued to come under attack from the White House and elsewhere, its internal rule-making procedures were praised and held up as a model for other agencies.[48] Reagan appointees, however, upon taking office, disagreed. EPA's Deputy Administrator John W. Hernandez, Jr. complained not long after assuming his position: "This is not an efficient organization. We've been careful not to bad-mouth our predecessors. But when you look at the backlog of work remaining to be done, and the lawsuits brought because of these delays, 'efficiency' is not one of the words that come to mind."[49] EPA Administrator Anne Burford was equally critical of what she called EPA's "nonmanagement" in defending her agency's 1983 budget cuts, since the "work can be done better and more efficiently without the same commitment of resources."[50]

There are, however, a number of problems that appear in the EPA's internal rule-making process and its direction by senior agency officials that go beyond partisan exchanges. One especially significant weakness has been the failure to integrate EPA rule-making efforts with the state units expected to implement them. While some programs, such as toxic substance regulation, involve only the federal government, the majority of EPA programs require close coordination between federal and state officials. Part of the problem lies in the diversity of local environmental protection agencies. Some are located in state public health organizations; others form independent units; and still others are part of superagencies which also promote economic development.[51] The EPA, in giving important responsibilities to state and local agencies, assumes that states will provide adequate financial support to fulfill these responsibilities. Often that support has not been provided.[52]

Early in 1985, the EPA announced that it would defer to state and local agencies for the regulation of most toxic air pollutants. The agency, in announcing the change in policy, argued that the regulation of large chemical plants was too complicated and varied to be pursued through national efforts.[53] Some state and local officials criticized the initiative, however, arguing that local agencies lacked the resources and analytic capability to replace the EPA.[54] Members of Congress were also critical of the plan: Some senators feared that allowing differences in state standards would cause some states to attract new industry by offering less stringent standards than could states that were already significantly industrialized.[55] Other members of Congress subsequently introduced legislation that specified 85 air pollutants for which the EPA was to formulate and enforce regulations, and specified for future regulation more than 400 other chemicals. The EPA countered by claiming that the congressional proposal was "unworkable,"[56] and eventually compiled a list of 403 very toxic chemicals and urged local governments to take actions to minimize the risks posed by them.[57]

Nor are state regulators usually anxious to enforce federal standards which threaten local employment and other economic activity.[58] Initial EPA standards issued under the Clean Air Act, for example, required the city of San Francisco to cut its automobile traffic by 97 percent in order to meet federal standards.[59] Competition between states has hampered EPA efforts as well: Pennsylvania has claimed, for instance, that Ohio's failure to meet air quality standards pollutes Pennsylvania air and gives a cost advantage to Ohio steel mills over the Pennsylvanian mills operating under more stringent laws. New England states complain that pollution from Midwest coal burning causes environmental damage in the Northeast.[60] A study of EPA decision making by the National Academy of Science emphasized the crucial responsibility of state governments in implementing EPA regulations, but found that " . . . there is only rarely a careful investigation of a regulation's immediate implications for EPA personnel levels, and almost never any formal attention either to the other impacts on EPA resources or to any of the resource implications for state and local implementing authorities."[61]

A second difficulty with EPA's rule-making procedures is that agency effort has been concentrated on specific actions, at the expense of broader efforts to set priorities and develop long-run strategies. General Accounting Office reports and other studies have criticized the EPA for its failure to manage its information systems—to develop the information necessary for a comprehensive effort in controlling pollution and for the formulation of specific regulations.[62] Much of the fragmentation in EPA rule making is a result of external pressures. The EPA's agenda is set by several statutes which are uncoordinated and do not reflect a comprehensive, systematic response by Congress to environmental concerns, as well as by a variety of court decisions. The EPA must respond to external demands accompanied by strict deadlines that render more systematic efforts extremely difficult.[63]

The EPA has begun exploring possibilities for integrating its pollution control efforts. Under the Carter administration, agency officials experimented with coordinating efforts to regulate air, water and hazardous waste pollution, rather than working through separate programs. The purpose is to improve the cost-effectiveness of regulations by focusing on the "accumulated economic impact" on industry of agency proposals. To enact such a program, however, would require congressional amendment of environmental laws to permit each to take into account the effects of the others, and Congress has not taken such action.[64]

A third consequence of the rule-making process is that it has inhibited experimentation with alternative strategies to regulation. Agency officials have been largely unwilling to experiment with effluent fees and other market-like approaches, which economists have argued are more efficient and effective in achieving reduced pollution. In contrast to the time-consuming process of setting standards and the threat of having to shut down noncomplying facilities, economists have proposed regulations that would give industries the responsibility for developing their own most efficient reduction of emissions.[65] In the last few years the EPA has begun to experiment with some market-oriented approaches such as the "bubble" approach, where the EPA sets overall emission limits on a facility and then leaves the firm free to set limits on each source,[66] and pollution "offsets", which permit firms to sell or trade "rights" to emit pollutants to other companies so that new sources of pollution are permitted as older facilities are abandoned without exceeding environmental standards.[67]

Rather than part of a systematic effort to improve the effectiveness of environmental programs, however, these limited approaches appear to have been an "ad hoc response to a political dilemma—how to permit new and expanding industry in areas exceeding national air quality."[68] In late 1984 the EPA did bring together environmentalists, trade association representatives, manufacturers of trucks and truck engines, state officials, and OMB officials to develop a proposal for a pollution tax on heavy trucks that failed to meet EPA standards. Even though the 1977 Clean Air Act Amendments had authorized such an approach, the tax had been widely attacked by environmentalists as a "license to pollute,"[69] and had not before been experimented with by the agency.

The EPA's actions are largely in response to external factors, but those factors are fragmented and often inconsistent. Congress has shown little interest in alternatives to extant regulatory mechanisms. Congressional staff members and members of environmental groups have been opposed to granting "licenses to pollute" and to setting prices for clean air or water, which they feel are priceless. Industry groups are opposed as well, since they fear their costs could significantly increase under such an approach.[70] In one proposed rule for chlorofluorocarbons, for example, which took a market-like approach to pollution control, over 2,000 comments were received. The agency subsequently decided against taking action.

Scientific and Economic Analysis in EPA Rule Making

EPA's rule-making procedures inhibit agency flexibility and adaptability to newly discovered scientific and technical information. New knowledge concerning threats to human health and the environment is continually developing, but agency procedures provide no way to quickly respond. EPA procedures are often actual obstacles to the development of new research findings, as such information poses difficult problems for agency decision makers. One EPA official argued that the "unscheduled and unpredictable character of the regulatory changes that new knowledge can require has fostered a tendency to resist new knowledge," and that changes were procedurally too difficult to make.[71] The EPA, for example, when it established its standards for sulfur oxide assumed that concentration of the pollutant near its source was the most major health threat. Therefore, the standard issued by the agency required the use of tall smokestacks to disperse the sulfur oxide. Further research, however, concluded that the real threat is from the transformation in the atmosphere of sulfur oxide into sulfates, which form acid rain and result in health and environmental hazards far from the sources. Other agency decisions have also been faulted for inadequate underlying information and the agency's inability to respond to change.[72] These failures are not just a consequence of agency procedures, but are also due to the lack of scientific and technical data underlying rule-making efforts.

The EPA confronts a number of problems in developing scientific and technical knowledge to serve as the basis of the regulations it issues. Most regulatory decisions rely on scientific knowledge that lacks certainty. Harmful effects of pollutants, for example, are usually based on epidemiological research, which can rarely control for other causal factors, or on clinical experiments, where calculations rely on interpolating effects of low exposures from high exposures and effects on humans from those on test animals.[73] Cancer-causing elements may have long latency periods, making prediction difficult. Synergistic factors, when chemicals are combined, may increase the likelihood of cancer by many times, but little information is available concerning these effects. Few toxic chemicals regulated by the EPA affect humans in isolation. The susceptibility of humans to carcinogens varies according to a number of factors that are also difficult to control for and are unlikely to be represented in the test population.[74]

The kind of model the EPA chooses to use also has important consequences for the standard actually developed. One chemical was evaluated using four different models, resulting in predicted cancer rates per million people exposed that varied from 210 to 5,200.[75] Under the Reagan administration, EPA officials have selected computer models which generally find chemicals to be less dangerous than do other models.[76] One example demonstrates well the kind of problem the agency confronts: "Tests on rodents have revealed more than 100 million-fold range in the potency of carcinogens. This means that one part of one of the most potent carcinogens per trillion parts of water can cause as much cancer in rodents as 100 parts of one of the weakest carcinogens per million parts of water."[77]

Some EPA officials state that the agency's decision-making process is "not a scientific process," and although they are "uncomfortable with it," they accept it as "the best we can do."[78] Decisions concerning agency regulations usually rest on the uncertainty as to whether there is "enough evidence of potential harm to take precautionary action, or is there enough evidence of safety to justify not taking this precautionary action?"[79] Agency exigencies often force scientists "to produce clear-cut statements that, however convenient for the regulator, may not have scientific justification."[80] There is a basic conflict in the EPA between restraints resulting from scientific knowledge and political imperatives. The National Academy of Science study of the EPA vividly portrays the dilemma:

> If there were no time pressure in the regulatory process, the normal accumulation and validation of scientific knowledge would dissipate much controversy. . . . Experiments would be replicated, alternative hypotheses explored and tested, and technical judgments checked against established theory and one or the other amended as necessary. Eventually the technical basis for decision making would emerge with greater clarity.

But regulatory decision making is hurried by the real or imagined urgency of environmental problems, by public demand for action and by the resulting statutory guidelines. Congress and the EPA are often forced to act before there is sufficient reliable scientific basis for action. This rush to regulate is not necessarily wrong: the decision not to regulate is also a decision. If there is no adequate scientific-technical basis for regulating, neither is there an adequate scientific-technical basis for the belief that no regulation is needed. The danger is that, under the pressure of adverse interests, the methods of science are bent, and tentative research results may be presented as proven fact.[81]

Cost-benefit analyses required for all major EPA regulations under the Reagan executive order compound the problems of inadequate scientific knowledge. Calculating the costs of compliance with EPA regulations has been relatively easy, compared to the problems in quantifying the benefits. Uncertainty over the risks associated with pollutants makes estimates of expected benefits from reduced emissions difficult to calculate. The EPA is dependent upon the regulated industries for much data and analyses concerning the costs and technical feasibility of pollution control devices. The industries, of course, have great incentives to withhold information whenever they expect the agency is considering actions against them. Industries are also reticent to release proprietary information. While such data is important for EPA decision making, it is also of interest to their competitors, who can use the Freedom of Information Act to gain access to the information submitted to the EPA.

Economic costs of compliance with environmental standards generally accrue during the short run while benefits may not result for years. Some regulations are to be based on considerations of "best available control technology," but as one scholar observed, "there is never a best technology but only successively more expensive and stringent technologies. . . . In practice, best available control technology embodies implicit assumptions about the benefits and costs of further abatement."[82] Cost-benefit analysis may also have a redistributive effect, as it determines who pays for pollution control.[83]

Cost-benefit analysis in environmental decision making requires judgments that go well beyond quantifiable variables and involve fundamental political decisions and tradeoffs. Some argue that it is inevitable; the EPA is forced to do this whether or not it admits it, and scarce pollution-fighting resources require comparing costs and benefits. Others have argued that an adequate cost-benefit calculation is simply impossible, or that it is merely added on to justify regulations already formed. The National Commission on Air Quality's report concluded that "it is fruitless to try to compare meaningfully the costs and benefits of air pollution control. There are too many uncertainties in the calculation of both sides of the situation, especially the benefit side."[84] While the debate continues, all major EPA rules must pass the cost-benefit test. The tests give an air of impartiality and precision to regulations that are, at best, based on rough estimates, and permit officials to reject standards for political reasons while claiming that they fail to satisfy analytic tests.

Finally, one of the greatest challenges to the EPA's regulatory efforts has been communicating with the public and the media concerning environmental hazards and the risks they pose. One study of the agency's regulation of the pesticide EDB concluded that the agency had both regulatory and public information responsibilities, and that these roles often conflicted. When the agency sought to inform the public of its concern with EDB, it used technical language, based on its risk assessment, that only produced "public confusion and rising anxiety."[85]

Due Process, Administrative Law, and the Rule-Making Process

The adversary process in EPA rule-making hearings is rarely applauded for making contributions to the quality of regulations produced, while attacks directed at it abound. Douglas Costle, EPA administrator under Jimmy Carter, attacked the legal profession's involvement in EPA rule making, arguing that lawyers use the Freedom of Information Law, lobby Congress and executive branch officials, and inundate the agency with massive comments to which it is required to respond, all to thwart agency efforts. Attention, he argued, is directed to procedural concerns rather than the development of an effective and appropriate regulation. One industry paid a Washington, D.C., law firm $1 million just to lobby against the EPA's advanced notice of the proposed rule for chlorofluorocarbons. Some seven feet of shelf space was required to hold the more than 4,000 comments submitted in response to another proposed rule.[86]

While EPA's public participation provisions in rule-making proceedings involve a variety of kinds of meetings, the informal hearing has become the most important kind of public involvement in rule making.[87] The adversary process provides the framework in which this takes place, where lawyers for all interested parties discuss agency proposals and sometimes have opportunities to cross-examine agency officials or those whom agency analyses rely upon.[88] The adversary process, however, provides little help in resolving the scientific and technical issues at the base of most EPA rules. Adversary proceedings exaggerate or minimize risks and suppress useful and relevant information. The National Academy of Science study found that "confrontation and the adversary process do not create an atmosphere conducive to the carefully weighing of scientific and technical information," and that the adversary process "distorts the state of scientific and technical agreement and disagreement on a given matter." Cross-examination, it argued, "can be (and has been) exploited as a delaying tactic, and is sometimes used by lawyers more with intent to discredit the witness on minor points than to probe the merits.'' Industries willing to cooperate with the EPA "did not, in the end, insist upon the use of the formal trial-type procedures''; instead technical issues were considered through exchange of documents and informal meetings between technical experts.[89] As one observer summarized the EPA's efforts to issue standards under the Toxic Substances Control Act:

> EPA officials know they have to build a framework of rules and standards that not only mediates the contending interests of the industry and the environmentalists, but can survive the lawsuits that inevitably follow any new regulation. One false procedural step and the agency might find itself sent back to the drawing board by a judge. . . . It is a cumbersome process, a system permeated by adversary contention, foot-dragging, and evasion. The industry has no incentive to cooperate with its new regulators, and the environmentalists don't want to give up any of the legal weapons the system affords them. As a result, an agency like EPA moves ever so tentatively, getting little or nothing done for years at a stretch.[90]

Judicial Oversight of EPA Rule Making

The role of the federal courts in imposing procedural restraints on EPA rule making has already been discussed here, and is generally credited with causing the agency to provide more access to its decision making to interested groups and to provide explanations of and justifications for the regulations it has issued. The courts, however, have disagreed among themselves over how the EPA is to implement specific statutes. Judicial decisions, in imposing responsibilities on the EPA, have not given much attention to the resources needed by the agency to comply with the court order or to the regional differences involved. This has forced premature agency decisions and has inhibited long-run planning.[91] Specific decisions have required the EPA to regulate additional pollutants to prevent the deterioration of air quality in areas where air is purer than the law requires, regulate vehicle use in metropolitan areas, issue rules in compliance with statutory goals, and establish standards for the quality of water flowing out of the nation's two million dams, and have struck down EPA regulations governing the most common forms of water pollution.[92]

The courts have played a major role in EPA decision making through citizen suit provisions which permit citizens to sue the agency for failing to perform nondiscretionary duties. Between 1970 and 1980, some 85 of these cases were decided by federal courts of appeals, and 68 percent were decided in favor of environmental groups.[93] Reviews of court decisions affecting the EPA in general, however, conclude that industry interests have been protected as often as have those of environmentalists; that "despite claims that either the industrial proponents or the environmental proponents have benefitted exclusively from judicial review, it appears that the review process has not systematically favored one group of litigants over another."[94]

Judicial review has been a significant factor in delaying EPA rule making. Former administrator William Ruckelshaus estimated that 80 percent of all rules issued by the EPA were subsequently challenged in federal courts, either by environmental groups who found the agency's initiatives too weak or by industry groups who sought to weaken or overturn them. He argued that Congress had "created so many checks and balances to prevent abuse that the process of enforcing laws has slowed to a crawl. Progress is stifled by substituting process for decisions." Judicial review itself serves to reduce agency responsibility, Ruckelshaus complained, because agency officials know they can always "pass the buck" to the courts.[95]

Political Oversight

Congress has not been formally involved in EPA rule-making proceedings. Legislative veto provisions were not included in EPA-enabling statutes until 1980, and have never been employed. One EPA official argued that Congress is rarely interested in EPA regulations, since they are generally highly technical.[96] Members of Congress have informally intervened in EPA rule makings where significant interests are involved, but the consequences of this ad hoc involvement in the EPA's rule-making process have not been well documented. There has, however, been great congressional interest in the enforcement activities of the EPA. During the height of the congressional concerns over the EPA under Anne Burford, five different congressional subcommittees were actively investigating charges of "sweetheart" deals, industry influence in agency decision making, and lax enforcement efforts.[97]

The OMB's review of EPA regulations to assure that they meet the standards set out under Executive Order 12291 appeared to have had little direct influence on agency regulations under the first Reagan administrator, Anne Burford. EPA officials indicate that Burford put on hold almost all rule-making efforts, except those aimed at reducing the costs of current regulations. Between the review of the administration and the OMB, "regulations that impose new costs are being blocked while those that reduce costs are going through."[98] According to OMB's deputy general counsel, the OMB "could tell Agencies to redo the analysis. But they couldn't hold something off to displace the agency's decision making authority."[99] Given the shared perspectives of OMB, EPA and other senior Reagan administration officials, OMB's review role in EPA rule making has added little except to review and curtail existing regulations. In his Senate confirmation hearings in the Spring of 1983, Administrator William Ruckelshaus vowed to enforce environmental laws "as written by Congress", but refused to agree to seek a bigger agency budget and increased personnel, steps that critics argued were essential in restoring the agency's effectiveness.[100]

Under Ruckelshaus, who resigned in 1984, and Lee Thomas, his successor, there was more tension between the EPA and the OMB. Members of Congress and environmentalists have criticized the OMB for blocking agency actions that the latter sees as too expensive or unwarranted. Other critics have charged that OMB officials were conduits for illegal industry intervention in agency decision-making procedures. In 1985 the EPA and OMB agreed that OMB interventions would become part of the formal rule-making record.[101]

Science, Law, and Politics in EPA Rule Making

The EPA's rule-making process, the central element of the agency's environmental protection efforts, has largely been unable to meet the demands placed upon it. The EPA has failed to produce a number of statutorily mandated regulations. For example, in 1972 the EPA was ordered to issue regulations for 129 toxic pollutants produced by 21 industries involved in water pollution; ten years later, the agency had issued only one regulation.[102] Under the 1976 Toxic Substances Control Act, the EPA was empowered to assess the risk of harmful chemicals and issue rules concerning the testing of all chemicals suspected to be hazardous. A 1980 report issued by the comptroller general found that the EPA had not issued any testing standards, that it would take about five years to issue each standard, and that at least nine years would probably elapse before a potentially harmful chemical was actually regulated.[103] Under another law, passed in 1976, the EPA was required to issue regulations for the dumping of hazardous wastes by 1978. Five years later, after being sued by environmentalists for not issuing the regulation and having received new court-imposed deadlines, the EPA had only issued three of the seven regulations required and argued that the rest of the rules could not be issued at that time, as it was wading through some 1,200 public comments related to its proposals. States, responsible for controlling hazardous wastes until 1976, have done nothing, waiting for the EPA to act. Industries have delayed developing treatment programs until EPA regulations are issued.[104]

Congress has been unwilling to address many scientific, economic and political issues associated with environmental regulation. It has provided little guidance for kinds of tradeoffs between economic and environmental concerns or the balancing of risks based on uncertain evidence that are fundamental elements of EPA rule-making decisions. And it has imposed overwhelming responsibilities on the agency to remedy an almost unlimited array of environmental problems, without providing adequate resources to even begin to solve these problems. As the agency pursues its statutory mandates, its discretion is constrained through congressional, presidential, and judicial influence, but these constraints are narrowly focused and fragmented. Insufficient attention is given to how the EPA should allocate its scarce resources and how it can effectively accomplish the policy tasks delegated to it.

Chapter 6 THE OCCUPATIONAL SAFETY AND HEALTH ADMINISTRATION

In 1970, Congress passed the Occupational Safety and Health Act, creating the Occupational Safety and Health Administration (as an agency within the Department of Labor), the Occupational Safety and Health Review Commission (as an independent commission which reviews OSHA enforcement decisions) and the National Institute for Occupational Safety and Health (as an occupational health research agency in the then Department of Health, Education and Welfare). OSHA was charged with the task of assuring "so far as possible every working man and women in the nation safe and healthful working conditions."[1] Its responsibilities include facilitating cooperation between employers and employees in reducing the number of health and safety hazards, formulating and issuing mandatory occupational safety and health standards, providing training programs to increase the number of qualified health and safety personnel, enforcing health and safety standards, assisting states in administering and enforcing their own job safety and health programs, and monitoring job-related illnesses and accidents.

As well as administering the 1970 legislation, OSHA oversees more specific legislation designed to promote health and safety among building and construction workers, longshoremen and harbor workers, and workers employed by federal contractors.[2] Under the OSH Act, the agency was ordered to issue, within two years of its establishment, any "national consensus standard"—established by industry or private standard-setting organizations—and any established federal standard that would result in improved worker safety or health. Within one month, OSHA had issued some 4,400 safety and health standards based on existing federal standards, industry codes, and work of the American National Standards Institute and the American Conference of Governmental Industrial Hygienists.[3]

OSHA was also empowered to promulgate additional occupational safety and health standards, and was authorized to issue emergency temporary standards, to take effect immediately upon publication in the *Federal Register*, whenever such action was necessary to protect employees "exposed to grave danger from exposure to substances or agents determined to be toxic or physically harmful."[4] Once an emergency standard is issued, OSHA must initiate a regular rule-making procedure, using the emergency standard as the proposed rule for the proceedings.

The OSH Act was passed during a period of great concern over environmental, safety, and health problems, although there was initially no strong support or intense lobbying for protecting worker health and safety. OSHA's roots have been traced to Robert Hardesty, a speechwriter for Lyndon Johnson, whose brother worked in HEW's Bureau of Occupational Safety and Health in the mid-1960s. Some intrafamily lobbying led to occasional references to occupational safety and health in the president's speeches that were interpreted by Department of Labor officials, on the lookout for new programs to administer, as presidential interest in an enlarged regulatory effort, and legislation was introduced in 1967 and again in 1969.[5]

The debate in Congress focused on the symbolic issue of where the rule-making and enforcement powers for occupational safety and health regulation would be located. The Nixon administration's bill called for the creation of an independent regulatory commission to promulgate regulations while the leading Democratic-organized labor proposal sought to delegate that power to the Department of Labor.[6] The compromise that was eventually fashioned gave to the Secretary of Labor the power to issue regulatory standards, and established an independent commission to review enforcement decisions and a separate research institute.

OSHA's safety and health standards have been widely attacked by business groups, members of Congress, and presidents. Much of the criticism has focused on OSHA enforcement efforts: Within one year of OSHA's effective date, some 100 bills had been introduced to abolish the agency.[7] Legislation was eventually passed that limited fines for employers charged with fewer than 10 violations and exempted businesses with fewer than 10 employees from OSHA regulations.[8] By 1977 public opinion polls found that OSHA had earned the title of most "hated" federal bureaucracy, although the agency had reported in 1975 that it had so few inspectors that it could inspect every workplace in America only once every 66 years.[9]

Since enforcement actions are based on OSHA health and safety standards, criticisms and complaints are eventually directed at those agency actions. Standards have been usually depicted as being either too "nit-picking" and marginally important or too expensive given the cost incurred. In 1971, Labor Secretary James Hodgson proudly proclaimed that OSHA regulations were "both comprehensive and comprehensible."[10] Less than one year later, the secretary reported that the agency was involved in a major effort to revise its safety standards. Some clearly useless or out-of-date regulations were deleted, but no comprehensive changes were made; most of the safety standards currently in effect were formulated before 1971.[11]

It was not until 1977 that OSHA began to review its safety standards and, after a lengthy effort led by Labor Secretary Ray Marshall and President

Carter, hundreds were revoked. In a speech given in 1978 Carter proclaimed: "We are beginning to eliminate the worst nit-picking regulations in agencies . . . like OSHA. In one day last year, 1,100 different regulations were wiped off the books."[12] In reality, however, OSHA had only announced its intention to revoke those regulations, since the process used to delete rules is the same as that for issuing new ones. Labor groups subsequently wanted to make sure that their members were not being forced to give up things they wanted, although OSHA inspectors were ordered not to enforce standards slated for revocation. Secretary Marshall, in a press conference, confided that: "The project has taught me an important and sobering lesson. . . . I discovered that the system makes it much easier for the government to promulgate new regulations than to get rid of outmoded or ineffective ones. Things are not impossible, however. Our efforts today indicate that with enough determination and creativity it is possible to beat the system."[13] Marshall's quote nicely demonstrates the tension between administrative procedures and political efforts to control bureaucratic discretion.

THE RULE-MAKING PROCESS AT OSHA: STATUTORY PROVISIONS

The Occupational Safety and Health Act outlines the process by which OSHA is to issue safety and health standards.[14] The process begins in response to petitions from individuals or groups, standard-setting organizations, NIOSH studies, requests from state or local officials, or information that otherwise comes to the attention of the agency. If the agency determines that a rule should be considered, it may appoint an advisory committee to review the proposed rule. Although an optional step, an advisory committee is routinely appointed for rule-making proceedings. Advisory committees are comprised of not more than 15 people, including at least one person appointed by the secretary of the Department of Health and Human Services, an equal number of individuals representing employers and employees, one or more representatives of state and local health and safety agencies, and others from related technical or professional areas or from standard-setting groups. The recommendations of the advisory committee are not binding upon the agency.[15]

The second step mandated by law includes publication of a proposed rule in the *Federal Register*, inviting any party to submit written comments within 30 days. Any person can request during this 30-day period that an oral hearing be held to discuss disputed issues. The hearing must be scheduled within 30 days of the close of the public comment period. Within 60 days of the completion of the above steps, the agency must either issue a rule or determine that none is needed. Employers may apply for a temporary order granting a variance from a standard if they meet certain conditions. Any person "who may be adversely affected by a standard" may file a petition challenging the action in a federal court of appeals for the circuit in which the person resides or conducts business. The reviewing court is to uphold the standard "if supported by substantial evidence in the record as a whole."[16]

Congress defined the goals of occupational safety and health standards to be those "reasonably necessary or appropriate to provide safe or healthful employment or places of employment."[17] Congress ordered that when standards for "toxic materials or harmful physical agents" were being considered, the Secretary of Labor

> shall set the standard which most adequately assures, to the extent feasible, on the basis of the best available evidence, that no employee will suffer material impairment of health or functional capacity even if such employee has regular exposure to the hazard dealt with by such standard for the period of his working life. . . . In addition to the attainment of the highest degree of health and safety protection for the employee, other considerations shall be the latest available scientific data in the field, the feasibility of the standards, and experience gained under this and other health and safety laws. Whenever practicable, the standard promulgated shall be expressed in terms of objective criteria and of the performance desired.[18]

OSHA Rule Making: Agency Procedures

OSHA's standard-setting process is organized around several different kinds of operating offices. The Health Standards and Safety Standards programs provide technical expertise in evaluating occupational safety and health problems and in developing standards. The health standards program focuses on the development of regulations for toxic substances and carcinogens; the safety standards program is divided into construction and civil engineering, electrical engineering, fire prevention, and maritime units. Two offices focus on reviews and evaluations of the agency's regulatory activities. The Office of Policy, Legislation and Interagency Programs coordinates OSHA activities with those of other agencies, and monitors OMB and congressional reviews of agency actions. The Technical Support Office conducts analyses of the costs and benefits of proposed standards and provides assistance in evaluating toxic substances and other workplace hazards.[19] Figure 6.1 describes the overall organization of OSHA.

Rule-making efforts revolve around project teams created for each proposed rule, directed by a representative of either the Health or the Safety Standards Offices and staffed by scientists, lawyers, and economists from agency offices. The project team is responsible for a proposed regulation from its initial formulation to its final publication in the *Federal Register*. Proposed health standards are usually based on a NIOSH criteria document which provides a review of the relevant scientific literature and provides recommendations for actions. Some proposals are based on information included in petitions submitted by private parties seeking OSHA action.[20] An

Figure 6.1. The Occupational Safety and Health Administration

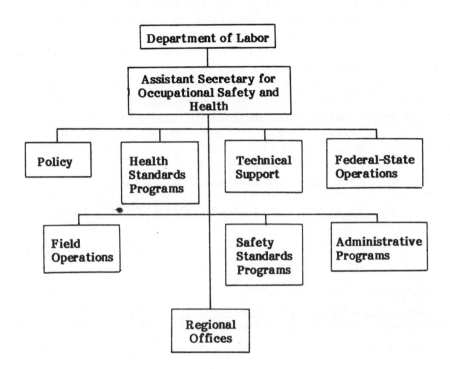

Source: Adapted from Congressional Quarterly, Federal Regulatory Directory, 5th ed. (Washington DC: Congressional Quarterly, 1986), p. 423.

advisory committee is usually appointed which meets informally to discuss the proposal, invites participation by other interested parties, and prepares a report providing recommendations for OSHA action. The project team then develops a proposed standard and publishes a notice of proposed rule making in the *Federal Register*. Comments are received by interested parties, and public hearings are held, conducted by an administrative law judge. OSHA officials, trade association representatives, employers, union officials, victims of occupational accidents and illnesses, manufacturers of safety devices, and members of public interest groups might be among the participants in a typical hearing. Protests and demonstrations have also been organized as part of the proceedings.

The hearings themselves are dominated by the legal staff of OSHA, industry and union representatives, who cross-examine witnesses and submit briefs. Hearings may last several weeks as a result of lengthy cross-examinations. Oral testimony is usually supplemented by extensive reports, and additional comments are received after the hearings. The project team then prepares the final standard, along with an explanation of each provision, and a response to objections raised against them in the public comment period.

Internal and External Review of OSHA Standards

The project team functions within a political environment that closely monitors its proposals for safety and health standards. An internal review mechanism and external executive, congressional and judicial oversight are all important elements of the rule-making process. Table 6.1 outlines the standard-setting process in OSHA.

Table 6.1. Steps in OSHA's Rule-Making Process

Action	Officials Responsible	
	Preparation	Review
Identify possible standards	Staff	Regulation Review Committee (RRC) Assistant Secretary (AS)
Preliminary research and analysis plan	Program Staff	RRC, AS
Formation of Preliminary Project Team	RRC	
Research and analysis plan	Preliminary Project	RRC, AS
Part I of assistant secretary's summary	Team	
Concept analysis paper	Preliminary Project Team	RRC, AS, Under Secretary of Labor's Review Panel
Formation of Regulation Team	Program Director	
Workplan	Regulation Team	RRC, AS
Part II of assistant secretary's summary		
Advanced notice of proposed rule making	Regulation Team	RRC, AS
Formation of Advisory Committee	Program Director	
Advisory Committee recommendations	Advisory Committee	
Notice of proposed rule package Regulatory impact analysis Regulatory flexibility analysis Paperwork reduction analysis Environmental impact statement Preliminary implementation plan Preliminary evaluation plan Options memorandum	Regulation Team	RRC, AS, Under Secretary's Review Panel, OMB
Public comment period	Regulation Team	
Public hearing	Administrative Judge	
Final rule package same as proposed rules	Regulation Team	Same as proposed rules
Final rule published in *Federal Register*	Solicitor's Office	

Adapted from Thorne Auchter, "OSHA Instruction RUL.1" (1 March 1982).

Within OSHA, the standard-setting process involves three levels of agency administration. The head of OSHA, the assistant secretary of labor for occupational safety and health, establishes priorities and objectives, allocates resources among projects, reviews and approves economic and technical analyses, and clears OSHA documents with the Department of Labor and with the OMB. The second level of agency officials in the standards-development process is the regulation review committee, comprised of a permanent executive committee and various officials who join the committee for agency actions relevant to their areas of expertise. The regulation review committee determines when a project team, the third level of administrative activity, is to be created; monitors the development of the standard; and supervises the preparation of a preliminary research and analysis plan.

OSHA regulations are ultimately the responsibility of the Secretary of Labor. The review process within the Department of Labor involves four offices. The Office of the Assistant Secretary for Policy, Evaluation and Research (ASPER) reviews the economic analyses accompanying proposed standards, and the Office of the Assistant Secretary for Administration and Management reviews the required paperwork, both in anticipation of OMB's review. The Under Secretary's Review Panel, comprised of the under secretary, the solicitor, the ASPER and a representative of the secretary, reviews all proposed and final standards, which must then be approved by the Secretary of Labor.[21]

In 1981, OSHA began sending all proposed and final regulations to the Office of Management and Budget for review. Beginning in 1985, it also began submitting to OMB's Office of Information and Regulatory Affairs a regulatory program, listing the standards OSHA plans to issue in the subsequent year. No standards can be issued that are not cleared through this process. Virtually every major standard issued by OSHA is then challenged by the federal courts, either by industry groups who find them too burdensome, labor groups who argue that they are too weak, and sometimes by both groups.[22]

Criteria for OSHA Health Standards

Five basic principles guide OSHA decision making for health standards. First, it must be clearly shown that proposed standards address a significant risk and that they are "reasonably necessary and appropriate to substantially reduce" the risk involved. Second, alternative approaches to reducing the risks, including nonregulatory options, must be considered. Third, standards must be shown to be both "technically and economically feasible on an industry-by-industry basis to the extent practicable." Fourth, the public must have an opportunity to participate in the process and those who are likely to be affected by the standards must be requested to submit information concerning the risks, feasibility, and cost-effectiveness involved. This information must be considered fully when developing standards. Fifth, and perhaps most important, the most "cost-effective" alternative must be selected.[23]

A number of documents, prepared during the standard-setting process, provide the framework for the economic and scientific analysis on which the standards are based. The research and analysis plan prepared by the regulation team is an "outline of the facts to be documented and the analyses to be made to justify a standard." It is designed to serve as a framework for an in-depth analysis of the risks involved and the evaluation of alternative agency actions, and describes the hazards involved, the extent of human exposure, a comparison of the risks involved with other hazards regulated by OSHA and by other agencies, the data available which document the risks, the antici-pated economic and technical impact on industry, factors which influence the level of risk (e.g., inadequate training, carelessness and poor equipment), a discussion of alternative strategies from voluntary techniques, such as educa-tion and training programs, to regulatory options (e.g., performance or design standards), and a discussion of the factual, legal, and overriding pol-icy issues that must be addressed.[24]

A related document, entitled "Part I of the Assistant Secretary's Sum-mary," is also prepared. It includes a description of the extent and severity of the hazard involved; the major legal, policy and factual issues to be addressed; possible agency actions, including the alternative most likely to be recommended; events leading up to the initiation of action by OSHA; and a discussion of the views of interested groups concerning the issues, including the White House, OMB, and the vice president's regulatory reform task force, other agencies, state and local government, Congress, labor, business, and public interest groups. The plan and summary are reviewed and approved by the regulation review committee and the head of OSHA. A con-cept analysis paper, an abbreviated version of the two documents described above, is then prepared to inform other offices in the Department of Labor of OSHA's regulatory initiatives.[25]

The Regulation Team next prepares a workplan and part 2 of the assistant secretary's summary, which are reviewed and approved by the Regulation Review Committee and by the assistant secretary. The workplan establishes deadlines for the actions required in the development of the standard, and schedules outreach efforts aimed at labor, industry and other groups. Part 2 of the assistant secretary's summary outlines the deadlines for completing the analyses and reviews required.

The assistant secretary may at this point order the Regulation Team to pre-pare an advanced notice of proposed rule making and a memorandum outlin-ing agency options. Legal issues raised by the proposed action are included here or may be included in a separate legal memorandum. These materials also pass through the review process described above. The standards director supervising the regulation team may also decide to form an Advisory Committee and directs the regulation team to prepare a decision document and a workplan which outlines the committee's responsibilities and issues it is to consider. The advisory committee is appointed by the assistant secretary, as outlined in the OSH Act. The decision document must be approved by the regulation review committee and by the assistant secretary; the workplan must be reviewed by the General Services Administration as required by the Federal Advisory Committee Act. The advisory committee eventually submits its recommendations to the project team, although they are not binding on the agency.[26]

The team then prepares a risk analysis which documents the significance of risk and the occupational situations involved, and examines feasible alternatives and their comparative cost-effectiveness. An action recommendation, based on these two analyses, is then prepared and submitted to the regulation review committee, the assistant secretary, and, in some cases, the under secretary of Labor.

The final phase of the rule-making process begins as the Regulation Team prepares a notice of proposed rule making, which, under various executive orders and statutes, includes a regulatory impact analysis, regulatory flexibility analysis, paperwork reduction analysis and an environmental impact statement. Other documentation required by the agency itself includes preliminary implementation and preliminary evaluation plans and an options memorandum. The NPRM is reviewed by Information and Consumer Affairs, the State Programs offices, and both internal and external experts. The entire proposed rule-making package is submitted to the regulation review committee, the assistant secretary, the under secretary's review panel and then the OMB. Once approved, it is published in the *Federal Register*.[27]

Economic Analysis in OSHA Rule Making

Economic and technical analyses have not been given high priority in OSHA standard-setting efforts until recently. The Reagan administration's emphasis on cost-benefit analysis, as translated by OSHA into cost-effectiveness analysis, has stimulated efforts to establish criteria for the agency's economic and technical analyses. The agency has begun to develop some guidelines for risk assessment and cost-effectiveness analysis, and, while only preliminary efforts, they demonstrate the kinds of criteria OSHA is likely to consider in developing standards. Thorne Auchter, OSHA administration between 1981 and 1984, outlined four broad considerations in issuing OSHA standards: "First, we make sure, as the Supreme Court directed in its decision on OSHA's benzene standard, that the substance we want to regulate poses a "significant risk" to workers. Then we verify that the rule we have in mind would substantially reduce that risk. Next we look at the best available data to set the most protective exposure limit that is both technologically and economically feasible. Finally, we figure out the most cost-effective means for employers to meet that level.'' Auchter argued that cost-benefit analysis was never expected to be the basis for establishing OSHA's safety and health standards, but only one factor to be considered. Thus, the Supreme Court's decision in 1981 that OSHA was not required to provide a cost–benefit analysis for the standards it issues would not require the agency to modify its goals.[28]

OSHA's occupational noise exposure standard, issued as a final rule in January 1981, required employers to provide hearing conservation programs for all employees exposed to 85 decibels or more during an eight-hour period, to include noise exposure monitoring, training, protective devices and record keeping.[29] In August, OSHA issued a regulatory impact analysis for the rule, in accordance with Executive Order 12291, which included an analysis of the costs and benefits involved.[30] OSHA's Office of Regulatory Analysis has described this analysis as "representative of the kind of economic analyses OSHA will be involved in in the foreseeable future"[31] and provides a useful example of how economic criteria are integrated into OSHA decision making.

The economic analyses of the hearing conservation rule were based on the projected costs for the six elements of the program required of employers— monitoring, audiometric testing, provision of hearing protectors, training, posting of warning signs, and record keeping—for firms in each of five groups, based on the number of production workers: 1–19, 20–49, 50–99, 100–249, and 250 + . The different-sized firms were assumed to incur different costs per employee. Firms with less than 250 employees, for example, were expected to use consultants to conduct monitoring activities, while establishments with more than 250 employees were expected to purchase equipment and provide their own monitoring.

The regulations, however, permitted employers to use whatever monitoring technique they wished, assuming it satisfied the monitoring requirements. Rental and purchase prices of measuring equipment and the salaries of employees conducting the testing were then calculated, assuming that up to 50 workers could be surveyed by monitoring a work area, and that employees would be monitored every two years. OSHA estimated that 5.1 million workers were exposed to more than 85 decibels of noise; the estimated costs of audiometric testing, when multiplied by the number of workers in each of the categories of firm sizes, yielded an annual cost of $76 million. The costs of hearing protectors for all employees exposed to over 90 decibels was estimated at $10 per employee, resulting in an annual cost of $45.5 million. Training costs were estimated at $20 million per year, based on one-half hour of training per employee each year. The requirement of posting warning signs was stayed pending further study. Record-keeping costs were estimated at $6 million. The total cost of compliance was estimated to be $170.6 million.[32]

The next element of the regulatory analysis sought to demonstrate, in response to the Supreme Court's 1980 and 1981 reviews of OSHA actions, that the hazard regulated posed a "significant risk" to workers, that the implementation of the regulation would significantly reduce the risk, and that the regulations were economically and technologically feasible. In arguing that noise was a significant workplace hazard, OSHA relied on a number of studies of the effects of noise on hearing summarized and presented to OSHA by NIOSH as well as on testimony from workers and labor leaders. OSHA projected that implementation of the noise conservation program would reduce the number of workers who were likely to suffer material impairment of hearing (in the absence of a program) from 1,060,000 to 162,000 workers. These figures were based on four studies, prepared for OSHA by consulting firms, which estimated the number of hearing impairments likely to occur under various regulatory approaches. Although the estimates provided by these consultants were criticized in public hearings and in post-hearing comments, no one submitted alternative figures, thus leading OSHA to accept the calculations. Other benefits projected, but not quantified, included reduced absenteeism, improved worker safety, and reduced medical costs.

Technological feasibility posed no problem, since the kinds of equipment needed were readily available. Economic feasibility was also defended since the total cost of the standard, if passed on to consumers in price increases, would only increase prices by 0.0148 percent. If firms absorbed the cost, that would represent only 0.1932 percent of profits. In determining the cost-effectiveness of the program, OSHA used discounting to evaluate health effects and costs occurring at different time intervals. At a discount rate of 10 percent, as recommended by OMB, OSHA calculated that it would cost $7,620 to maintain a lifetime of adequate hearing for a worker who would otherwise suffer hearing impairment.[33]

The hearing conservation program is particularly amenable to regulatory analysis, since the calculations of the costs are relatively straightforward and the risks involved are well recognized. The effect of workplace noise on hearing capability has been widely recognized and regulation is not likely to force many businesses to close operations. Industry concerns focused on costs and technical feasibility of implementing various elements of the programs, but did not offer alternative figures to those used by OSHA. The regulatory analysis does demonstrate an effort by OSHA to describe and, when possible, quantify the costs involved in complying with a regulation. More difficult than describing the costs, however, is gauging the extent to which the proposed regulation reduces the risks involved. Again, the calculation in the above case was quite straightforward, given a general level of confidence in the scientific information available. In other areas, such as carcinogens, the risk assessment underlying OSHA's regulatory analyses has been much more problematic.

Risk Assessment in OSHA Rule Making

In January 1980, OSHA issued a carcinogen policy which outlined the criteria to be used by the agency for identifying and regulating occupational carcinogens.[34] The policy did not seek to regulate any specific substances, but provided a procedural framework for subsequent regulations of carcinogens as well as technical and scientific guidelines for the analyses involved. The policy was immediately challenged in court by several groups, and in January 1982, OSHA announced that it was reevaluating the policy and was considering changes to assure its consistency with recent Supreme Court decisions, to consider more cost-effective approaches, and to comply with the requirements of Executive Order 12291. OSHA has indicated that revision of its cancer policy is included in its regulatory plan for the 1986–87 year.

While the agency's overall risk assessment approach is still uncertain, OSHA has regulated several carcinogens under the Reagan administration. The risk assessment it provided for in its proposed standard for arsenic gives some idea of the way in which scientific analysis is incorporated into the standard-setting process. In 1971, OSHA adopted an already existing standard for exposure to arsenic in the workplace, and then began reviewing the standard after a 1973 NIOSH study found significant evidence that occupational exposure to arsenic caused cancer. In 1978 a final standard was issued, sharply reducing the permissible exposure level permitted under the original standard. The standard was immediately challenged in several appeals courts, and the cases were eventually consolidated in the Ninth Circuit. The court remanded the case to OSHA for reconsideration in light of the benzene decision, since the arsenic rule did not include any estimates of the degree of risk at low levels of exposure.[35]

In reopening the rule-making process in April of 1982, OSHA prepared a preliminary risk analysis. OSHA's interpretation of the Supreme Court's benzene decision found four principles to guide its regulatory efforts to reduce risk:

1. Before issuing a standard, OSHA must "make a threshold finding that a place of employment is unsafe—in the sense that significant risks are present and can be eliminated or lessened."
2. OSHA's power to reduce workplace risks was limited to "requiring the elimination of significant risks."
3. Mathematical estimates used in risk assessments were appropriate means of demonstrating significant risk since the agency was "not required to support its finding that a significant risk exists with anything approaching

scientific certainty," and OSHA was to be given "some leeway where its findings must be made on the frontiers of scientific knowledge."

4. OSHA was to be free "to use conservative assumptions in interpreting the data with respect to carcinogens, risking error on the side of over-protection rather than under-protection."[36]

The preliminary risk analysis for arsenic was based on three studies, conducted between 1969 and 1974, of workers at copper smelter and chemical plants, and three risk assessments prepared by consultants, including the EPA's Cancer Assessment Group. The studies concluded that a standard limiting exposure to inorganic arsenic of 10 micrograms per cubic meter ($\mu g/m^3$) would "significantly reduce" health risks. The studies projected that at levels of exposure near the original 1981 standard of 500 $\mu g/m^3$ level there was a risk of from 334 to 425 additional cases of cancer for each 1,000 employees exposed, while at the proposed standard of 10 $\mu g/m^3$ only 7 to 10 additional cases of cancer per 1,000 employees exposed were projected. This level of risk was below that of high-risk occupations, calculated by the Bureau of Labor Statistics to range as high as 27.45 deaths per 1,000 employees, and above the risk in manufacturing occupations of average risk of 2.7 deaths per 1,000 employees.[37]

The studies themselves were based on epidemiological studies of workers who had contracted respiratory cancer. The data developed demonstrated the dose–response relationship at high levels of exposure, and then extrapolated the relationship for exposure levels below those directly observed by assuming a linear relationship. The risk assessments based on these epidemiological studies cited them as being "exceptionally" well done, and appropriate for the analysis upon which they were based. OSHA rejected the risk assessment based on one of the three epidemiological studies, since the quality of its data was considered inferior to those of the two other studies, even though it would have led to higher estimates of risk; the agency also rejected the high-side estimates of one of the risk assessments. OSHA defended its standard for arsenic on the following grounds: (1) the underlying data was of high quality, (2) the risk assessment was based on epidemiological studies of workers actually exposed to arsenic while working, and (3) evidence from the statistical significance of the dose–response and other relationships calculated, the seriousness of the risk involved, and the significance of the risk predicted that proposed action would significantly reduce risk.[38]

Political and Legal Oversight of OSHA Rules

The two Supreme Court cases—benzene and cotton dust (see p. 134)—have required that the agency engage in risk assessment, while affirming the agency's long-held view that it was not required to demonstrate that benefits of proposed rules exceed costs. In rejecting OSHA's benzene standard, the Court interpreted the OSH Act's requirement that standards be "reasonably necessary or appropriate to provide safe or healthful employment and places of employment" to require first that the agency "make a finding that the workplace in question is not safe. But 'safe' is not the equivalent of 'risk-free' . . . a workplace can hardly be considered 'unsafe' unless it threatens the workers with a significant risk of harm." OSHA, then, was required, for each standard, to "make a threshold finding that a place of employment is unsafe—in the sense that significant risks are present and can be eliminated or lessened by a change in practice."[39]

In the cotton dust decision, the Court prohibited the agency from issuing a standard "based on a balancing of costs and benefits . . . that strikes a different balance than that struck by Congress." The court concluded that "Congress itself defined the basic relationship between costs and benefits, by placing the 'benefit' of worker health above all other considerations save those making the attainment of the 'benefit' unachievable."[40]

OMB review of OSHA's proposed and final standards have also had an important impact on several standards. At least four of its proposed and final rules have been rewritten in response to OMB criticisms. In its final standard for ethylene oxide, for example, OSHA removed the short term exposure limit (STEL) from the regulation after OMB criticized it, simply scratching it out by hand in the material sent to the *Federal Register* for publication. The standard was challenged and the Court of Appeals for the District of Columbia rejected OSHA's deletion of the STEL as unjustified, given the rule-making record, but did not rule on the question of the legality and constitutionality of the OMB review, which had been raised by the plaintiffs.[41]

More important than OMB's review process itself is the commitment of OSHA heads to the administration's regulatory relief efforts, thus making conflicts between OSHA and the White House less likely. In two cases, however, OSHA and OMB officials squared off in a battle that was ultimately resolved by the vice president's task force on regulatory relief in favor of OSHA. OSHA had proposed, during the final days of the Carter administration, a standard which required labels on toxic-chemical containers indicating the contents, hazards involved, symptoms of overexposure, and measures to limit exposure. When the Reagan administration assumed office, the proposal was included in the freeze on "midnight" regulations, and a weaker proposal was eventually proposed. OSHA estimated that the revised rule would cost industry $582 million initially and $228 million annually, rather than the $2.6 billion initial cost and $1.25 billion annual costs projected under the Carter proposal, and that 4,000 cancer deaths would be avoided each year.

OMB officials branded as "wildly optimistic" OSHA's estimate of cancers that would be avoided, countering with a figure only one-tenth of the 4,000 estimate. The officials attacked the effectiveness of labels in general, claimed that there was no evidence that labeling would increase safety, and argued that OSHA had "no effect" on workplace health and safety. The proposal was rejected by OMB since the prevention of 400 cancers did not justify such a "highly prescriptive" regulation.[42]

The Department of Labor warned the White House that a failure to issue the rule would present serious political problems in giving labor "a cudgel with which to beat this Administration." The department hired an independent economist to study the proposed rule. His report, finding the proposal a "clear demonstration of benefits far exceeding costs," was received by the White House staff on March 16. A congressional subcommittee had scheduled hearings on OMB's actions for March 18 and 19. Chemical manufacturers, who had opposed the Carter version, joined the painters' union in lobbying for the proposal, as business groups preferred one national standard over the 50 or more likely under state and local laws. All of these factors came together on March 17, when the White House suddenly authorized OSHA to publish the rule.[43] OSHA's victory was short-lived, however, as a federal court of appeals in 1985 remanded the rule to the agency for further development.[44]

OSHA's experience with OMB review demonstrates that there is some tension among Reagan appointees concerning regulatory initiatives. OMB's primary concern appeared to be the fact that the labeling proposal would be the first substantial new regulatory burden imposed by the Reagan administration. OSHA was primarily concerned about adverse labor reaction to not issuing the proposal as well as the expected benefits of the rule itself. In the end, the apparent impact of the OMB review was limited to delay of the rule-making process by four months.

The threat of congressional hearings was an uncertain factor in the decision. The hearings were held, attended only by Representative Collins, chair of Government Operations' Manpower and Housing Subcommittee, who has shown a general interest in the role of OMB's review in the rule-making process. Congress as a whole has not played a major role in OSHA's rule-making efforts, concentrating instead on the enforcement actions of the agency. OMB intervention in OSHA rule making has raised the ire of members of Congress, however. In June 1985, the chairmen of five congressional committees joined with public interest and labor groups in a suit challenging the last-minute intervention of OMB officials in the ethylene oxide rule. The members of Congress charged the OMB with "systematic usurpation of legislative power" and with a violation of the constitutional prerogatives of Congress to delegate rule-making power to administrative agencies.[45]

THE COTTON DUST STANDARD: A CASE STUDY OF OSHA RULE MAKING

Between 250,000 and 800,000 workers in the United States are exposed each year to cotton dust and the risk of contracting byssinosis, or brown lung, a debilitating respiratory disease that can be fatal.[46] Cotton dust is produced throughout the processing of cotton and the manufacturing of cloth and other products. Almost 15 percent of the production workers in the cotton industry suffer from brown lung disease in some stage. Victims of brown lung suffer from shortness of breath, wheezing and coughing. In its final stage it becomes irreversible, disabling workers and leading to death through infection, breathing failure, or heart attacks from strain caused by the impaired lungs.[47]

The federal government first began regulating worker exposure to cotton dust in 1965 under the Walsh-Healey Public Contracts Act, setting an exposure limit of 500 micrograms per cubic meter ($\mu g/m^3$) of respirable dust. It was not until 1976, however, that OSHA issued its own proposed standard, based on a review of NIOSH and other studies, requiring that exposure be reduced from 500 $\mu g/m^3$ to 200 $\mu g/m^3$ in seven years. The proposal required that employers install air-cleaning equipment and that employees be given respirators until exposure levels were reduced. OSHA estimated the initial cost of compliance to be $2.7 billion initially and $810 million in annual costs.[48]

After extensive hearings and reviews, OSHA issued a final rule in 1978 which set different levels of exposure for different workplaces from 200 $\mu g/m^3$ to 750 $\mu g/m^3$—depending on the prevalence of byssinosis—which reduced the annual compliance costs to $200 million. An acrimonious battle, between OSHA and the AFL-CIO on one side and White House economic advisers on the other, eventually resulted in the personal intervention of President Carter.[49] The American Textile Manufacturers Institute and other industry groups immediately challenged the rule in court, and were eventually joined by the AFL-CIO, which found the standard too weak. The standard was upheld by the Court of Appeals for the District of Columbia in 1979. In March 1981, under the Reagan administration, OSHA asked the Supreme Court to defer a decision on the case pending an agency reconsideration of the issues; the Court ignored the request and upheld the standard in June 1981. The head of OSHA subsequently announced that the rule would be reviewed anyway as part of the agency's regulatory relief efforts. Some changes were eventually proposed by the agency but rejected by OMB as too expensive. After a five-month dispute, administration officials overruled OMB and accepted the OSHA position, which still eased some of the provisions of the cotton dust standard.[50]

Three elements of the rule-making process for the cotton dust standard deserve attention here: the analysis of the economic and scientific issues conducted by OSHA, the role of White House officials in the formulation of the final rule, and the decision of the Supreme Court and its impact on the agency.

Economic and Scientific Analyses of Cotton Dust Hazards

For more than one hundred years, epidemiological studies from throughout the world have demonstrated a close relationship between respirable cotton dust and byssinosis. The disease progresses from an initial reversible, acute stage of chest tightness and minor irritation to a permanent, chronic condition similar to chronic bronchitis or emphysema. Several studies have examined differences in risk of byssinosis between smokers and nonsmokers; one recent study concluded that nonsmokers and ex-smokers were unlikely to contract chronic, disabling byssinosis when exposed to normal workplace levels of cotton dust.[51]

In issuing its cotton dust standard, OSHA found that inhalation of cotton dust was clearly associated with some form of respiratory disease, but there were widely varying definitions of disease. It was also unclear whether different sizes of particles posed different levels of risk. Despite these problems, the dose–response relationship that was calculated, based on epidemiological studies, indicated that exposure to even very low levels ($50-60 \mu g/m^3$—a level only slightly higher than background dust in rural areas) was likely to cause early stages of byssinosis. As a result, the agency decided that the standard should reflect the lowest level of exposure that could be achieved.[52]

The cotton-processing industry was financially strapped, burdened with old buildings and equipment, competitively weak, and had recently been required to reduce noise levels in its factories. Not only were there questions about the feasibility of engineering controls, but it was feared that high regulatory costs would cripple the industry. Compliance costs were limited by two decisions made after meetings with union and management groups. First, compliance would be based on engineering controls, phased in gradually over a seven-year period. In the interim, workers would wear respirators and be closely monitored. Second, since the studies OSHA relied on found different levels of risk for different stages of manufacturing processes, three sets of standards were developed for the various stages. The agency also concluded that the standard could be met with existing technology.[53]

In considering the economic feasibility, OSHA expressly avoided a cost-benefit analysis. In its preamble to the standard, the agency found that "the costs of compliance are not overly burdensome to industry. Having determined that the benefits of the proposed standard are likely to be appreciable,

OSHA is not obligated to carry out further exercises toward more precise calculations of benefit which would not significantly clarify the ultimate decision."[54] The cost of engineering controls was estimated at $42,767 for each case of brown lung avoided, compared to $555 for monitoring and respirators. For workers in the cotton-ginning industry, the less expensive approach was ordered. The agency has generally ruled that personal protective devices are to be used as a last resort, preferring instead engineering controls. While some argue that such an approach is favored because OSHA can more easily monitor levels of dust than it can the wearing of protective devices, others argue that the OSH Act only provides for regulations aimed at the workplace environment, not at worker behavior.[55]

In 1979 OSHA submitted to Congress a study on the cost-effectiveness of the cotton dust standard and its alternatives. Congress had requested the report in order to encourage OSHA to consider alternatives that would be less costly, more technologically feasible, and have minimum impact on the international competitive position of the U.S. cotton and textile industries. The report argued that in providing different standards for different sectors of cotton processing, OSHA could provide all workers with "essentially the same health protection, but at substantial cost savings." The agency, however, rejected the use of personal protective devices—in this case respirators—since wearing them was described as "fatiguing, uncomfortable, and stressful, especially in a hot, humid textile mill" and they were especially unsuitable for workers already suffering from respiratory problems.[56]

OSHA emphasized the cost-effectiveness of its final standard by comparing its reduced costs with the much higher costs of the proposed standard published in 1976 (which set an exposure level of 200 $\mu g/m^3$ for all workers), rather than by analyzing the standard itself. The agency concluded that 23,490 cases of byssinosis would be prevented at a cost of from $7,540 to $8,658 per case. It attacked industry estimates of compliance as overstated for several reasons, and identified a savings of $100,852 in brown lung disability payments for each case prevented. A number of nonquantifiable benefits such as reduced pain, suffering, and death, as well as other financial benefits such as reduced worker absenteeism and turnover, were identified but not discussed in detail.[57]

In terms of the impact of compliance costs on inflation, OSHA calculated that cotton products would increase in price by 1 percent, yielding a 0.074 percent increase in the Consumer Price Index. This, however, would be a one-time increase only. Some 1,256 jobs were expected to be lost due to higher production costs and lower output, although new ones would be created in firms manufacturing and installing control equipment. Finally, while the standard was expected to increase cotton textile imports by 1.3 to 1.7 percent and reduce exports by 1.7 percent, OSHA concluded that the industry was "well protected by import quotas and tariffs" and the impact would "probably be even smaller."[58]

The key element of the standard was the setting of the exposure levels. OSHA assumed a linear dose-response relationship, based on existing studies, assuming that no threshold level existed. The actual exposure levels set were based on existing epidemiological studies, including those done by NIOSH, and would bring the risks in the cotton production industry in line with those of other industries. Medical criteria appeared to be the decisive factor in setting the initial level, although financial considerations were also important. The Amalgamated Clothing and Textile Workers Union sought a 100 $\mu g/m^3$ level, but OSHA estimates concluded that the costs of that standard would be $6.5 billion initially and $1.9 billion in annual costs.[59]

Oral and written testimony submitted to OSHA, after the proposed rule was published, apparently convinced the agency that the same general level of protection could be provided for all workers by varying the standard for different elements of the manufacturing process, since the disease occurs at different rates for workers in those different elements. This reduced initial compliance costs from $2.7 billion to $655.1 million, and annual costs from $808.3 million to $205 million, while reducing the number of projected cases of prevented byssinosis from 28,750 to 23,490.[60]

Presidential Review of the Cotton Dust Standard

Despite OSHA's enthusiastic defense of its cotton dust standard, economic advisors to President Carter found the rules running counter to the president's inflation-fighting priorities. The costs projected in the economic impact statement accompanying the proposed cotton dust standard had already alerted the White House, and just before the final rule was issued, OSHA discussed the regulation with the Council on Wage and Price Stability. The CWPS then prepared an informal memorandum criticizing the proposed standard and requesting that it not be issued until further study could be conducted. The CWPS evaluation argued that the standard requiring engineering controls, which required the installation of ventilation equipment, was less cost-effective than "performance standards," which might include the use of respirators or increased monitoring by medical personnel.[61]

OSHA argued in response that performance standards were difficult to enforce, since agency inspectors could monitor plants to see that equipment was installed but could not assure that protective devices were used. Battle lines were eventually drawn within the Carter administration. Charles Schultze, chairman of the Council of Economic Advisers and the head of the administration's regulatory oversight effort, asked the Secretary of Labor to postpone issuing the standard. Rejected there, Schultze then met with the president, who agreed to relax the standards as recommended in the CWPS memorandum. The Secretary of Labor, upon learning of the Carter decision, met with the president and convinced him to change his mind. The rule was then issued, with one modification—a four-year lead time provision to soften the rule's economic effects.[62]

The president's decision was widely attacked by industry, which felt the standard was too expensive, and labor, which viewed it as too weak, and criticism was focused on the president himself and his role as mediator.[63] Congress eventually intervened in the course of reviewing OSHA's appropriations bill, but its only action was to require the agency to provide Congress with a study of costs and technical feasibility for the cotton dust standard. This report concluded that the proposed rule indeed represented the most cost-effective alternative, and congressional interest faded.[64]

While President Carter never indicated the reasons for his decision in the cotton dust controversy, one observer surmised that the technical and political understanding of the proposed rule by the Secretary of Labor was more convincing than the limited economic arguments offered by the CWPS.[65] In any event, the action shifted to the judicial branch: Labor groups challenged the weakness of the rule as well as the intervention in the rule-making process of the White House, while industry groups challenged the standards as too stringent.

The Supreme Court and the Cotton Dust Standard

In its challenge to the cotton dust standard, the cotton industry argued that OSHA failed to demonstrate that there was a reasonable relationship between the costs and benefits of the standard and that the agency did not show that the standard was economically feasible. The Supreme Court ruled, in a 5–3 decision, that OSHA was not required to provide a cost-benefit analysis in issuing regulations.

Writing for the majority, Justice Brennan argued that OSHA standards were to assure that

> "no employee will suffer material impairment of health," limited only by the extent to which this is "capable of being done." In effect then . . . Congress itself defined the basic relationship between costs and benefits, by placing the "benefit" of worker health above all other considerations save those making attainment of this "benefit" unachievable. Any standard based on a balancing of costs and benefits by the Secretary that strikes a different balance than that struck by Congress would be inconsistent with the command set forth in [the Occupational Safety and Health Act].[66]

Brennan's argument relied on his reading of legislative history, which he found provided no "indication whatsoever that Congress intended OSHA to conduct its own cost-benefit analysis before promulgating a . . . standard." In many other statutes, he argued, Congress had expressly provided for cost-benefit analysis. Brennan reviewed the studies used by OSHA in calculating the projected compliance costs and found that since nothing in those studies "indicates that the cotton textile industry as a whole [would] be seriously threatened . . . OSHA's estimated compliance cost of $656.6 million is 'economically feasible.' "[67]

The three dissenters disagreed with their brethren for different reasons. Justice Stewart found that the rule-making record included no "substantial evidence" supporting the standard, that it was based on "unsupported speculation."[68] Justice Rehnquist and Chief Justice Burger reiterated the Rehnquist dissent in the benzene case that the OSH Act was an unconstitutional delegation of power to the executive branch to make the " 'hard policy choices' properly the task of the legislature." Instead of making those hard choices, Congress used words like "feasibility," which Rehnquist characterized as a "legislative mirage, appearing to some members [of Congress] but not to others, and assuming any form desired by the beholder."[69]

The cotton dust case was heard by the Supreme Court during the first full day of the Reagan administration. The new Labor Department found itself on the opposite side of the old department, and in March of 1981, three months before the Court's decision was eventually made public, OSHA, in an extraordinary move, asked the Court to vacate the lower court decision that had upheld the standard and to remand the case to the agency.[70] The Court rejected the request and issued the decision in June; OSHA then announced that it would review the standard to assure its compatibility with Executive Order 12291.[71]

The scientific and economic analyses upon which OSHA based its cotton dust standard were plagued with uncertainties, although less than for other OSHA standard-setting efforts. Among them were political forces involved, from Carter administration inflation fighters seeking to weaken the proposal to Reagan appointees seeking to overturn a Supreme Court decision. Economic analyses captured the attention of industry and of administrations anxious to control inflation. In practice, the cotton dust standard, according to one study, "has proven to be much more cost effective than was anticipated originally," although its actual costs were still "extraordinarily high by comparison with any value that can be reasonably placed upon its achievements." The original industry costs of compliance were, according to that study, "greatly exaggerated."[72]

At best, cost-benefit analysis helped identify some of the benefits and some of the costs, while political factors determined who would pay the costs—industry and consumers through higher costs, or workers through increased illness and death if no regulations were provided. That determination was then coupled with the decision of an administration which tried to limit the aggregate costs it imposed, by cutting costs where the opposition was weakest and political gains most likely. Perhaps the cotton dust standard is a wrong-headed approach to a real problem; the debate of the last eight years has done little to provide definitive answers. As much as the problem has been framed in terms of what Congress intended, Congress has actually played a minor role in helping to resolve the conflict. Congress has shown an unwillingness to make the specific decisions required, yet it refuses to grant to OSHA the authority to issue definitive regulations. The courts, in turn, seek to bridge the gap between their unearthing of legislative intent and decisions that are reasonably defended in the rule-making record. The process is a long, drawn-out drama, which, in the case of cotton dust, goes on, while workers continue to suffer and die of brown lung.

EVALUATING THE OSHA STANDARD-SETTING PROCESS

In the mid-to-late 1970s, OSHA began giving increased attention to health hazards. Some health standards had been issued among the 4,400 adopted in 1971 that were based on existing industry codes and guidelines. By 1985 OSHA had issued 26 safety regulations, all of which were changes in the 1971 rules. Safety standards have not imposed particularly expensive burdens on industry, and while they have often been criticized as "nitpicking" and meddlesome, most of the controversy has focused on OSHA health standards. By 1985, 18 health standards had been issued. Twelve health standards provided new or revised restrictions for 24 substances and one physical agent. Three standards produced generic guidelines for keeping records of health hazards and making them available to workers, labeling hazardous materials to which workers were exposed, and regulating carcinogens. Three standards modified existing standards. A final standard for asbestos was issued in January of 1986. Table 6.2 lists the health standards issued by OSHA.

OSHA was given authority in its enabling statute to adopt national consensus standards, and did so in 1971 by adopting health standards formulated by the American Conference of Governmental Industrial Hygienists (ACGIH) in 1968. ACGIH annually updates its health standards, and has added more than 200 substances since 1968. Its standards are, overall, stricter than OSHA's and OSHA has added only a handful of new chemicals to its regulated list since 1971. The exposure limits recommended by the National Institute of Occupational Safety and Health also exceed OSHA standards.[73]

The slow pace of the standard-setting process (which has produced about three rules every two years), the relative weakness of the 1971 standards when compared with those suggested by professional organizations, the gap between known workplace health hazards and the standards that have been issued, and other indicators have caused many people inside and outside of OSHA to argue that too few rules have been issued.[74] Several reasons for this seem apparent.

Table 6.2. OSHA Health Standards

Standard	Year Issued
Asbestos[a]	1972, 1986
Fourteen Carcinogens	1974
Vinyl Chloride	1974
Coke Oven Emissions	1976
Benzene[b]	1978
DBCP	1978
Inorganic Arsenic	1978
Cotton dust/cotton gins[c]	1978
Acrylonitrile	1978
Lead	1978
Cancer policy[d]	1980
Access to employee exposure and medical records	1980
Occupational noise/hearing conversation	1981
Lead—reconsideration of respirator fit-testing requirements	1982
Coal tar pitch volatiles—modification of interpretation	1983
Hearing conservation—reconsideration	1983
Hazard Communication (labeling)	1983
Ethlyne Oxide[e]	1984

[a]Osha proposed a revision to this standard in 1975; in 1983 it issued an emergency temporary standard that was subsequently vacated by a court of appeals in 1984. A new proposal was issued in 1984 and a final rule was issued in January of 1986.

[b]standard deleted in 1981

[c]parts of this standard have been vacated by federal courts

[d]revised policy listed in 1986-87 regulatory plan

[e]the permissible exposure level upheld by Court of Appeals in July of 1986; standard remanded for inclusion of short term exposure level

Source: Office of Technology Assessment, *Preventing Illness and Injury in the Workplace* (Washington, DC: Government Printing Office, 1985), p. 363.

First, OSHA has been given very modest resources, given the variety and sheer magnitude of the health and safety threats to workers. If Congress was really serious about accomplishing the broad, expansive goals it had delegated to OSHA to assure a safe and healthy workplace for all workers, it would have appropriated many times the funds actually provided. These goals have created unrealistic expectations of what OSHA was to be able to accomplish. Members of Congress happily claimed credit for taking a bold and aggressive stand to protect workers, but gave little attention to how the inevitable costs of regulation were to be allocated. They placed OSHA in a highly volatile environment by delegating to it the difficult and controversial choices that they refused to address. OSHA has been expected to defuse political pressures Congress found too strong to deal with; the agency has been buffeted and tossed by political pressures ever since, and has been given little guidance concerning the means of achieving the goals given to it and the costs those goals impose.

Second, the Reagan administration has appointed agency heads who have clearly been unsympathetic to OSHA's statutory purposes. This, combined with an OMB review process that has sought to block every OSHA regulatory initiative, has dampened regulatory activity. In the words of one agency official, "it is amazing that OSHA can get anything out at all." The few rules that have been issued are a result of court orders and congressional pressure. Neither have previous administrations been much more willing to permit OSHA to be more aggressive in issuing new standards.

Third, the paucity of standards is also a result of the opposition that they have engendered. To some extent, of course, regulations would naturally be opposed by the regulated industries, although many scholars argue that agencies are inevitably captured by the industries they are expected to regulate and used to reduce competition. Economists, policy analysts, and industry representatives, however, have argued that OSHA rules have often been overly severe and less cost-efficient than regulations issued by other agencies, and have imposed costs that are not justified given the benefits promised. OSHA has sought to impose maximum limits on exposure, rather than to balance small increases in protection with the significant increases in costs that occur under extreme exposure limits. While many firms argue they would accept modest standards, and sometimes even lobby for national standards rather than permitting states to issue their own regulations, they revolt against standards that, in a marginal analysis, are not justified.

Critics have also attacked OSHA for favoring engineering rather than performance standards. Engineering standards are favored by OSHA rule-writers since compliance with them can generally be determined more easily by inspectors. This, however, often results in the rejection of more flexible performance standards, which might permit employers to develop their own solutions. OSHA's past interpretation of its statutory mandate has been to require that the workplace be made as safe as is feasible, while industry tends to focus on reducing accidents and illnesses through altering worker behavior. Thus, employers may believe that protective devices worn by workers are much less expensive than engineering controls while still protecting worker health and safety, while OSHA standards focus on the workplace environment. Until some consensus is developed or imposed on this issue, workers and employers, and OSHA and industry trade associations, are likely to remain far apart.

The conflict between proponents and opponents of a vigorous OSHA effort also rests on a fundamental difference in perspective. Proponents are motivated by a commitment to guarantee the "right" to a safe workplace. Like other rights to be guaranteed by government, they argue, a safe workplace is a primary value to be furthered without a utilitarian balancing of costs and benefits. Opponents, while generally agreeing that workers should not be injured or killed at work, state that all efforts to protect them should be firmly rooted in the market system. In their view, the role of government is to intervene to assure the operation of the market, so that workers in dangerous occupations will receive higher pay and employers responsible for employee injuries will bear the costs involved. The difficulties in trying to satisfy both those who seek significant changes in the economic system and its underlying values and those who seek to maintain and reinforce the system can overwhelm narrow issues of risk assessment and scientific and technical analysis.

Risk assessment is further undermined because the information available to OSHA, upon which it is expected to base its standards, is often incomplete or inconclusive. OSHA (like other agencies) allocates few resources to long-term research needs. The research available usually requires quantitative and qualitative extrapolations that are rough estimates at best. Occupational safety and health professionals usually favor as much protection as possible, reflecting their commitment to worker protection. Providing a safe margin of protection also helps avoid any catastrophe that could be blamed on them. The courts, for their part, have required that agencies respond to all of the comments submitted to them, and industry groups have become increasingly sophisticated in their ability to delay regulatory action by inundating agencies with studies and arguments to which they must respond. Since so many agency resources are consumed in each case, only a few standards will ever be issued.

Delays in OSHA rule making are not due simply to economic or technical uncertainty, however. The agency has been trying to decide since 1972 whether or not to issue a rule requiring toilets and clean washing and drinking water for farm workers. Hearings and court rules have filled more than 4,000 pages, yet there has been little progress in bringing together representatives of farmers who oppose the proposal and worker and other groups who favor it. The costs are clearly identifiable, but disputes concerning states' rights, human dignity, and worker health have been difficult to reconcile.[75] In September 1985, the Department of Labor announced that states would be given 18 months to develop their own standards; if they failed to act, OSHA would then impose federal standards. That decision reversed an earlier department announcement that no federal action would be taken.[76]

OSHA has moved from being one of the most often criticized regulatory agencies by regulated industries to one of the most popular ones. One official of the U.S Chamber of Commerce explained the reversal of perceptions: "I don't think there's a regulatory agency in Washington that has delivered more on candidate Reagan's promises on regulatory reform—OSHA's way out in front in that respect. . . . OSHA, really for the first time, has widespread acceptance in the business community."[77] The Reagan administration has not been able to eliminate the conflicts and inconsistencies that are at the base of OSHA but has been able to submerge them.

The lack of scientific research and data on occupational health risks has weakened even further the ability of OSHA to pursue aggressively its statutory mandate. Risk assessment calculations are always susceptible to manipulation, because of the uncertainty of scientific knowledge in this area and the importance of the assumptions on which the analysis is built. When the scientific evidence is unambiguous and health risks are clearly identifiable, OSHA is able to act aggressively and in that sense risk assessment can drive risk management.

What is more likely, however, is just the opposite. Decisions are made for political reasons and in response to ideological and policy considerations; then, risk assessment is ordered to provide justification and legitimacy for those decisions. There is no procedural prevention for any particular actions if decision-makers really want to take them. This, of course, is not surprising, given the political clout of policy analysts and scientists compared to the interests affected by agency initiatives.

The integrity of risk assessment, however, is threatened by such decisions and they can weaken the ability of agencies to generate the best scientific information available to serve as the basis for risk management decisions. This danger seems especially likely in OMB review of OSHA standards. OSHA officials deny that provisions in agency standards are ever dictated by their OMB overseers, but proposals produced within the agency and then sent over to OMB often differ from those ultimately issued. Instead of stating openly that agency proposals were inconsistent with the president's policy of regulatory relief, much time and effort is spent generating technical justifications for the policy decisions.

Recommendations for alternative approaches to and reforms of current OSHA practices depend on how one defines the agency's problems. If OSHA issues too few health standards, the solution lies in increasing the ability of OSHA to issue more of them. OSHA could likely do so if it decided to issue more regulations that were less strict.[78] Scarce agency resources could be used to formulate more standards that permitted greater levels of exposure. The guidelines set by ACGIH, NIOSH, and others could be more widely adopted by OSHA. Marginal analysis should be central to OSHA decision making, as efforts to provide absolute or maximum protection would be replaced by careful comparisons of the costs of incremental increases in protection with the increased benefits, and standards set where the benefits most outweigh the costs.

Unions, industries, and others would have to suppress their inclination to litigate over each standard OSHA issues. Such a shift in strategy toward regulation is not politically infeasible, however. Unions and other advocates of worker health might conclude that workers are better protected by more widespread and moderate regulations than by fewer, more extreme ones. Industry officials would probably be willing to accept increased breadth of regulations to avoid extremely costly standards and the uncertainty that is endemic in current proceedings. Congress could do much to encourage these reforms by explicitly writing them into the OSH Act, but much progress can be made independent of statutory reform. OMB's review process might not provide a major barrier to increased regulatory activity if it did not raise the ire of the administration's constituencies.

There is great potential for tangible regulatory reform in OSHA. Regulatory reform need not be equated with regulatory relief or regulatory euthanasia, but can produce efforts that more efficiently and effectively address the threats to worker health posed by toxic chemicals.

Chapter 7 THE CONSUMER PRODUCT SAFETY COMMISSION

The Consumer Product Safety Commission, created as an independent regulatory agency in 1972, is empowered to establish mandatory safety standards for the design, construction, contents, performance and labeling of tens of thousands of consumer products. Products posing unreasonable risks for consumers, where such risks cannot be effectively minimized through the promulgation of safety standards, may be banned. Voluntary, industry-established safety standards are also encouraged and fostered by the CPSC. Consumer goods which present a "substantial product hazard," fail to comply with a product safety standard, or create a "substantial risk of injury to the public" may lead to commission action. Such action might require that manufacturers notify the public, repair or replace unsafe items, or refund the purchase price of such items. When the commission identifies consumer goods that are found to be "imminently hazardous," it may initiate judicial proceedings to require immediate recall, repair, replacement, or refund. And manufacturers can be required to notify the commission whenever they learn of hazards identified with items they produce.

The CPSC is one of the smallest of the federal regulatory agencies. Its staff and budget grew from 586 employees and $19 million to its peak in 1978 of 900 employees and a 1981 budget of $44 million.[1] It has been singled out by the Reagan administration for budget and personnel cuts. Its 1984 budget authority was only $35 million, and was expected to fall to $34 million by 1986.[2] The Heritage Foundation's *Mandate for Leadership II*, considered to be the Reagan administration's blueprint for regulatory reform, called for the abolition of the commission, arguing that product liability laws "make redundant much of the work of the Consumer Product Safety Commission."[3] Its enabling statute is one of the broadest given to a regulatory agency, and its jurisdiction extends to virtually every kind of consumer product. While much of the attention directed at the CPSC is a result of its actions to require manufacturers to recall unsafe products, the commission has issued several product safety standards that have generated controversy. Three aspects of the CPSC's rule-making activity are deserving of particular attention: (1) the agency's autonomy as an independent regulatory commission and the consequence of that for political oversight of its rules, (2) its openness and emphasis on public participation, and (3) its reliance on economic analysis in evaluating alternative courses of action. These procedural considerations have had important effects on particular rules, and, more significantly, on the commission's ability to pursue its regulatory agenda.

STATUTORY AUTHORITY OF THE CPSC

The Consumer Product Safety Commission is empowered to issue consumer product safety standards whenever such an action is "reasonably necessary to prevent or reduce an unreasonable risk or injury." Standards can prescribe requirements for performance, composition, design, danger warnings, and operating instructions. If the commission finds that "no feasible consumer product safety standard . . . would adequately protect the public from the unreasonable risk or injury," then it may issue a product ban. There may be little practical difference between a ban and a safety standard. A product ban might prohibit outright the manufacturing and marketing of a product with particular characteristics or elements, while a product standard might have the same effect by prohibiting a product component which is determined to be hazardous. Indeed, the rule-making processes for bans and standards are somewhat similar, and a proposed standard can be recast as a ban, or vice versa.[4]

Rule-making proceedings may be initiated by petitions from any interested persons requesting that the CPSC issue a product safety standard or by commission officials themselves. Under the 1972 act the commission was required to respond to petitions within 120 days; the 1981 amendments deleted this time restriction, thus conforming the CPSC's process to the petition requirement in the Administrative Procedure Act. This petition provision has had, according to one study of the CPSC for the Administrative Conference, a "major role in determining which substances the Commission selects for regulatory action."[5] Petitioners whose initiatives are rejected by the commission may seek review of that decision in a federal district court.

Once the commission decides to proceed with the development of a standard, it publishes its intentions in the *Federal Register*. Under the 1972 law, consumer groups, industry groups, or other government agencies could submit existing standards or offer to develop new ones; the commission was required to accept any reasonable offer to provide or develop a standard, and was authorized to provide commission funds to assist groups that could not otherwise afford to take part in the process. The commission was given more discretion in 1978 in deciding whether to issue standards itself or accept the proposal of an offerer. In 1981, the offerer process was limited to the preparation of voluntary standards, as part of the CPSC's redirection toward voluntary rather than mandatory efforts. The commission could also issue standards under the Hazardous Safety and the Flammable Fabric Acts, which involve procedural provisions less elaborate than those under the Consumer Product Safety Act. The 1981 amendments, however, required that all regulations issued by the commission be developed according to the same procedures.[6]

The publication in the *Federal Register* of the commission's intention to issue a safety standard or ban must now take the form of an advanced notice of proposed rule making which must include a description of the product to be regulated, the nature of the risk involved, the alternatives for commission action, an invitation to interested persons to propose or develop voluntary standards, and a request for comments on the proposed action. A copy of the notice is required to be sent to the House Committee on Energy and Commerce and the Senate Commerce, Science and Transportation Committee. If the commission finds that a voluntary standard is likely to eliminate or adequately reduce the risk of injury and that there is likely to be a substantial compliance with a voluntary standard, then it must terminate the rule making and notify the public, through the *Federal Register*, that the commission will rely on the voluntary standards.

Sixty or more days after the issuance of the advance notice of proposed rule making the commission then publishes the proposed rule, which must be accompanied by a preliminary regulatory analysis, to include a description of the potential benefits and costs of the proposed rules, an explanation of why a voluntary standard would not eliminate or sufficiently reduce the risk of injury, and a description of any reasonable alternatives to the proposed rule along with their potential costs and benefits. This analysis must also be sent to House and Senate committees. The commission is required to ''give interested persons an opportunity for the oral presentation of data, views or arguments, in addition to an opportunity to make written submissions'' and must keep a transcript of all oral presentations.[7]

The 1981 law also established guidelines for commission decision making once the proposed rule is announced. The CPSC is to consider available data concerning product safety research and testing in general as well as engaging in specific investigatory activities, and is to take into account how proposed rules might adversely affect the special needs of the elderly and handicapped. The commission must also consider the degree and nature of risk involved, the number of products affected, the need of the public for the product and the ''probable effect of such rule upon the utility, cost or availability of such products to meet such needs,'' and how the rule could minimize the adverse effects on competition or the disruption of commercial practices.[8]

Within 60 days after the publication of the proposed rule (which can be extended for good cause) the commission must issue a final rule, or withdraw its proposal if it is not ''reasonably necessary to eliminate or reduce'' the risk associated with the product or not ''in the public interest.'' If the CPSC issues a rule, it must be accompanied by a final regulatory analysis, to include a description of the potential costs and benefits, identification of those who would probably bear the costs and receive the benefits, description of the costs and benefits of any alternatives to the rule that the commission considered (with an explanation of why each was rejected), and a summary of all significant issues raised during the public comment period (with the commission's assessment of each issue).[9]

The rule itself must include findings which demonstrate that:

1. The rule is "reasonably necessary to eliminate or reduce an unreasonable risk of injury."
2. Issuance of the rule is "in the public interest."
3. Voluntary standards would not be likely "to result in the elimination or adequate reduction" of injuries (or "substantial" compliance of voluntary standards would not be likely).
4. "[B]enefits expected from the rule bear a reasonable relationship to its costs."
5. The rule "imposes the least burdensome requirement which prevents or adequately reduces the risk of injury for which the rule is being promulgated."

All rules must go into effect within 180 days of the publication of the final rule unless a later date is in the "public interest."[10]

Several other provisions deserve some attention here. If the commission finds that no product standard "would adequately protect the public from the unreasonable risk of injury associated" with a product, then the rule issued may take the form of a product ban. The CPSC is authorized to contribute to costs incurred by individuals who assist it in developing product safety standards. Standards are required to be expressed in terms of performance requirements (rather than design standards) and are expected to require warnings and labels rather than more restrictive provisions.[11] The CPSC may not issue an advanced notice of proposed rule making for any product that is suspected of causing cancer, birth defects, or genetic mutations until the scientific evidence and other information upon which the commission relies have been reviewed by a chronic hazard advisory panel. A panel is appointed for each proposed rule by the commission from a list of scientists nominated by the president of the National Academy of Sciences and who "have demonstrated the ability to critically assess chronic hazards and risks to human health presented by the exposure of humans to toxic substances." The findings of the panel, however, are nonbinding upon the CPSC.[12]

Under the 1981 law, once the CPSC publishes a final rule in the *Federal Register*, it must submit the rule to Congress. The rule does not take effect if a resolution of disapproval is adopted by one house within 60 days and that resolution is not subsequently disapproved by the other house within 30 days, or if both houses adopt a concurrent resolution of disapproval within 90 days.[13] This procedure is referred to as a "one and one-half house" legislative veto and is patterned after the veto provisions included in amendments to the Federal Trade Commission's enabling legislation. However, in the first congressional action after the Supreme Court declared the legislative veto unconstitutional, the House passed two amendments modifying the rule-making process. Under one proposal, CPSC regulations are to take effect after 90 days unless vetoed in a bill passed by both houses and signed by the President. The other amendment requires that all regulations be enacted in the regular legislative process before they can take effect. House-Senate conferees were to then choose which version they preferred for the actual amendment. Thus, at least in the House, members of Congress seem anxious to circumvent the Court's rejection of a favorite congressional tool for monitoring the rule-making process.[14]

In creating the Consumer Product Safety Commission in 1972, Congress experimented with a number of procedural innovations and also included devices and arrangements it had developed elsewhere. A 1976 review of the CPSC by the House Commerce Subcommittee on Oversight and Investigations found that the commission's rule-making process "represented in many respects the most advanced congressional thinking on the techniques of federal regulation. The Act incorporated a number of concepts of regulatory reform. Indeed, many current proposals for regulatory reform appear to be its progeny."[15]

Congressional intent in creating the CPSC as an independent regulatory commission was a result of a combination of factors, including rivalry between Congress and the president over control of the new agency, partisan differences, and an interest in insulating the commission from industry pressure. The administration's proposal to put the new consumer safety program in the FDA was rejected by members of Congress who found the FDA ineffective in regulating food and drug safety and insisted on an independent commission. In the House there was strong support, bolstered by consumer group lobbying, for an independent commission. The Senate, backed by industry groups, wanted the new consumer safety agency placed in the Health, Education and Welfare Department.[16] The House committee report defended the decision to establish an independent body:

> This decision reflects the committee's belief that an independent agency can better carry out the legislative and judicial functions contained in this bill with cold neutrality that the public has a right to expect of regulatory agencies formed for its protection. Independent status, and bipartisan commissioners with staggered and fixed terms, will tend to provide greater insulation from political and economic pressures than is possible · · · in a cabinet-level department. The Commission's decision under this legislation will necessarily involve

a careful meld of safety and economic considerations. This delicate balance, the committee believes should be struck in a setting as far removed as possible from partisan influence.[17]

The House version of the bill, which was generally accepted by the conference committee and by the Congress as a whole, sought to assure that the commission would be free from presidential influence by requiring that the chair of the commission not serve at the pleasure of the president, but, once confirmed, serve out the entire term as chair. The vice-chair was to be elected by the commissioners, commissioners could not be removed for "inefficiency" as was true in other agencies, and all CPSC budgetary and legislative proposals were to be submitted directly to Congress as well as the OMB. Although some of these provisions were later eliminated in reauthorizing amendments (such as permitting a newly elected president to appoint the chair of the commission), new requirements were added requiring that the appointment of no officer besides the commissioners be reviewed by anyone in the Executive Office of the President, thus giving renewed emphasis to the independence of the commission.[18]

A second major congressional purpose was to provide for increased public participation in commission proceedings. The Senate report in 1972 emphasized that the basic concern was "to encourage consumer participation in the procedures and processes of the agency." The offerer process for the development of product safety standards, time limits for commission responses to petition, public financing of citizen participation, requirements that all meetings involving the commissioners be open to the public, public access to logs of all meetings between commissioners and those affected by regulations, provisions for hearings for "interested persons, including consumers and consumer organizations," and the granting of standing to challenge commission regulations "by any person affected by such rule, or any consumer or consumer organization" are all manifestations of congressional efforts to assure that consumers be able to monitor and be involved in CPSC decision making.[19]

Congressional intent in assuring industry and consumer access to the CPSC decision-making process reflects the view that Congress expected the commission to be a referee between consumer and business interests.[20] In 1972 Congress rejected the creation of a consumer advocate within the federal government. Some members of Congress assumed that the CPSC would take that kind of role while others saw the commission as an umpire to settle disputes between consumer and industry groups.

A third objective of Congress was to be able to monitor itself the regulations issued by the CPSC. In creating the commission, Congress authorized it for only three years, to assure that the CPSC would be subject to periodic congressional scrutiny. In 1975 and 1978 the CPSC was reauthorized for additional three-year periods, in order to give Congress "the discipline of some oversight" and enable congressional committees "to assess thoroughly the Commission's performance."[21] In reauthorizing the CPSC in 1981, the commission was granted authority for only two years so that Congress would be able to review the commission's progress. In 1976 Congress also began requiring that all proposed CPSC rules be sent to House and Senate committees. By 1981 Congress authorized a legislative veto provision over all commission regulations.[22]

A final congressional intent has been to specify the criteria to be used by the CPSC in establishing product safety regulations, although the criteria were not a subject of significant debate. They reflected an effort by Congress to give some guidance to the commission without imposing any substantive decisions. The 1981 amendments, however, included a number of criteria for CPSC rules expressly designed to constrain commission decision making and assure that all rules issued had passed a cost-benefit test. In so doing, Congress sought to impose upon the CPSC some of the standards applicable to executive agencies under Executive Order 12291, President Reagan's regulatory relief order, although it rejected a formal cost-benefit requirement in favor of a more flexible standard that had been developed by reviewing courts and approved by the Supreme Court.

Although the CPSC's rule-making process has been centered around the statutory provisions discussed above, additional procedural steps have become part of the process. These have developed primarily in response to the internal organization and dynamics of the CPSC as well as additional statutory requirements. All of the rules issued by the CPSC have originated in petitions received by the commission, although the commission was already considering taking action on several of the products involved when the petitions were received. The initial decision made by the commission is based upon the identification of the problem, a preliminary risk assessment which examines the number of injuries and the frequency of product use, a profile of the relevant industry and a preliminary economic analysis, and a review of research and literature in the product area. The Office of Program Management was created in 1976 and charged with the responsibility of analyzing all petitions received by the CPSC, identifying other potential projects and preparing the initial analyses. The commissioners review each petition and make the final decision to terminate or continue commission action.[23] Figure 7.1 is an organization chart depicting these offices in the commission.

Commission options include the development of a product safety standard, an outright ban, or an enforcement action against a specific product. An ad hoc project team is established for each proposed regulation, comprised of individuals from two different kinds of offices. The project head comes from one of the following program areas within the Office of Program Management: acute chemical and environmental hazards, electric shock haz-

Figure 7.1. The Consumer Product Safety Commission

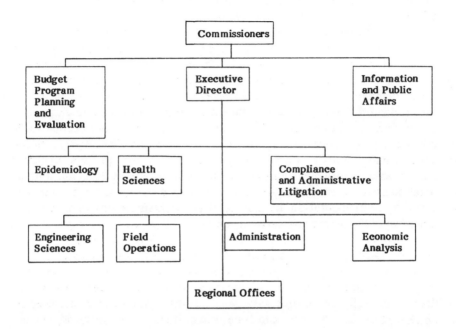

Source: Adapted from Congressional Quarterly, Federal Regulatory Directory 5th ed. (Washington DC: Congressional Quarterly, Inc., 1986), p. 95.

ards, emerging hazards, fire and thermal burn hazards, household structures, mechanical hazards—children's products and mechanical hazards—powered equipment. The Office of Program Management is responsible for directing and reviewing all projects and coordinating involvement with groups setting voluntary standards.

Members of the project team also come from the relevant program area and from the technical resource directorates, including epidemiology, engineering sciences and health sciences, and from the administrative directorates of compliance and administrative litigation and field operations. The technical resource directorates are comprised of engineers, economists, and scientists who conduct studies of the economic impact of proposed standards on industry and consumers, develop and evaluate product performance standards and operate product-testing facilities, collect and evaluate data concerning physiological effects of products, and conduct tests and review research in the area of toxicological and chemical hazards. Representatives of the compliance and administrative litigation directorate assist in developing standards that are consistent with enforcement imperatives. This approach has developed as a result of the small size of the commission and the need for flexibility, as well as from a desire to direct staff member commitment to the project at hand rather than to a product category. Table 7.1 depicts this matrix structure for the organization of project teams.

The project leader prepares an operating plan for the project that must be approved by the commissioners, or, in some cases, the commission's executive director. Once the project team begins work, there is a continual, informal review of the team's efforts in place of a structured review mechanism. Team members raise problems or concerns with the team head as well as with the heads of the technical and administrative directorates, all of whom then attempt to resolve the conflicts. For major regulations, the project team usually prepares guidance briefings for the commissioners. The small size of the commission permits this less structured internal review process. Officials from other directorates such as field operations, communication, and administration assist the project team in developing standards consonant with concerns of implementation by area officers, consumer information and commission budgetary and personnel policies.[24]

Economic Analysis and CPSC Rule Making

An important element of the CPSC's rule-making process has been the development of economic and scientific analyses for each proposal. During the first several years of operation there was little expertise within the commission in the areas of cost and benefit identification and risk assessment. The CPSC's enabling statute required only that the commission find that regulations it issued achieved their objectives while "minimizing adverse effects

Table 7.1. Organization of CPSC Project Teams

Office of Program Management

Program Areas
  Acute Chemical and Environmental Hazards
  Electric Shock Hazards
  Emerging Hazards
  Fire and Thermal Burn Hazards
  Household Structures
  Mechanical Hazards—Children's Products
  Mechanical Hazards—Powered Equipment

Technical Directorates

  Epidemiology
  Engineering Sciences
  Health Sciences

Administrative Directorates

  Compliance and Administrative Litigation

---

on competition or disruption or dislocation of manufacturing and other commercial practices."[25] The legislative history of the 1972 legislation did not require cost–benefit analysis: The Senate report indicated that the commission was to balance the risks involved and their seriousness with the effect of commission action on product utility, availability, and cost, while the House report concluded that a formal cost–benefit analysis was not required, but that "no standard would be expected to impose added costs or inconvenience to the consumer unless there is reasonable assurance that the frequency or severity of injuries or illnesses will be reduced."[26]

In reviewing CPSC standards in the mid-to-late 1970s, federal courts found the commission's economic analyses to be weak, prompting a commission effort to improve its analytic methods. In 1978 one court of appeals ruled that the "Commission does not have to conduct an elaborate cost–benefit analysis", but that it was required to "examin[e] the relevant factors and produc[e] substantial evidence to support its conclusion that they weigh in favor of the standards." The "crucial question," according to the court, was "whether the benefit has a reasonable relationship to the disadvantages" posed by the regulation.[27]

In December 1980 the commission issued a proposed rule which described its methodology for the regulatory analyses it was required to perform when issuing regulations. This was perhaps the first time any regulatory agency had made public the criteria it used in its rule-making deliberations. Although the 1981 amendments to the CPSC established additional criteria for the analyses accompanying product safety standards and bans, the primary requirements—that benefits of a rule must "bear a reasonable relationship" to the costs—was already an element of the commission's methodology, and was part of the proposed rule introduced in 1980. Commission officials have emphasized, however, that such a requirement does not entail a formal cost-benefit test, where the quantifiable benefits must exceed the quantifiable costs.[28]

The first finding that the commission must make is an assessment of the degree and nature of the risk involved. This involves an estimate of the number of injuries and illnesses involved from the CPSC's National Electronic Injury Surveillance System and from other sources. The commission then estimates the number and kinds of injuries that would be prevented, the expected level of industry compliance, and the indirect costs (lost wages, pain and suffering, etc.) and direct medical costs that would be avoided through compliance with the regulation. Numerical figures are used whenever possible, but qualitative descriptions are expected to be part of the analysis.[29]

The CPSC differentiates between acute injuries or illnesses, those likely to occur at or immediately after exposure, and chronic injuries and illnesses, those expected to develop over a long period of time. In determining whether or not products are likely to cause chronic illnesses, the commission examines the experience of workers and others who are exposed to the substance, laboratory experiments with animals that have been exposed, and predictive tests based on the chemical structures of the substance being evaluated and other chemicals viewed as hazardous. The CPSC generally relies on the work of outside organizations and, in particular, bases its actions on research conducted by the EPA, OSHA, and the National Cancer Institute. The Interagency Regulatory Liaison Group's policy statement on the identification of potential carcinogens and the estimation of risk provides additional guidance to the commission.[30]

While the CPSC relies to a great extent on other agencies and institutions in identifying the risks of substances, the commission alone focuses on the nature and extent of consumer exposure to suspected chronic hazards. Its risk assessment may include the development of a model describing typical consumer exposure, which is then combined with the potential hazard posed by the substance in generating an estimate of the number of injuries, illnesses, and deaths that would be prevented by adopting the regulation. The assessment may also reflect consideration of other factors, such as the susceptibility of certain groups within the general population (such as children or the aged) and how consumer use affects the level of risk involved.[31]

The second kind of finding required in CPSC rule making involves the determination of the levels of production and sales of the regulated products, including current levels and expected changes, in order to calculate the impact of proposed regulation on producers and consumers. The commission relies on industry-provided data, as well as government and other private sources, and on surveys and observations conducted by commission officials. The commission determines the extent to which the product is used, the availability of substitutes, and the probable effect of the proposed regulation on the product's marketability and appeal to consumers. The costs associated with the proposal are then estimated, including the costs of manufacturing and distributing products that comply with the regulation, the losses that are incurred through ceasing production of the hazardous products, and other production and distribution costs, such as shifts in product lines.

Costs to consumers are also estimated, in terms of anticipated changes in price, availability, quality, durability and required maintenance. Other associated costs are estimated, such as changes in sales and employment, "effects on international trade, competitive disruptions, or other changes in normal business practice," and increased sales and employment for firms offering substitutable products. Finally, the commission considers exemptions to the proposed rule for small businesses and possible alternatives to minimize adverse effects while protecting public health and safety, such as labeling requirements, voluntary standards, information disclosure or changes in the substantive requirements initially proposed.[32]

The third finding is the central element of the CPSC's regulatory analysis. The commission reviews the degree and nature of the risk; the expected effectiveness of the proposed rule, including "engineering, scientific, behavioral and enforcement considerations"; and the costs involved. If the commission finds that the "expected benefits of a rule bear a reasonable relationship to the anticipated costs," then it issues the regulation. The CPSC may, however, find that a rule meets this test but is not in the public interest, as a result of environmental, energy or international trade considerations, and not issue the regulation.

Finally, if the CPSC decides that no "feasible" consumer product safety standard would protect the public, it may issue a product ban. The commission must show here that no standard is "technically and economically possible" within a reasonable time period, given current technology or technology expected to be developed in the near future.

The commission's statutory and self-imposed procedures and guidelines for issuing rules have been among the most innovative in the federal government. The commission has, in recent years, sought to rely on voluntary rather than mandatory safety regulations. Between 1978–1981 the CPSC won 17 of 21 major lawsuits that were directed at overturning commission regulations. Regulatory critic Murray Weidenbaum, when he was chairman of the Council of Economic Advisers, praised the CPSC as "the only [regulatory] body I know that is really weighing costs imposed against benefits that might be gained—and trying to behave rationally."[33] Nevertheless, the commission and its supporters have had to fight off a number of efforts to abolish the agency or to place it in a cabinet department. Its budget and personnel have been reduced under the Reagan administration by more than any other major regulatory agency. Yet a 1983 Harris poll found that Americans think the CPSC is doing a better job of protecting consumers than any other governmental agency.[34]

UFFI: A CASE STUDY OF CPSC RULE MAKING

Urea-formaldehyde foam insulation (UFFI) accounts for less than 10 percent of the total use of formaldehyde, but none of the other uses of the chemical has generated such controversy. Unlike other types of insulation, which are prepared in factories, UFFI is prepared on the job site and appears much like shaving cream as it is pumped into spaces between walls. It was especially popular in the mid-to-late 1970s as rising energy prices and tax incentives stimulated insulation installations. Because it could be injected into spaces that were otherwise hard to reach, UFFI was widely used in older homes where the installation of other kinds of insulation was usually difficult and expensive. In 1977 the industry reached a peak of 32 manufacturers of the foam, 1,500 dealers, and over 170,000 installations.[35]

The CPSC was first made aware of the potential health hazards of UFFI in a 1976 petition filed by the city of Denver's Consumer Office. Since the mid-1970s the CPSC received some 2,200 complaints, involving 5,700 people, of illnesses, irritations or forced displacement from residences.[36] By 1981, installations had dropped off to 8,320, manufacturers had declined to three and only about 200 dealers remained.[37] In 1979, the Formaldehyde Institute, a trade association of manufacturers of formaldehyde, notified the CPSC that a study conducted by the Chemical Institute for Toxicology had linked formaldehyde with nasal cancer in rats that had been exposed to 15 ppm of the chemical. The CPSC and other agencies then sent a team of government pathologists to review the Chemical Industry Institute's research and they confirmed the preliminary findings. In January of 1980 the CPSC asked the National Toxicology Program, comprised of four agencies in the Department of Health and Human Services (HHS) involved in toxicological research and testing, to organize a task force to review the Institute study.[38]

The responsibility for conducting the commission's analysis of UFFI was given to the household structural products team composed of staff members from the directorates for health science, engineering, economic analyses, and compliance and administrative litigation. The CPSC also held hearings in four cities between 1979 and 1980, and met with experts from the United States and eight foreign countries concerning foam insulation and formaldehyde. In June of 1980 the CPSC issued a proposal which would have required manufacturers of UFFI to provide to purchasers information concerning the suspected health hazards. The proposal described the ongoing evaluation of the chemical industry's research and indicated that the CPSC was considering issuing a rule which would require a cancer warning to accompany sales of the foam insulation. In issuing the proposal, however, the commission found that adverse economic effects of a disclosure rule would be small and made no attempt to estimate the costs that would be required to provide the warning statements.[39]

In February of 1981 the commissioners rejected the proposed labeling rule and proposed, instead, a rule which would have banned the manufacturing or selling of UFFI and its installation in homes, commercial buildings, recreational facilities, schools, and other public buildings. The underlying basis of the ban was the report of the National Toxicology Program's special panel which had been submitted to the CPSC in November of 1980. The panel concluded that formaldehyde "should be presumed to pose a carcinogenic risk to humans", since it caused cancer in rats when inhaled at doses "not greatly different from those to which consumers are exposed." The panel found that there were no "significant qualitative metabolic differences between rats and humans with regard to formaldehyde", and that while available epidemiological studies were "inadequate to permit a direct assessment of the carcinogenicity of formaldehyde to humans," review of other experiments in the scientific literature confirmed the suggestive evidence of the health hazards of formaldehyde. The panel also found evidence of genetic mutations and chromosome damage from exposure to formaldehyde, and recommended that additional tests be conducted to assess the risk of cancer from other kinds of exposure to formaldehyde such as exposure through the skin or through ingestion from food products, but did not recommend that additional testing of inhaling formaldehyde gas was needed.[40]

CPSC scientists then reviewed the panel's study and agreed with its conclusions. The commission rejected epidemiological studies presented to it by the Formaldehyde Institute as inconclusive. Commission scientists also concluded that there was no threshold or dose level below which formaldehyde could be considered noncarcinogenic, so that consumer exposure to the chemical should be eliminated to the extent possible. Commission scientists also examined research concerning the amount of formaldehyde gas released under optimal installation conditions as well as in residences where UFFI had been installed, and found that in some cases the levels of exposure were similar to those in the laboratory experiments. Finally, the scientists concluded that the release of formaldehyde gas could continue over several years, thus prolonging consumer exposure to the health hazard.[41]

The CPSC also sought to assess the risks of acute injury and illness. It contracted with the National Academy of Science to investigate the level of formaldehyde in homes insulated with UFFI and its effects on humans. The NAS panel concluded that since part of the population would suffer some irritation even at levels of formaldehyde gas below 0.25 ppm, indoor residential exposure should be maintained at the "lowest practical level." Human exposure was tested in both controlled exposure studies and in homes where health complaints had been noted. In homes where the level of formaldehyde gas measured was less than 0.5 ppm, residents suffered from eye irritation, upper respiratory difficulties, headaches, skin problems, and gastrointestinal tract disturbances. Research reported in the scientific literature confirmed these and other acute effects of exposure to formaldehyde.[42]

The second step taken by the CPSC's project team was an assessment of the degree of risk of injury or illness from exposure to formaldehyde gas. The commission found that existing epidemiological studies were not useful in predicting the magnitude of risk associated with exposure to formaldehyde gas, and prepared its own estimate of the risk of cancer from UFFI insulation. The assessment estimated that as many as 150 persons out of the 1.75 million exposed to the UFFI that had been installed in 500,000 homes between 1975 and 1980 might develop cancer, and that 23 people could be expected to develop cancer as a result of installations during the years to follow. These estimates were generated from a "multistage" model, a widely used approach found by the CPSC to be consistent with chemical theories of carcinogenicity. At low doses, the model predicts that the relationship between exposure and carcinogenic response is linear. As the level of exposure increases, the relationship shifts to a new "stage" of increased carcinogenicity. At high levels of exposure the dose–response curve shoots upward since the effects of carcinogenicity are expected to be cumulative.[43]

The data used in generating the dose–response curve came from the Chemical Industry Institute's study, since the levels of exposure in that experiment were similar to those found in homes where UFFI had been installed. The level of household exposure was calculated through a simulated UFFI installation and a measurement of the resultant concentration of formaldehyde gas as well as a sample of actual homes insulated with UFFI. These exposure levels were then put into the model, which generated a range of values for the number of cancers likely to result. The CPSC used the highest value in the range, 150 cancers, to be "on the side of safety," which meant that a person living in an average home with UFFI for seven years after installation would have an additional cancer risk of 1 in 10,000. This data was then applied to future installations at the 1980 projected rate and generated the estimate of 23 additional cancers. And the commission emphasized that since the data used came from highly controlled laboratory experiments, the risk of cancer was probably underestimated, since an exposure to several potential carcinogens may be more likely to cause cancer than each substance in isolation.[44]

In assessing the degree of risk of acute illness, staff members investigated over 400 complaints and found that over 90 percent of the consumer complaints were associated with UFFI installation. In about half of the households involved, medical attention was sought, and in about 50 cases medical professionals linked the health complaint with exposure to formaldehyde. The level of formaldehyde gas was measured in about 100 of the investigations; many of the residences had levels at or below 0.1 ppm and one-third had levels over 1 ppm.

The third step in the commission's analysis considered the extent to which product safety standards would be able to reduce sufficiently unreasonable risks associated with UFFI. Staff members examined standards proposed by the Department of Energy and the National Insulation Certification Institute and found that the standards would not result in reduced formaldehyde levels. The staff argued, in addition, that even if standards might theoretically reduce the level of formaldehyde gas, variations in preparing and installing practices and in the kind of structure in which the UFFI is installed would likely render any standards ineffective. Unlike other consumer products produced in factories where product quality control is possible, UFFI is "manufactured" on the job site and its chemical composition is likely to vary greatly.[45]

Since the staff was unable to identify an acceptable safe level of formaldehyde exposure, it rejected the feasibility of a product standard. Nor did it find that warnings and instructions were appropriate regulatory alternatives, since no label could be affixed to the foam itself and subsequent buyers of buildings insulated with UFFI might be unaware of the risks involved. Further, since the insulation was permanent and nonreturnable, it prohibited consumers who might not understand or be aware of the potential hazards from easily obtaining redress.

Once the staff concluded that there was no feasible standard that would adequately protect the public from the risks of exposure to formaldehyde gas, it then prepared an analysis of the economic effects likely to result from a product ban. Three primary effects of the proposed ban were identified: for UFFI manufacturers, lost revenues and employment; for insulation contractors, similar losses; and for homeowners, lost energy savings, reduced real estate values, and benefits from eliminating exposure to the hazardous chemical. The cost to manufacturers was estimated at from $12- to $20 million per year. Staff members estimated that from 60- to 80 thousand homes would be insulated if there was no ban, and that the maximum impact of a ban would be a loss in employment from 250 to 300 persons, although they recognized that a number of manufacturers and suppliers of UFFI had already gone out of business. The analysis, however, made no attempt to estimate the effects of previous commission action on the UFFI industry.[46]

The CPSC staff estimated that the annual retail value of the insulation ranged from $43- to $120 million for 60- to 80 thousand installations, but that estimates of effects on individual contractors were not available, since lost revenues might be recovered through increased sales of substitute products. While the number of contractors had dropped from between 1,500 and 2,000 to between 600 and 800, the staff did not attempt to estimate the loss in employment associated with CPSC actions, since some contractors had reported to the commission that they were able to use employees in other activities.[47]

The staff then examined the economic effects on consumers. Energy savings from the installation of 75,000 installations were estimated at $16- to $20 million in 1980 energy prices. But since only 5 to 10 percent of the wall cavities of homes were so narrow that UFFI was the only available insulation, the estimate of foregone energy savings was reduced to from $204,000 to $518,000. No cumulative estimate of lost energy savings was made, since the staff concluded that there was inadequate information concerning the number of houses that would be insulated if no ban were issued and no way to include the possibility that new materials could be found to insulate narrow wall cavities. Decreases in real estate values were considered by the staff as secondary costs, since the ban would only apply to future installations, and were not calculated since the staff found "insufficient information to accurately estimate the magnitudé of [those] effects." The staff was also unable to estimate the cost of litigation and remedial efforts which manufacturers and contractors might incur if the ban were issued and consumers who had had the insulation installed tried to have it removed.[48]

The final step in the CPSC's analysis was the conclusion that the benefits of banning UFFI outweighed the costs imposed. The potential benefits described by the staff report were the 23 cancer cases that were projected to be prevented by banning UFFI, and the nonquantifiable benefits of avoiding the loss of life and the medical costs associated with cancer as well as avoiding subsequent treatment or removal costs of the UFFI. The costs included in the analysis were limited to the foregone energy savings of from $1.6- to $5.2 million for 10 years. Reduced values of homes already insulated with UFFI were dismissed as being not directly attributable to the ban, since it was not retroactive. Nor did the analysis consider the lost revenues and employment of manufacturers and installers a cost, since those losses would be offset by increases for firms dealing in other kinds of insulation. Thus the commission concluded the cost per cancer avoided was from $70,000 to $226,000 per year. The staff report concluded that "when the benefits of avoided incidences of cancer and the additional benefits are considered in relationship to the facts that the ban is likely to result in a relatively minor impact to the economy as a whole, and will result in minimal energy losses because of the ready availability of substitute types of insulation for most applications, the Commission preliminarily concludes that the benefits of the ban do bear reasonable relationship, and do in fact justify, the costs of the regulatory action."[49]

The CPSC then invited public comments for 60 days, and held a public meeting on March 20, 1981. The commission received extensive written comments (270 on the proposed ban of February, and 68 additional comments after a supplemental scientific, technical and economic report was published in November of 1981) as well as 21 comments presented orally from industry representatives, consumers, consumer groups, consultants, scientists, and other federal, state and local agencies. Consumers who supported the ban complained of health problems and economic losses from the installation of UFFI, while consumers opposed to the ban complained that if it were issued, their homes would be significantly devalued even though they suffered no health effects. Almost all of the industry representatives opposed the ban and favored the development of a product safety standard instead.[50]

The commission was required by law either to issue or withdraw its proposed ban by October 6, 1981. It extended that deadline to February 15, 1982, in order to give staff members more time to respond to the comments received. In November 1981 the CPSC published in the *Federal Register* additional economic and technical findings concerning its proposed ban on UFFI. The findings presented the results of additional tests conducted for the

CPSC, on the levels of formaldehyde gas emitted, which supported the conclusions of previous studies. The staff also issued a revised risk assessment, based on the additional research of contractors and a study from the chemical industry's Institute for Toxicology, which concluded that the upper range of cancers to be expected from present installations was 89 cases, and that 13 cases could be expected in each year of subsequent installations, or 1.8 additional cases for every 10,000 homes insulated.

A revised economic assessment was also issued which found that fewer installations had been made in 1981 than had been predicted and that 40 percent of the 200 to 250 firms installing UFFI would go out of business if the ban were enacted, an additional 31 percent reporting that they would have great difficulty in making up the lost revenues. The assessment also concluded that because of the possible development of alternative insulating materials, the estimated cost of a ban, in terms of foregone energy savings, "may be overestimated" and that information on real estate values was still insufficient to generate estimates of costs.[51]

The project team prepared a briefing package for the commissioners in January 1982 which presented its analysis of the comments submitted to the CPSC. The team recommended that the commission reject a petition by the Formaldehyde Institute to initiate a product safety standard proceeding. After responding to the major technical and economic criticisms of its risk assessment and economic analyses, the team concluded that

> none of the information that has been received subsequent to the proposal regarding major issues such as toxic health effects, potential risk of cancer to humans, feasibility of a product standard, and economic considerations would cause the team to alter its original position regarding these major issues. Further, the information that supports the team's position on these issues is considered to be more extensive now than at the time of the proposal. Thus, the Household Structural Products team recommends that the Commission finalize the ban of urea formaldehyde foam insulation as it is described in the draft *Federal Register* notice.[52]

The CPSC was scheduled to make a final decision on its proposed ban on February 8, but postponed the decision for two weeks after it received a large amount of scientific material just before the commissioners were to meet. On February 11 the National Insulation Certification Institute, the trade association of UFFI installers, petitioned the CPSC to adopt a mandatory product safety standard that would set a maximum level of formaldehyde gas released from UFFI installation, provide for a massive consumer education and information program, and require that installers remove the installation if necessary to achieve the required decrease in levels of the gas.[53]

The commissioners voted on February 22, four to one, to put the ban into effect. The CPSC's chair at that time, Nancy Harvey Steorts, argued that she favored "a voluntary solution—one that would protect the consumer from unreasonable risk of injury. But, unfortunately, at this time, I have concluded there is not a voluntary solution to this problem." She indicated that her major concern was that once the insulation was installed, any problems were "virtually impossible to eliminate," thus making the ban the only feasible alternative.[54]

Other commissioners based their decisions on other factors. Commissioner Edith Barksdale Sloan was convinced by the conclusions of government scientists that UFFI "presents an unreasonable risk of acute and often traumatic health problems."[55] Commissioner R. David Pittle defended the ban after evaluating the laboratory studies relied upon by the project team, and explained in some detail his understanding of the process by which cancer had been induced in test animals. He emphasized that no feasible standard to protect consumer health had been established and that "given the ready availability of substitutes for UFFI, and the potentially serious health consequences of long-term exposure to formaldehyde by persons who cannot afford to remove UFFI from their homes or, if necessary, to move from their homes" there was no alternative to the product ban.[56] Commissioner Sam Zagoria, who voted against the proposed ban in 1981 and favored a warning requirement, reversed his vote in 1982, concluding that since UFFI could not be inspected in advance to identify problems and future occupants of a residence insulated with UFFI might react differently to the gas emitted or be unaware of the potential hazard, a product ban was needed.[57]

The only commissioner to oppose the ban, Stuart M. Statler, argued that the commission had failed to demonstrate that low levels of exposure to formaldehyde gas posed an unreasonable risk, although at levels above 0.25 ppm the gas was clearly a source of acute and chronic adverse health effects. He defended the industry's plan of development of a product safety standard, disclosure of potential risks to customers, and a program of redress of consumer complaints—including removal of the insulation if the level of gas emissions persists. He favored such an approach since it retained consumer choice, avoided damaging repercussions on the value of residences already insulated with UFFI, permitted UFFI firms to continue operating and "reduced, if not eliminated" the level of acute and chronic health risks.[58]

As soon as the CPSC announced its decision, the president of the National Insulation Certification Institute vowed to challenge the CPSC's ban in court and in Congress, claiming that the ban would hurt "500,000 satisfied customers, who will find their homes devalued by 25 to 30 percent."[59] In April 1983, the Court of Appeals for the Fifth Circuit vacated the ban, finding that the commission failed to provide the "substantial evidence necessary" to support its action. The Court found that the studies of rats that developed nasal carcinomas after inhaling formaldehyde gas were insufficient to support a ban.[60] One commission official well expressed the dilemma that the CPSC found itself in as it decided whether or not to appeal the case: "To get the Supreme Court to hear the case, you argue that it has far-reaching impact. But if the ruling stands, you have to say that it has limited impact."[61] The commission eventually decided not to appeal the decision.

Several aspects of the CPSC's ban on UFFI are noteworthy. First, given Commission Chairman Steort's often-expressed commitment to the Reagan administration's position that new regulatory burdens should not be imposed, the ban was somewhat unexpected. One former CPSC official expressed surprise at the decision, but offered, off the record, a number of explanations. The industry itself was weak, having already been reduced significantly from 1979, when concerns about the safety of UFFI first surfaced. By early 1982 it was estimated that there were only three manufacturers and from 100 to 200 installers involved in UFFI, not a particularly powerful political force. The head of the industry association had also apparently offended commissioners and staff members, in his attacks on the staff's research and through threats to have commission decisions overturned. The commission was thus probably impatient with his counterproposals and willing to directly oppose him. Perhaps more importantly, the commissioners appeared to be frustrated by a feeling that no one took them seriously and that they had been largely ignored and dismissed as weak and ineffective, and they wanted to assert themselves by taking some action.

Second, the commission's risk assessment was notable in its reliance on research done outside of the commission and in the creation of an expert panel to advise the agency on whether formaldehyde should be considered carcinogenic. It appears to be a conservative assessment except in its projection of future UFFI installations, which had been based on a 1980 estimate of 30,000 installations; by 1981, however, the number of installations had fallen to less than 10,000. Based on that lower projection, the number of expected cancers was only about two per year if the ban was not issued. Thus, the commission probably overstated the number of cases of cancer that were likely to develop in the absence of a ban. The commission's economic analysis, too, was problematic since it was based on the position that since the ban was not retroactive, only the costs incurred after it was put into effect were to be counted. Such a calculation ignored the costs resulting from previous commission press releases and proposed actions, which clearly had been a primary factor in the industry's meteoric fall from 170,000 installations in 1977 to 8,320 in 1981.

The risk assessment clearly demonstrated some acute and chronic health effects. Alternatives to UFFI insulation were available, except for a small percentage of homes with inaccessible spaces. Removal of hazardous insulation was expensive. All of the commissioners cited at least one of these factors in justifying their decision; not one of them discussed the costs, or claimed that the costs and benefits appeared to bear a reasonable relationship. It is hard to see how the commission's decision was based on anything approaching an analysis of costs and benefits. While estimating the benefits of health and safety regulation is usually a difficult task because of the human values involved, estimating the costs seems almost as difficult, since some costs are imposed whenever the commission proposes an action or announces that it is investigating a product because it may pose a hazard. Calculation of industry losses before any formal action was taken is not included in commission procedures; if it were, it could not be anything more than a vague guess.

In addition, the economic analysis provided little help in indicating who should bear the costs of regulatory actions. A primary decision to be made by the commission is who is to bear the costs of a health or safety hazard—consumers, industry, or government and the public as a whole. Identifying those costs is the first step, but the political decision that follows is not one that can be answered through economic analysis. It is clear here that the choice was not a particularly difficult one, since the industry involved was already almost exhausted financially—as a result of CPSC action—before the commission began to evaluate the effect of additional action on the industry.

Finally, the CPSC's decision to ban UFFI demonstrates some of the features of decision making under a commission. Different commissioners were attracted to different arguments. They based their votes on different criteria, thus weakening the appearance of decision making based on an analytic model. While it is not clear whether or not a single-headed agency would have come up with the same conclusion, the number of decision makers appears to increase the importance of political considerations over analytic ones. There is at least some independence of the CPSC from presidential pressure. Nancy Harvey Steorts, the only Reagan appointee on the commission at that time, voted for the ban. She resigned from the commission, however, in November 1984, after learning that she would not be reappointed when her term expired—apparently because she was frequently at odds with the White House over consumer protection.[62]

EVALUATING CPSC RULE MAKING

The CPSC was created with great expectations for regulatory rule making. It promised to formulate some 100 mandatory product safety standards between 1977 and 1982.[63] The commission, however, only issued 20 rules during its first decade of activity, banned seven products, and imposed reporting requirements on three products. Table 7.2 lists all of the CPSC rules issued during this period. The CPSC has been widely criticized for taking on relatively unimportant and even trivial product safety concerns. Between 1974 and 1980, only 1 percent of the major regulatory costs imposed by government were a result of CPSC rules.[64] Much of the criticism aimed at the commission has come from consumer groups, members of Congress, and others who have been dissatisfied with its lack of aggressiveness. As the commission

Table 7.2. CPSC Rules: The First Decade

Consumer Product Safety Standards

    Architectural glazing materials
    Matchbooks
    Walk-behind power lawnmowers
    Swimming pool slides
    Cellulose insulation
    Gas-fired space heaters
    Toy ingestion and choking
    Electrical toys
    Baby-cribs—full size and non-full size
    Baby rattles
    Clothing—textiles
    Vinyl plastic film
    Children's sleepwear
    Carpets and rugs
    Small carpets and rugs
    Mattresses
    Poison prevention packaging
    Refrigerators

Product Bans

    Unstable refuse bins
    Extremely flammable contact adhesives
    Lead-containing paint
    Patching compounds with asbestos
    Artificial emberizing materials
    Fireworks
    UFFI

Information Requirements Standards

    Chlorofluorocarbons
    CB and television antennas
    Cellulose insulation

Source: 16 *Code of Federal Regulations* 1201–1750.

has improved its performance in recent years, it has attracted increasing criticism from manufacturing and other business groups.[65]

It should be emphasized that much of the criticism directed at the CPSC has focused on its imminent hazard actions, involving product recalls and other corrective actions. The commission may seek injunctions against manufacturers producing imminent hazards, although the process involved is time consuming and rarely used.[66] The commission may require manufacturers of products covered by regulations that fail to meet the standards to notify consumers of hazards, or to repair or replace those products. The commission usually negotiates with manufacturers in developing a recall strategy and an order can be issued in a matter of weeks. The CPSC's annual report emphasizes the advantage of this recall authority: "While developing a mandatory standard can take years and cost hundreds of thousands of dollars, implementing a [recall] action can, if need be, occur within weeks."[67]

Manufacturers have been especially concerned about this power of the CPSC, as the uncertainty it generates makes financial and production planning more difficult. They see few constraints on commission decision making under the recall authority. It has been widely suggested that the CPSC only be permitted to recall products covered by commission rules, thus replacing the uncertainty surrounding its regulatory activities, except in the case of imminent hazards.[68] Such a proposal renders all the more important the CPSC's rule-making process and the need to evaluate how well it works.

Developing a Regulatory Agenda

In 1976, the House Commerce Committee's Subcommittee on Oversight and Investigation asked the CPSC to respond to the following question: "How in the past five fiscal years, has your commission translated its basic policy into significant rulings, regulations or programs? Give those examples you believe best illustrate such efforts." The commission's primary response was that it had issued rules concerning its policy for Freedom of Information requests.[69] The commission, during its first several years of operation, was unable to narrow or define its broad mandate. As Paul Weaver noted in 1975,

> The problem is that the commission doesn't seem to have a clear idea of how to go about its job. Given the size of its task—reducing the 20 million annual injuries associated with an estimated 10,000 kinds of consumer products—there are only two sensible ways to proceed. Either the commission could take upon itself the Sisyphean job of identifying the thousands of risks, redesigning all the products, and systematically enforcing compliance with its every regulation; or it could organize itself to provide the information and incentive needed by industry to improve the safety of products on its own.
>
> The first approach would require an enormous bureaucracy endowed with sweeping expertise. The second would require only a lean staff, a sophisticated data system, and a discriminating regulatory touch to stimulate private initiative rather than stifle it. The commission tries to use both of these approaches, but in fact its current setup is suited to neither. The aim is to have the best of both worlds; the effect is more often like falling between stools. . . . [70]

Since then the commission has made some progress: By 1978 it reduced its number of top-priority goals from 150 to 15, and had developed a product injury data base to help identify potential actions. Earlier problems in deciding when to initiate rule making resulted from a variety of factors, such as a lack of knowledge of how to get manufacturers to redesign products that would be safe despite consumer ignorance or misuse, difficulties in breaking down products into smaller categories to facilitate the focusing of commission efforts, a lack of licensing or pre-market testing requirement to identify problems, and the requirement that the commission respond to all petitions within 120 days. Commission officials found the petition requirement particularly inhibitive of planning and priority setting, a "noose" around the agency's neck subjecting it to the influence of groups who were able to "force their agenda" on the CPSC.[71]

The internal development of proposed rules has been flexible and informal: the matrix scheme for forming project teams seems to be a reasonable approach, since agency resources are insufficient to establish a permanent team for all major consumer product categories even if an appropriate categorization could be constructed. However, the commission suffers from an inability to develop alternative ways of addressing concerns other than the few basic approaches that had been used since the first years of operation, as well as from a lack of coordination between the engineering, science and epidemiology sections, as they sometimes based their work on different timetables.[72]

Finally, the tension between the staff and commissioners has been a source of confrontation, delays and inefficiency. Staff members have felt they were alone in really understanding the technical issues while commissioners saw themselves as the only ones with an adequate understanding of the "big" political picture. Each commissioner presented a different perspective and set of priorities to the staff. Different commissioners supported different kinds of analyses and emphases. Staff members developed allies among the commissioners, who then supported their analyses or asked for more studies. Many decisions were postponed while particular studies were requested by individual commissioners. There was little continuity among commissioners—eleven of them during the first six years—which meant that 3–2 votes could be reversed within a short period of time. Commissioners often viewed their tenure on the commission as short-term; they were often gone by the time a rule they supported was challenged in court and no one commissioner could be held accountable for a decision of the agency. Thus, the difficulty of providing guidance to an organization by a group of diverse individuals, each with different political priorities and professional biases, explains much concerning the problems encountered by the CPSC in its rule-making efforts.

Economic and Technical Analyses

The CPSC's economic and scientific analyses rest on the fragile base of a small staff with little in-house expertise in many areas, limited control or technical review of the analyses done by contractors, and information that has generally been supplied by the industries being regulated. The analyses supporting commission rules were widely attacked in early years as careless and inadequate. As in other agencies, the commission's choices about how to assess the risk of hazardous substances, which assumptions are to provide the basis for decisions, to what extent the findings of scientific studies can be relied upon, how the benefits of regulatory actions should be determined, and how the real costs of such actions can be identified are difficult, controversial and subjective.

Some observers, however, credit the CPSC with improved analytic efforts. Its lawnmower safety standard, for example, was upheld by the U.S. Court of Appeals for the Fifth Circuit, a court not noted for its sympathy for federal regulations and the same court that rejected the UFFI ban. Since reviewing courts have generally taken a "hard look" at the analyses behind CPSC standards, judicial approval has been an important indicator of improved analytic efforts. And commission lawyers have insisted on increased staff analyses of rules in an attempt to prevent judicial reversals.[73] Despite the progress, the CPSC is continually hampered by inadequate data and a staff too small to develop the data needed to address effectively the kinds of consumer hazards that are in its jurisdiction. This is true particularly in the area of chronic hazards. The commission's use of scientific research and analysis from outside its own staff shows some promise for improving the analytic foundation of its regulations.

Administrative Law and Due Process in CPSC Rule Making

The requirement that all meetings involving the commissioners be held in public has generated some significant difficulties. All meetings between staff and commissioners are required to be public, a requirement that some have found inhibits full and frank consideration of the commission's options. Some decisions have been based on consideration of the public statements of commissioners as much as on an analysis of the relevant issues.[74] The openness of commission deliberations has also posed a problem for the industries subject to CPSC regulation: The commission's proclivity to release information, either through press releases or public meetings, or when sought through Freedom of Information requests, has been widely attacked by business because competitors have been among the recipients of commission disclosures. Businesses try to avoid turning over information needed by the agency, since they fear competitors will be able to gain access to it as well. Voluntary efforts have also been inhibited by fears of releasing confidential information in a public setting. Commission mistakes in releasing confidential information have not assuaged corporate officials. As one commissioner stated:

> Instead of weighing the competing values of consumer protection and open decisionmaking, the commission simply assumed that total openness could be obtained without detracting from its safety mandate. It was felt that openness could only enhance the quality of decisions affecting consumer health and safety. . . .

When a formal regulatory decision is at hand, openness should be preserved to the extent possible. . . . But when an agency is simply exploring issues devoid of any immediate regulatory impact—and especially at an early or preliminary stage—unfettered discussion should be encouraged.[75]

Thus, openness, combined with eventual judicial review of agency decisions, poses a difficult problem for the CPSC; while public involvement may increase the number of views presented to the agency and improve the quality of regulations, it may also provide ammunition for the subsequent attacks of opposing lawyers, and may lessen the willingness of regulated firms to help resolve the problems being addressed. Although the CPSC recognizes the problems inherent in its policy of openness, it has not been able to strike an appropriate balance between administrative effectiveness and public participation.

Political Oversight

Congress has intervened in a number of rule-making proceedings in order to redirect commission actions, at times regarding them as too slow and at other times as too restrictive on industry. In 1978 the House Commerce Committee's Subcommittee on Oversight and Investigations accused the CPSC of being "derelict in failing to set safety standards for various types of [cellulose home] insulation."[76] The high demand for insulation along with a number of inexperienced firms installing the cellulose had led to home fires and other problems. The commission had been petitioned in 1976 to develop a mandatory standard but had failed to act as of 1978. Senator Wendell Ford, chairman of the Commerce Consumer subcommittee, then introduced legislation to establish mandatory safety standards which were eventually passed by Congress.[77] In 1981 Congress amended a CPSC rule for power lawnmowers, in response to business complaints that the regulation was unfair, and exempted amusement park rides from CPSC jurisdiction, also in response to industry pressure.[78] Thus, Congress has shown a willingness to intervene in CPSC rule-making decisions, but the concerns of the relevant commerce committee subcommittee chairmen have been the determining factor in shaping the intervention, rather than a general effort to oversee and give guidance to the CPSC's efforts.

The CPSC narrowly escaped being placed within a cabinet department in 1981. Some members of Congress sought to abolish the commission, while industry groups and the Reagan administration favored putting it into the Commerce Department. The head of the Senate commerce committee's consumer subcommittee criticized the CPSC for having "clearly overstepped the bounds of cost-benefit analysis."[79] OMB Director David Stockman argued that the commission had "largely accomplished its task" and had developed a "tendency for misguided activities."[80] Since the CPSC was to be the first

regulatory agency to come up for reauthorization under the Reagan administration, it was expected to be a target of major administrative concern in demonstrating how it would deal with regulatory agencies in general. Proponents
of an independent CPSC feared that a strong administration effort to end the
commission's independence was likely to succeed.[81] A vigorous defense of the
CPSC by Representative Waxman, chairman of the House subcommittee
with jurisdiction over the commission, who vowed that a bill ending the commission's independence would pass only "over my dead body"[82], and—perhaps more importantly—the administration's slowness in pushing for
placement of the commission in the Commerce Department resulted in the
reauthorization of the CPSC as an independent commission.[83]

THE CONSEQUENCES OF MISMATCHING RESPONSIBILITIES AND RESOURCES

The CPSC has been targeted by the Reagan administration for significant
reductions in operation. Its budget has been cut more than any other regulatory agency, resulting in the dismissal of 150 of its 850 employees, and the
cancellation of a variety of research projects, investigations and consumer
outreach programs.[84] The commission's budget has never borne much relationship to its broadly defined mandates. The CPSC was designed to take, as
a study for the Administrative Conference noted, a "predominantly reactive
posture: in responding to hazards brought to its attention by outside parties
rather than taking initiatives in developing a comprehensive regulatory program for consumer safety."[85] A former chair of the CPSC echoed this view:
"The Consumer Product Safety Commission has never, in my opinion, had
the advantage of an adequate base budget. It has never received funding from
the Congress which would permit it to address on its own initiative those can-
didates for regulation which score high on our priority list. We have found
ourselves continuously in a reactive stance."[86]

The CPSC, much like other regulatory agencies less formally independent
from the White House, suffers from a lack of direction. It carries a history of
high expectations and little success in achieving them. CPSC rule making has
lacked the resources that would have permitted it to escape the need to set
priorities and make choices; the choices made for it by Congress and by the
White House, however, have not gone beyond efforts to reduce agency
expenditures or eliminate regulations aimed at specific industries. As a result,
the rule-making efforts of the commission have been unable to meet the
expectations created for them by consumer advocates and their allies in Congress. The CPSC has begun to use more and more case-by-case proceedings,

such as product recalls, as an alternative to rule making, to escape the procedural limitations placed on it by Congress and the White House. As it relies on adjudicative proceedings, its actions become harder to predict and anticipate.[87]

Chapter 8 THE FOOD AND DRUG ADMINISTRATION

The Food and Drug Administration, created in 1931 as a part of the Agriculture Department, has jurisdiction over food, cosmetics, drugs, serums and vaccines, blood, food preparation facilities, medical and veterinary devices, and products emitting radiation (such as televisions and microwave ovens). The agency, now located in the Department of Health and Human Services, is empowered to issue regulations for food quality, drug efficacy and food and drug labels; review and approve new drugs before they are marketed; inspect and monitor food, cosmetics, drug and medical device manufacturers; and order product recalls or the seizure by federal marshals of unsafe products. More than a dozen statutes define FDA powers and responsibilities.[1]

Although a number of the statutory provisions under which the FDA functions are relatively specific, the agency exercises great discretion in many of its regulatory activities. Much attention has been directed toward the agency's enforcement activities, which often begin with on-site inspection of food, drug, cosmetic and medical device manufacturers. When inspectors detect violations of the law, enforcement proceedings begin, which may include sending a regulatory letter to top management asking for voluntary compliance. The FDA may request that a manufacturer recall a defective product from the marketplace; if voluntary actions are not sufficient, the FDA can seek a court injunction ordering compliance with an agency decision, or ordering federal marshals to seize the products. Criminal actions may also be filed by the agency in federal court against violators.[2] In setting standards and in evaluating products falling within those standards, the FDA confronts difficult issues of how to assess the risk, benefits and costs associated with food and drug production processes, as well as how to function in a highly political arena.

To some extent, the FDA's regulatory efforts for food and drugs are similar. Both include the issuance by the FDA of general standards for the labeling, safety, and quality of food and drugs and rule-making proceedings that are designed to evaluate specific food and drug products. The agency also issues regulations for the manufacturing of foods that contain substances

174

hazardous to human health and rules on applications for approval of new drugs. These actions are taken during administrative procedures that are somewhat like informal rule-making proceedings, but are often directed at a small number of manufacturers. However, the issues raised in FDA decision making of legislative purpose, the effect of procedural provisions, and the compatibility of scientific, economic and political criteria can be examined and compared with the rule-making efforts of the other agencies described in the preceding chapters. This chapter follows a somewhat different format than that of earlier chapters; several brief case studies will be presented, rather than one in-depth study, due to the variety of FDA proceedings.

The regulations and standards most often issued by the FDA involve food standards, which establish guidelines for food and food products; current good manufacturing practice regulations, which provide for quality controls such as inspections of materials and finished products; and new drug regulations, which set requirements for the approval of new drugs and the monitoring of the safety and effectiveness of drugs already in use. The FDA's responsibilities for food and drug regulation are examined separately in the sections below, since the statutory bases and regulatory process of the agency differ significantly for the two areas. Figure 8.1 presents an organization chart of the FDA which outlines its major program areas.

REGULATION OF FOOD SAFETY

The FDA's regulation of food safety rests upon a patchwork of statutes that require different procedures and provide different guidelines for the categories of food within the agency's jurisdiction. Congress has addressed a variety of food hazards through the enactment of various statutes, beginning in 1906, but has made little attempt to integrate new provisions with existing requirements. These provisions can be classified into four general categories of food constituents—natural constituents, environmental contaminants, food ingredients or additives, and substances used for other purposes such as food packaging material or pesticides that become part of food—that pose risks to human health and safety and have been the subject of congressional action. Although several food constituents may fall into more than one category, the statutory frameworks within which the FDA regulates these constituents differ in a number of ways and will be examined individually.[3]

Natural Food Constituents

The basis of the FDA's regulation of natural and environmental food contaminants is the 1938 Food, Drug and Cosmetic Act. Under the law, food is considered adulterated, and thus subject to FDA regulation, "if it bears or contains any poisonous or deleterious substance which may render it injuri-

Figure 8.1. The Food and Drug Administration

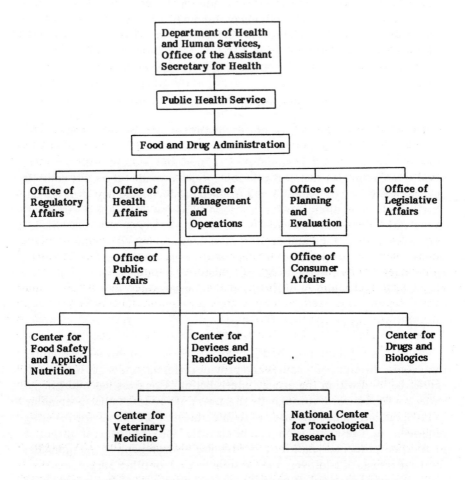

ous to health; but in case the substance is not an added substance such food
shall not be considered adulterated under this clause if the quantity of such
substance in such food does not ordinarily render it injurious to health."[4]
Examples of foods in this category include spinach, which contains nitrates, a
carcinogen; oranges, which contain ascorbic acid; and poisonous mush-
rooms. The FDA has the authority to issue a regulation or standard which
identifies a naturally occurring food constituent as an adulterant. In regulating the sale of a food that naturally contains a carcinogen, the FDA would

have to demonstrate that the food presents a serious risk when consumed in ordinary quantities. The FDA, however, has rarely taken such an action. Instead, it has generally seized dangerous foods through court action. The law does not require that food composed of only natural constituents be approved before marketing; as a result, the FDA has generally relied on a case-by-case approach in dealing with such foods.[5]

Environmental Contaminants

Environmental contaminants are dangerous substances unavoidably added to food during production or harvesting. Examples include aflatoxins (a carcinogen) found on peanuts and grains, and mercury in swordfish. Environmental contaminants are also regulated under the statutory provision discussed above. The provisions applicable to such contaminants require the FDA to act if the food "bears or contains any poisonous or deleterious substance which may render it injurious to health."[6] In practice, this statutory provision provides a more rigorous standard for environmental contaminants than for naturally occurring toxins, requiring the FDA to show a greater level of harm before regulating natural contaminants.

Judicial interpretation of the provision has indicated that the FDA must show that the food itself, and not merely the contaminant, is dangerous. In demonstrating that the food should be regulated, the agency is required to prove that there is a significant possibility that the food is "injurious to health": "[If] it cannot by any possibility, when the facts are reasonably considered, injure the health of any consumer, such [food], although having a small addition of poisonous or deleterious ingredients, may not be condemned under the act."[7] The level of exposure is also considered; the agency must show that the quantity of the adulterant is sufficiently great to present a hazard.

As has been true for naturally occurring contaminants, the FDA has generally regulated environmental contaminants on a case-by-case basis, rather than through rule making. Once it identifies food suspected of being unsafe, the agency conducts tests and has the burden of proof in demonstrating in court that the food is harmful to consumers. However, a subsequent statutory provision permits the FDA to consider whether poisonous or deleterious substances provide some benefit to food production or else cannot be avoided in important foods. The statute provides that: "Any poisonous or deleterious substance added to any food, except where such substance is required in the production thereof or cannot be avoided by good manufacturing practice shall be deemed to be unsafe . . . but when such substance is so required or cannot be so avoided, the Secretary shall promulgate regulations limiting the quantity therein or thereon to such extent as he finds necessary for the protection of public health, and any quantity exceeding the limits so fixed shall also be deemed to be unsafe."[8] The statute provides little guidance for the regulations or tolerances to be issued: the FDA is to determine " . . . the extent to which the use of such substance is required or cannot be avoided in the production of each such article, and the other ways in which the consumer may be affected by the same or other poisonous or deleterious substances."[9]

The FDA did not begin establishing formal tolerances until the 1970s. It had developed some informal tolerances for pesticide residue on raw agricultural products and, although producers and distributors of food were aware of them, they were never published.[10] As studies in the 1960s and 1970s increasingly identified contaminants such as polychlorinated biphenyls (PCBs), mercury and mycotoxins, the FDA sought to regulate these and other environmental and unavoidable food contaminants. It is required to establish standards for any dangerous substance that can't be eliminated through "good manufacturing practices," while assuring that levels do not threaten health. However, in some cases the lowest levels achievable still exceed amounts considered to be safe. As a result, the agency has in effect ignored these statutory requirements in favor of a more generalized consideration of the value of the food, its level of toxicity, and the extent to which the risk can be limited.[11]

Until 1954 the FDA was required to hold a formal hearing for every rule-making proceeding to set tolerances for unavoidable poisonous ingredients in food. In 1954 the law was amended to require a formal hearing only when requested by an affected party.[12] The process is nevertheless quite elaborately defined by Congress. The agency is required to issue a notice of proposed rule making in the *Federal Register* which describes the proposal. Interested persons may submit written comments to the agency, which, after considering the comments, publishes an "order" (or rule) that becomes final unless objections are filed by any person adversely affected.[13] Most rule-making proceedings in the past have terminated at this point, since objections have often not been raised or those raised have been dismissed for an insufficient legal basis.[14]

If the proceedings continue, a formal trial-type hearing must be held before an administrative law judge. The administrative law judge prepares a report and forwards that along with the record of the hearing to the commissioner, who then issues a tentative order. This can be challenged by any party involved, and the commissioner may request oral arguments by the parties before issuing a final order, based "only on substantial evidence of record." Any party adversely affected by the order can seek review in a court of appeals. The reviewing court is to defer to all agency findings the fact "supported by substantial evidence," but may otherwise order the FDA to issue, amend, repeal or not issue any rule.[15] The formal process is cumbersome and costly and has been replaced, in most cases, by an informal rule-making process that is described later in this section.

Food Additives

Food additives include both natural and synthetic substances intentionally used in food production, from those used in packaging and processing to those which directly alter the food itself. Different kinds of food additives are treated differently: color additives, additives that are "generally recognized as safe," and substances that were permitted prior to 1958 fall under different statutory guidelines than those for other food additives.

Congress considered a number of bills throughout the 1950s in response to recommendations of the "Delaney Committee," a select committee established in the House of Representatives in 1950 (chaired by Representative James Delaney) to investigate the use of chemicals in food. After three years of hearings, four reports were issued, including a study on food safety which called for the pre-market testing of food additives rather than the time consuming and difficult process of monitoring additives already on the market.[16] Two issues were particularly divisive: how to regulate additives already on the market, and whether to accept Representative Delaney's proviso banning all additives shown to induce cancer in man or animals. The way in which Congress responded to these issues, in the amendments to the Food, Drug and Cosmetic Law passed in 1958, has since shaped much of the FDA's regulatory efforts for food safety.[17]

Representatives of food manufacturers sought to exempt additives already on the market from regulation, but some members of Congress feared that such an exemption would leave too many potentially dangerous substances on the market. A compromise was eventually reached which provided that substances generally shown to be safe after years of repeated use would not have to be approved by the FDA. Ingredients that are generally recognized as safe (GRAS) were defined by the law as food additives that have been "adequately shown through scientific procedures (or, in the case of a substance used in food prior to January 1, 1958, through either scientific procedures or experience based on common use in food) to be safe under the conditions of [their] intended use."[18]

This provision of the law has been implemented through the issuance of a list of ingredients considered by the FDA to be GRAS. Food manufacturers are free to determine for themselves whether an additive they seek to use is GRAS. If the FDA disagrees, it may seek court action against the manufacturer, but the burden of proof is on the agency to show that the additive is not safe. Ingredients that are GRAS may be regulated by the FDA if later shown to be dangerous. Cyclamate, for example, was widely believed to be GRAS until research in the 1960s indicating that it might cause cancer in animals led to an FDA ban in 1969.[19] Similarly, the use of saccharin, another former GRAS substance, was regulated by an interim food additive regulation during the late 1970s and early 1980s. A number of additives escape regulation under the FDA's "grandfather clause," where food ingredients approved earlier by the FDA or the USDA, before the 1958 amendments took effect, cannot be regulated as food additives even if new evidence questions their safety. They can only be regulated through the FDA's general food adulteration provisions.[20]

All food additives not included in the categories discussed above fall within the FDA's general mandate for regulating food additives. The FDA must issue a regulation authorizing the use of any food additives not generally recognized as safe before they can be used in food. Food safety statutes provide several criteria to be met before approving an additive, including evidence that it is safe and that its use will not "promote deception of the consumer." The FDA may issue a regulation specifying the conditions under which the additive may be used, limits on the quantity to be used, and packaging and labeling requirements.[21]

Congress gave some indication of how the FDA was to determine if a food additive was "safe" in the House and Senate reports accompanying the 1958 amendments. A determination that an additive was safe required "proof of a reasonable certainty that no harm will result from the proposed use of an additive." Congress rejected a standard of zero risk: "The concept of safety . . . does not—and cannot—require proof beyond any possible doubt that no harm will result under any conceivable circumstance."[22] It also rejected a balancing of risks and benefits in regulating food additives. Any benefits associated with a food additive would be irrelevant, as long as there was reasonable certainty that a danger existed. The well-known Delaney Clause reflects this intent of Congress: The FDA was instructed that "no additive shall be deemed to be safe if it is found to cause cancer when ingested by man or animal, or if it is found, after tests which are appropriate for the evaluation of the safety of food additives, to induce cancer in man or animal."[23]

The process prescribed by statute for regulating food additives is as intricate as that involved in issuing tolerances, outlined above, although the specific proceedings involved differ. Food manufacturers initiate the process by petitioning the FDA for approval of a particular additive, and then submitting data which demonstrate the additive's safety. The FDA must publish in the *Federal Register* a notice indicating that a petition has been received. The agency then reviews the petition and publishes a final order of approval or disapproval. Any person adversely affected by the final order may request an oral hearing to challenge the agency and decision. The agency's approval goes into effect immediately, even if a hearing is forthcoming. The final decision following a hearing is subject to review by a federal court of appeals.[24] The FDA, however, approves most food-additive petitions and only a few have required a formal hearing.[25]

Indirect Food Constituents and Substances

The final category of food constituents regulated under the Food, Drug and Cosmetic Act involves substances that become constituents of food in processing, production and distribution. The FDA has estimated that there are some 10,000 substances that are part of food packaging, processing equipment, and food storage that might become part of the food itself. Animal drugs that leave residuals in meat, eggs and milk and pesticide residuals on raw and processed foods are also regulated as indirect food additives. The statutorily prescribed process and criteria for approving these indirect food additives are the same as for direct additives, as discussed above.[26] Recent technological developments have permitted the measurement of increasingly small quantities of materials, and have identified a number of substances previously thought to be safe as possible carcinogens. As a result, the FDA will be under increased pressure to ban such materials, under both the Delaney Clause and the general safety clause for food additives.[27]

Animal drugs and animal feed are also treated as food additives and are subject to the same statutory provisions as other additives, as well as additional legislation expressly enacted for this category of additives in 1962. Congress ordered that the Delaney Clause "shall not apply with respect to the use of a substance such as an ingredient of feed for animals which are raised for food production, if the Secretary finds (i) that . . . such additive will not adversely affect the animals for which such food is intended, and (ii) that no residue of the additive will be found . . . in any edible portion of such animal after slaughter or in any food yielded by or derived from the living animal."[28] Thus, before approving a new animal drug or feed additive, the FDA reviews manufacturers' data to determine if the additive may be carcinogenic. If carcinogenicity is demonstrated, the additive may still be permitted as long as unsafe residuals do not remain in the food produced.[29]

Rather than instructing the FDA to develop a comprehensive approach, which maximizes consumer benefits and minimizes risks, Congress has provided different and sometimes contradictory standards for different kinds of food ingredients. In some cases Congress has sought to provide a relatively specific balancing of risks and benefits, while clearly indicating in others that safety is to be the determining factor. To some extent, these statutory differences are not irrational or haphazard, but are indicative of congressional interest in dealing with a complex issue: regulating substances that may pose some risk but are widely used and popular. Other statutory provisions, however, such as those distinguishing between carcinogens in food additives and animal drugs and pesticides, appear to make less sense, since the risk to humans is the same regardless of the source of the dangerous substance. Recent proposals introduced in Congress would limit the FDA's regulatory reach to only those food additives posing a "significant risk" to consumers,[30] while counterproposals backed by consumer groups have also been introduced.[31] The Reagan administration began writing its own version in 1981, but insufficient interest was generated for statutory change.

FDA RULE MAKING AND FOOD SAFETY REGULATION

The provisions of the food safety laws have posed a number of problems for the FDA. The rule-making provisions require formal proceedings which are expensive, time consuming, and have largely been replaced by the FDA with a more informal process. Some of these informal efforts, however, permit almost no public participation and involve little more than an announcement in the *Federal Register* of the agency's intention. Congress has not provided for hybrid or informal rule-making proceedings to guide the FDA, as has been done for other agencies. Nor does the law provide for rule making for some kinds of food ingredients. When the agency wishes to demonstrate that a natural ingredient renders a food product dangerous, for example, it must take each distributor to court separately. As it reviews applications for food additives and issues tolerances or standards for natural and environmental food contaminants, the FDA determines whether consumers are to have products that are safer and more expensive, whether some products will not be available at all, or whether they are to have popular products that may increase health risks. Some procedural guidelines and general criteria have been developed by the Bureau of Foods for approving food additives and for issuing tolerances, but much of the bureau's operating procedure is informal and ad hoc.

Regulating Environmental or Unavoidable Food Contaminants

Between 1938 and 1970, the FDA did not issue a single formal tolerance for any toxic substance that was classified as an unavoidable or environmental contaminant.[32] Instead, the agency developed an informal rule-making process designed to produce "action levels," standards for pesticides and other environmental contaminants that, when exceeded, would trigger FDA enforcement action. While action levels do not carry the same weight as formal rules, they do represent agency decisions concerning how its prosecutorial discretion is likely to be exercised. The process of issuing action levels involves little more than publishing the proposed level in the *Federal Register* once it has been developed within the FDA.[33]

By the 1970s, however, the FDA found that the increasing importance of action levels required an increase in public participation. In 1974, the agency issued proposed regulations outlining the procedures and criteria to be used in establishing action levels. The FDA argued that since "industrial practices were improving so quickly [and] that the extent to which [a] substance is avoidable changes significantly from year to year, there is little justification for the use of [formal rule making] procedures." The agency then proposed that the traditional informal rule-making process be used for each of the 10 to 20 contaminants dealt with each year.[34]

By 1977, however, when it issued the final rule for establishing action levels, the FDA found that the "establishment of action levels through informal rulemaking would still involve a substantial amount of time and agency resources. Because of the time required to promulgate an action level and the dynamic circumstances in which action levels are used, the possibility exists that an action level will be outdated soon after it is promulgated, in which case the process would begin anew. The potential for wasteful expenditure of agency resources has persuaded the agency that a simplified procedure for adopting action levels should be used."[35] The process defined by the agency involves publishing a proposed action level for a specific substance in the *Federal Register*, inviting public comments on the proposal and providing for public inspection of all related data used in developing the standard, and publishing a final action level, revised if necessary, in response to received comments. And even this process would sometimes be broached: "Because of the dynamic circumstances in which action levels are used, it will frequently be necessary to revise a particular action level before a notice can be published in the *Federal Register*."[36] Although there is no public discussion of the agency's decisions, there is, at least, publication of the allowable levels of contamination. By 1981 the FDA had issued some 200 action levels for food contaminants, most of which were developed with little or no public participation.[37]

The criteria used by the FDA in setting action levels is not clear. Statutory guidelines include the effect of the substance on public health, the extent to which it is avoidable, and other ways in which it affects consumers.[38] The ability to detect and measure the contaminant is also considered an important factor. One former chief counsel indicated that the agency's primary criterion is the lowest level of contaminant that is technologically or economically attainable. The agency then attempts to reconcile that level with the health data describing the risks involved.[39] A former commissioner, in contrast, stated that the FDA first estimates the highest level of exposure that would not adversely affect consumers, based on published research. (This has not been particularly controversial for noncarcinogens, since it is generally assumed that a minimum safe or threshold consumption level exists.) Once this exposure level is established, the agency then divides by a "safety factor" which yields a "safe" level of contamination.[40] For carcinogens, however, the dominant view, as expressed in the Delaney Clause, is that no safe level of exposure exists for these substances. When not bound by the Delaney Clause, the FDA establishes action levels for food ingredients that, while they are assumed to have no safe level of consumption, may pose relatively insignificant risks at some levels.[41]

The FDA's effort to regulate carcinogenic environmental contaminants is limited by the difficulties, similar to those in other regulatory efforts, of extrapolating from animals to humans and from high test doses to low human consumption doses, as well as additional difficulties inherent in food regulation. Since these food contaminants are unintended, for example, manufacturers have not done any testing to assess the potential risks. No premarketing approval is required, thus providing no mechanism or incentive for industry testing. Nor is information available concerning the impact on food prices of regulations limiting these contaminants or on consumption levels of products that are most likely to be contaminated.[42]

The Bureau of Foods has found the formal tolerance-issuing process "basically unworkable" and has rarely used it. The bureau has responded to most demands for action on an ad hoc basis, gathering together agency officials with relevant expertise and experience who are required to make decisions based on little information. That lack of information, coupled with the sense of emergency usually involved, generally results in an informal agency decision characterized by one FDA official as the "best judgment at this point in time."[43]

The FDA's use of action levels to establish limits on the amount of harmful substances permitted in food is conducted informally, without the kinds of rule-making procedures used elsewhere. In 1985, however, the federal court of appeals in Washington, D.C., found that such informality was contrary to congressional intent, and ordered the FDA to use formal proceedings to increase public participation and to develop a rule-making record that would include the scientific information on which the agency based its action.[44]

Regulating Unavoidable Contaminants: The FDA and PBBs

The FDA's regulatory efforts of the chemical group known as PBBs demonstrate some of the agency's difficulties in regulating environmental food contaminants. Polybrominated biphenyls (PBBs) are chemical compounds used as fire retardants in plastics. Chemical companies had identified them as potentially toxic in 1972. In 1973 a major producer of PBBs shipped bags of a fire retardant containing PBBs to a Michigan feed company by mistake. The fire retardant and the feed supplement ordered by the feed company looked almost identical, and both were shipped in brown paper bags with stenciled labels. The retardant was added to feed supplement and distributed to farmers, who eventually noticed sickness and reduced milk production in cows.[45]

By April of 1974 scientists identified PBBs as the cause of the problem and in May the FDA set action levels of one ppm in meat and dairy products, based on the smallest amount of PBB residue the agency was able to detect. By November of 1974 the FDA was able to detect residues at 0.3 ppm and the action level was lowered accordingly, since the FDA had concluded that no safe level could be established for PBBs. Because good manufacturing practices could have prevented the problem, the agency acted under its statutory mandate to prevent possibly "injurious" food from being marketed. Some 20,000 cattle containing residues of PBBs exceeding the FDA's standard were subsequently destroyed.[46]

By the end of 1975, the FDA had used refined analytic methods to identify traces of PBBs as low as five parts per billion in milk and meat. Almost nine million people in Michigan had become exposed to the contaminant by this time, and it became clear that if the FDA again lowered its standard, a great part of Michigan's livestock and produce would have to be destroyed. In the interim, agency officials had also become skeptical of the health hazards of PBBs. As a result, the agency reclassified PBBs as environmental or unavoidable food contaminants, arguing that they had become an inextricable part of the food supply in Michigan. Thus, the agency would regulate PBBs under another statutory provision, for unavoidable contaminants, which permitted a balancing of risks and economic costs. As a result the agency maintained the 0.3 ppm action level, despite pressure for a lower level from a panel of scientists appointed by the governor of Michigan and from a Michigan congressman.[47]

In only one case has the FDA issued a formal tolerance for environmental contaminants through the formal rule-making process required by statute. In 1979 the FDA issued a tolerance for polychlorinated biphenyls (PCBs), toxic chemicals similar to PBBs found in significant amounts in the lakes and streams of industrial regions. The agency was able to base its decision on much more scientific information concerning the risks posed by PCBs than it had for PBBs. The final decision, however, rested on a sort of cost–benefit analysis that the agency made in 1974: "Consideration of the amount of food loss caused by a tolerance helps to ensure that the direct economic consequences of the tolerance (in this case, decreased sales and employment in the commercial fishing industry) will not be disproportionate to the increased degree of public health protection accomplished by the tolerance; but the agency considers secondary economic consequences, such as potential impact on the recreational fishing industry."[48]

Food Additives

The FDA approves almost all requests for new food additives and for new uses of additives already approved. The extremely high rate of approval is largely due to the informal review process within the Bureau of Foods. Before actually submitting a petition to the FDA, food manufacturers usually meet with officials of the Food and Drug Additives Division to discuss the data required to accompany the request for approval of the new substance. Requests that are not likely to meet the agency's requirements are usually not submitted.

Once a petition is received, it is given a quick review by a consumer safety officer from the Division of Food and Color Additives, who becomes responsible for the application. A notice of filing is then published in the *Federal Register* and public comments are invited. By law the agency is to take final action within 180 days of the filing date. If additional information is requested, the manufacturer is notified and the 180-day period is stayed until the manufacturer responds. Review of the application also involves officials from the Division of Chemicals and Toxics, who are asked to review the claims of chemical effectiveness and safety made by the petitioner. The heads of all three divisions must sign the final order, which is then sent to the Regulation Review Office and the director of the Bureau of Foods. At the agency level, the general counsel and the assistant commissioner for regulatory affairs review the final order before it is published in the *Federal Register*.[49] The process is considered quite routine and rarely generates much controversy. If anyone adversely affected requests a hearing, however, the statutory-defined formal rule-making process is triggered. For color additives, the final order is stayed while the hearing takes place, while for all other additives the order takes effect immediately.

The FDA has banned a number of food and food color additives under the general safety clause. Only two additives have been banned under the Delaney Clause. Table 8.1 lists some of the major substances banned by the FDA. The decision to ban a food additive usually begins with either a petition from a consumer group or information generated within the agency. A proposal is published in the *Federal Register* explaining the reason for the proposed ban. Comments are usually submitted to the agency by interested parties. Before the final decision is published, it must be approved by the office of the Secretary of Health and Human Services.[50]

The FDA initiated in April of 1982 an effort to outline the criteria to be used in assessing health risks of food ingredients. The agency issued an advanced notice of proposed rule making for a policy on regulating carcinogenic chemicals in food and color additives, which gives some indication of the FDA's effort to move away from its case-by-case approach to regulating food and food color additives.[51] The policy seeks to develop a uniform standard for environmental contaminants and food and color additives that rejects, to some extent, the Delaney Clause's flat prohibition of carcinogenic food ingredients. The proposed policy would integrate previous FDA decisions, which have approved food ingredients containing lead and arsenic (proven carcinogens categorized as unavoidable or environmental contaminants, subject not to the Delaney Clause but to exposure levels set by the

Table 8.1. Selected FDA Food Additive Bans

Year	Substance	Function	Comment
1950	Dulcin P-4000	artificial sweetener	decision made because other artificial substances available
1954	Coumarin	ingredient in cacao products	causes liver damage in test animals
1960	Safrole and related compounds	flavoring agent	carcinogen, but prior sanctioned substance
1968	Oil of Calamus	flavoring agent	causes malignant intestinal tumors in rats
1969	Cyclamates and related compounds	artificial sweeteners	carcinogen, but GRAS substance
1972	Diethylpyro-carbonate	beverage preservative	byproduct, urethan, is a carcinogen; formerly GRAS
1973	Mercapto-imidazoline	packaging component	carcinogen, but GRAS; byproduct of ethy-lenethiourea
1973	FDA Violet #1	coloring agent	provisional listing revoked
1976	Red #4	coloring agent	provisional listing revoked
1976	Carbon black	coloring	provisional listing revoked
1967	Flectol H	packaging material	carcinogen in test animals; banned under Delaney Clause[a]
1969	4,4'-Methylenebis (2-chloraniline)	packaging material	carcinogen in test animals; banned under Delaney Clause

[a]The FDA decided to ban saccharin in 1977, under the Delaney Clause, but was overruled by Congress.

Source: Congressional Research Service, "Food Safety Policy Issues" Report No. 81–155 SPR (June 1981), pp. 32–33.

agency), with those coming under the Delaney Clause ban.

The first step in assessing the risk associated with the use of a food additive would involve generating and analyzing test data from animal experiments and calculating a maximum exposure level. The agency has not decided, however, which model it would use—linear, multistage or some other model—to extrapolate the test data to human exposure. Nor has the agency defined the risk standard—the level of the risk to human health and safety—that would be tolerated.[52]

Once the maximum exposure level is established, the agency would then determine the actual level of exposure and would, if necessary, establish standards to assure safe consumption levels. This risk assessment procedure would, according to the FDA, "yield such low acceptable levels that nothing but minor levels of carcinogenic chemicals would pass the screen." The procedures would be "conservative to compensate for the weakness in scientific rigor" and would "likely overestimate the risk."[53] The analysis would also include the economic and environmental impact of the regulatory action resulting from the risk assessment, along with the cost-benefit analysis required under Executive Order 12291.

The agency gave three primary reasons for its shift in policy. First, analytical capabilities had greatly increased in terms of identifying carcinogens and in terms of the ability to detect extremely minute traces of chemicals. As a result, there were many more substances considered to be carcinogenic, and they could be identified at levels as small as one part per billion. The FDA found that many additives containing carcinogenic constituents do not appear to cause cancer themselves. Thus, additives composed of ingredients that include carcinogens should not be banned if they are not themselves carcinogenic.[54]

Second, the agency sought to respond to a 1979 ruling by the Court of Appeals for the District of Columbia which interpreted the food safety legislation to grant "administrative discretion" to the FDA "to deal appropriately with *de minimis* situations." Thus the agency could approve of a food additive containing a carcinogenic element if there was a "reasonable certainty of no harm."[55]

The third reason for the issuance of the new policy was the agency's confidence in its ability to assess the levels of risk involved in the use of a food additive containing carcinogenic elements. It argued that in using conservative extrapolation models, upper limits of risk could be estimated, and be used with confidence to demonstrate a "reasonable certainty that no harm [would] result from the intended use of an additive."[56]

The FDA's carcinogen policy is not likely to result in a major shift in agency decision making. The agency could continue to regulate additives on a case-by-case basis. The proposal does not constitute a frontal attack on the Delaney Clause, only partially addressing the difficulty of regulating carcinogens. It does, however, represent a willingness to consider the costs imposed by its regulatory decisions. One FDA official attributed the shift to the Reagan administration's emphasis on cost-benefit analysis and explanations of agency actions, although some FDA decisions, since they are not considered rule makings, do not formally come under Executive Order 12291.[57] In 1985, the FDA rejected a petition by a consumer group to ban 10 food dyes, claiming that the threat they posed was "de minimis"—too insignificant for legal action—even though six of the chemicals had induced cancer in laboratory animals. Critics argued that the agency's failure to act was a violation of the Delaney Clause.[58] The experience of the FDA in regulating saccharin under the Delaney Clause provides some important background for better understanding the FDA's regulation of food additives and its regulatory efforts in general.

Saccharin and the FDA's Regulation of Food Additives

Saccharin is a food additive 350 times more potent than ordinary sugar when used as a sweetener and contains no calories. An estimated 50 to 70 million Americans are saccharin consumers. In 1977, some 6.4 million pounds of saccharin were consumed in the U.S. As early as 1907 there were concerns over possible adverse health effects of its use, and in 1912 it was banned by the Department of Agriculture. Sugar shortages during World War I, however, led to the lifting of the ban, and by the early 1950s saccharin was widely used as a cheap substitute for sugar. The FDA began to reexamine the safety of saccharin use in 1955 and asked the National Academy of Sciences to review the scientific literature related to saccharin. The NAS concluded that up to one gram per day of saccharin should be considered safe, and when the 1958 Food Additives Amendment was passed, saccharin was classified as a "generally recognized as safe" substance. The NAS reviewed the safety of saccharin again in 1967 and, although a little more cautious in its approval of saccharin, maintained its view that consuming one gram per day was safe. In 1970 the FDA banned cyclamate after tests indicated it might be a carcinogen in animals, which left saccharin as the only artificial sweetener.[59]

The FDA had attempted to avoid banning cyclamate and saccharin by classifying artificial sweeteners as drugs, and thus not within the scope of coverage of the Delaney Clause. Congressional charges that the agency was ignoring the law caused the agency to reverse direction, and a new category was created—"interim food additive"—for substances previously classified as GRAS but undergoing additional testing. After another review by the NAS, saccharin was classified as an interim food additive and restricted to special dietary use. The FDA began its own testing of saccharin, as did a private organization financed by the sugar industry. The NAS again was asked to review these and other studies and found in 1974 that research did not conclusively demonstrate that saccharin was a carcinogen. The FDA extended the interim classification of saccharin through 1976 pending further research.[60]

In the spring of 1977 the Canadian government banned saccharin after a Canadian study concluded it was carcinogenic. FDA officials reviewed the study, concurred with the findings, and in April of 1977 published a proposal to ban the use of saccharin except as a "drug" to be used by diabetics. In November of 1977 Congress enacted the Saccharin Study and Labeling Act, which ordered the FDA to delay its ban for 18 months and to require that products containing saccharin bear the following warning label written by the FDA: "Use of this product may be hazardous to your health. This product contains saccharin which has been determined to cause cancer in laboratory animals."[61] Congress extended the moratorium on the FDA's ban of saccharin in 1980, 1981, and 1985, assuring that saccharin can be used until at least 1987.[62]

FDA officials have offered a number of explanations for the decision to ban saccharin. The commissioner, in announcing the agency's decision, stated that the decision was based on the general safety clause as well as the Delaney Clause: "The focus on the Delaney Clause led many people to believe that we would not have acted against saccharin in foods and beverages without this strict provision. This is not true. General provisions of the Food,

Drug and Cosmetic Act say that food additives must be safe. And with the accumulated evidence we now have against saccharin, including cancer findings in each of the last three animal studies, our judgment is that it is not safe for continued use as a food additive. We therefore would have moved to end the general use of saccharin even without the Delaney Clause."[63] The FDA's general counsel, writing three years after the decision, indicated that the decision "did not result from careful comparison of saccharin's risks and benefits. . . . The Delaney Clause made legally unnecessary though not politically irrelevant, quantification of saccharin's risk or reexamination of the relevance of animal experiments as evidence of human risk."[64]

A number of factors came together in 1977 to force the FDA to act. The agency had a significant amount of data amassed over more than a decade, much more information than it normally had before making decisions. The data was indefinite enough, however, to cause the agency to waver. The epidemiological studies reviewed by the NAS gave either conflicting results or were rejected for methodological reasons. The animal tests reviewed indicated that high saccharin doses—7.5 percent of the total diet of the animals—caused bladder cancer in rats. (The level of exposure of the test animals in the Canadian experiments was the equivalent of a human drinking some 800 12-ounce cans of diet soda each day.) The NAS report concluded that saccharin should be viewed as a "potential carcinogen" in humans, but that "the state of the art in extrapolation does not permit confident estimation of the potency of saccharin as a cause of cancer in humans."[65] Once the NAS study was published, the FDA had no choice but to ban saccharin, as members of Congress, the press and consumer groups attacked the FDA for failing to protect the public's health, and lawsuits were threatened if the agency did not act.[66]

Once the proposed ban was announced, attention shifted to Congress. Some members reported that more mail from constituents had been received concerning the proposed ban than for any other recent issue.[67] Lobbying by the soft drink industry, diet food manufacturers, dieters and diabetics convinced members of Congress that the ban should be postponed. Debate then shifted to the health warnings that were to be required in all advertising of products containing saccharin. The final vote permitted members to respond to the demands of industry lobbying, vote for strong warning labels to protect public health, and support continued research.[68] In 1980, when the 1977 action expired, Congress reviewed a number of studies, including three studies of the National Cancer Institute, Harvard University's School of Public Health, and the American Health Foundation, which found little support for classifying saccharin as a carcinogen, and voted to renew the extension.[69] In 1985, Congress again extended its ban on FDA action to regulate saccharin,[70] as the controversy over the safety of artificial sweeteners continues. Food producers continue to call for FDA approval of cyclamate, while consumer groups have charged that aspartame (NutraSweet), the newest widely used sugar substitute, is not safe.[71]

Evaluating Food Safety Regulation in the FDA

In the past, the FDA's food safety efforts have generally ignored costs in seeking to maximize the protection of public health. One former FDA official argued that agency decision making was (and should be) guided by "common sense" rather than analytic formulas. Once top agency officials came to a decision, they would turn to the person responsible for assessing the impact of the decision on inflation, who would be instructed to prepare a report showing that the impact would be less than $100 million, thus freeing the agency from the constraints imposed by the (Carter) executive order. Attention would then turn to the person responsible for the environmental impact statement, who would be instructed to prepare evidence that the intended action would not have a significant impact on the environment. Another FDA official emphasized the difficulty of creating analytic and economic rules to guide agency decision making, arguing that each case brought before the agency involves unique factors and requires individualized decisions.[72]

Since most of the FDA's regulatory activities have been applied on a case-by-case basis, it has escaped much of the regulatory relief action of the Reagan administration. If significant opposition arises to an agency action, a formal rule-making process is initiated, but such a process is exempt from Executive Order 12291. And decisions made by the FDA in the area of food safety usually have a relatively minor economic impact, with a few notable exceptions, such as saccharin. The FDA has traditionally enjoyed a great degree of autonomy within the Department of Health and Human Services (previously the Department of Health, Education and Welfare). Almost all regulatory powers had been delegated to the commissioner, although the secretary of the department was always alerted when a major decision was forthcoming. In 1981, however, the secretary of HHS began to retract some of this delegated authority.[73]

By 1985, critics charged that the FDA was being illegally constrained by the Department of Health and Human Services and the Office of Management and Budget from regulating food additives. As discussed above, the FDA's interest in regulating 10 widely used color additives, including Red Dye #3 and two others that represent half of all dyes consumed in the United States, has generated significant controversy. In 1963 the agency first considered banning the dyes; by 1985, the agency had postponed making a decision 28 times. FDA scientists favor the ban, but it has been blocked by the HHS Secretary's office. Congressional critics charged then-Secretary Margaret Heckler with violating the Delaney Clause and with permitting the OMB to influence FDA decision making.[74] *The New York Times* reported that the FDA was still considering banning some 120 food additives. A variety of "animal experiments, several lawsuits, a special hearing by a congressional oversight committee, and pressure both from consumer groups . . . and from industry lobbyists" are part of the regulatory history of just one food color additive, Red Dye #3.[75]

The FDA has been the subject of a number of significant court cases which have forced the agency to explain the bases of its decisions.[76] Congress has also had an important impact on the FDA's food safety regulatory actions, usually focusing on a particular substance, such as saccharin, where public opinion galvanized Congress into challenging the agency. Although the FDA has been frequently criticized for issuing regulations unpopular with the public, or failing to provide careful analyses to justify its decisions, one study conducted for the Administrative Conference concluded that "it is difficult, however, to point to an instance in which the agency failed to discover or heed evidence about risk or avoidability that would have dictated a different decision."[77]

The FDA's complex scheme of food safety laws, the uncertainty of scientific analyses used in decision making, and the highly charged political environment in which many decisions develop result in food safety decisions that are based upon a rough, imprecise balancing of the costs and possibilities of limiting exposure to products that may be a risk to public health. The costs of food to be destroyed and the ability of the agency to detect levels of contamination are both factors in a decision that ultimately rests on the political judgment of the officials involved. Scientific analysis pales here in significance, when compared to political calculations and concerns. And although the political environment shapes the efforts of the FDA in regulating drugs as well, the agency's experience has differed in several areas as discussed below.

DRUG REGULATION AND CONGRESSIONAL INTENT

The FDA's responsibilities for the marketing of drugs in the United States have developed over 75 years and rest on a number of statutory provisions. The 1906 Food and Drugs Act banned from interstate commerce drugs that contained impurities, were otherwise adulterated, or failed to meet the recognized standards of the pharmacological industry under which they were sold. Misbranded drugs—those whose labels were false, misleading or failed to identify specified ingredients such as alcohol or narcotics—were also prohibited.[78] In 1938, Congress, after more than 100 deaths caused by the use of "Elixir of Sulfanilamide," a patent medicine that had been tested for flavor and appearance but not for safety, established detailed drug-labeling requirements including ingredients (for those drugs not listed in the pharmaceutical industries' compendia of official drugs), directions for use, and warnings against possible habit formation. The most important shift in statutory provisions was the requirement that all new drugs be approved by the FDA. Drug manufacturers were required to submit reports to the FDA demonstrating the safety of new drugs before they could be marketed. Drugs already on the market were not affected unless the FDA initiated a court proceeding to demonstrate that they were dangerous.[79]

In 1951 another amendment was passed, defining categories of drugs requiring a prescription before sale and providing regulations for the dispensing of prescription drugs. Habit-forming drugs, drugs not safe for self-medication and new drugs limited to prescription dispensing were included in the law. Over-the-counter drug sales were given additional labeling requirements to assure safe and effective use.[80] Between 1938 and 1962, new drugs were developed at a rapid pace, and the FDA's review of the new drug applications took, on the average, seven months. Attention shifted to drug safety in 1962, after the use of thalidomide had resulted in birth defects in children born in several European countries where the drug was widely used. Congress quickly passed amendments to the drug laws requiring that drug manufacturers demonstrate the efficacy as well as the safety of new products. Prior to 1962, drug manufacturers were required to show only that their products were safe; the FDA, if it challenged the marketing of a drug, had the burden of proof in demonstrating that the drug was unsafe. After 1962, drug companies were required to prove that their products effectively achieved the claims made about them.[81]

The 1962 amendments also required drug manufacturers to submit a new drug investigational plan, which provided the results of tests of the proposed substance on animals, before testing on human subjects could begin. New drug applications were no longer automatically approved unless the FDA rejected them, but instead required agency approval before they could be marketed. FDA powers were strengthened and expanded in still other areas as the agency was empowered to issue regulations for "good manufacturing practices" for the production of drugs, to monitor compliance with additional requirements for drug labels, and to regulate prescription drug advertising. (The Federal Trade Commission was given responsibility for regulating the advertising of over-the-counter drugs in 1938.) The drug laws were amended again in 1972, requiring manufacturers to submit to the FDA an inventory of all drugs, their current labeling, representative samples of advertising and package inserts, and to update the inventory every six months.[82]

In 1979 the Senate passed a drug regulatory reform act, introduced by the Carter administration and the FDA. The proposal sought to increase public involvement in the drug approval process, reduce delays in approving significant new drugs, stimulate competition from generic producers of drugs after patents expire by reducing testing requirements, and extend FDA authority in monitoring drug use after the initial approval. Many of the provisions of the bill would have codified FDA rules and policy guidelines developed by the agency over the past several years. The bill, however, was never reported out of committee in the House, and died as Congress adjourned in 1980.[83] The Reagan administration has not pushed for any statutory changes in the FDA, preferring instead to pursue reform through administrative efforts.

Regulation of Drug Safety

The FDA has developed an elaborate drug approval process in response to its statutory authority and responsibilities. Figure 8.2 presents the process involved in developing a drug under the FDA's supervision. Once a new drug has been developed and tested in animals, the manufacturer submits to the FDA an investigational new drug (IND) application which must be approved

Figure 8.2. Drug Development and Approval under the FDA

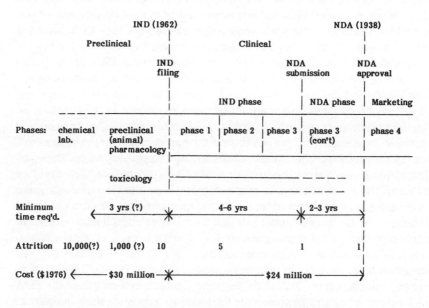

Average Effective Patent Life (from NDA approval date):　　1966: 13.8 years
　　　　　　　　　　　　　　　　　　　　　　　　　　　　1977: 9.5 yrs

Source:　Henry G. Grabowski and John M. Vernon, The Regulation of Pharmaceuticals: Balancing the Benefits and Risks (Washington DC: American Enterprise Institute, 1983), p. 22, from an article by William M. Wardell, "The History of Drug Discovery, Development, and Regulation : Issues in Pharmaceutical Economics, Robert I. Chien, ed. (Lexington, Mass.: Lexington Books, 1979).

before the drug can be tested on human subjects. The Bureau of Drugs evaluates the application in terms of the protection afforded the human research subjects involved, the results of the animal testing already conducted, and the overall danger of the research project and the qualifications of the researchers. The drug manufacturer may begin human testing 30 days after the application is submitted to the FDA unless the agency rejects the application.[84]

Testing by drug manufacturers generally proceeds through three phases. The drug is first tested on healthy research subjects in highly controlled conditions. Phase two involves testing the drug on a limited number of patients. If these two steps yield positive results and the manufacturer believes the drug is likely to be marketed successfully, phase three begins, involving studies of large groups of patients treated with the new drug. If the tests are successful and marketing potential remains significant, the firm then submits a new drug application (NDA) to the FDA. The manufacturer must submit the results of all tests conducted, which generally consist of from two to 15 volumes of summary information and 10 to 100 volumes of raw data. The FDA is required to review and act upon an NDA within 180 days. In practice, however, the process has taken, on the average, almost three years. As is indicated in Figure 8.2, for every 10 new drugs approved at the IND stage, only about one will be submitted as an NDA. However, a drug reaching the NDA stage enjoys a 90 percent chance of being approved by the FDA.[85]

The Bureau of Drugs' Office of the Associate Director of New Drug Evaluation initially reviews all NDAs and creates a team to evaluate each NDA. Team members come from the six divisions within this office representing various categories of drugs, and are usually comprised of a medical officer who evaluates the data from the clinical tests, a pharmacologist who reviews the data from animal tests, a chemist who reviews the chemical and manufacturing processes, and occasionally a statistician, microbiologist, or other specialist. The team is headed by a medical officer. During the review process, the team often requests additional information from the drug manufacturer and may meet with industry representatives. Drug manufacturers are given the right, by statute, to a formal administrative hearing to contest scientific decisions made by the FDA, but rarely do so, since the process is expensive, time consuming, and likely to damage industry relations with the agency.[86] The review team meets with the head of the division under which it operates; with the bureau director; and, when necessary, with the manufacturers of the drug, to resolve conflicts over scientific information or to request additional data. If it appears that the FDA will approve the application, the agency and company officials meet to determine what information will be included in the package insert—the official labeling used by physicians and pharmacists.

The Bureau of Drugs has established a number of public advisory groups to assist it in reviewing NDAs. The committees, which do not review all applications but only those given to them by the agency, usually meet only two to four times a year, often delaying the review process even further.[87] A recent GAO study of the FDA's drug approval process found that advisory committees were used "to provide advice on problems or questions FDA may have concerning selected drug applications" but applications were not "submitted routinely to the committees."[88] Outside consultants are also occasionally used in reviewing specific applications.

The process terminates with a decision approving or rejecting the application, or the agency may formally request additional information and the process continues. The FDA has recently begun classifying NDAs as they are received to identify those drugs that are likely to yield "an important advance" in treatment and give priority to those applications. NDAs chosen for this "fast-track" review process are then likely to be approved for public use more quickly.[89]

Once a drug is approved, the FDA assumes a relatively minor role in monitoring its use. The FDA has no authority to regulate the way in which physicians prescribe approved drugs, although the agency monitors the advertising of prescription drugs. Manufacturers are required to notify the FDA whenever they learn of negative or adverse reactions from the use of drugs they produce, and the agency may subsequently remove from the market or order changes in labeling for drugs previously approved.[90]

Evaluating the Drug Approval Process

The process of reviewing new drug applications takes much longer than the time allowed by the Food, Drug and Cosmetic Act. A GAO study of 132 new drug applications filed in 1975, for example, found that by the middle of 1979 only 52 percent had been approved or otherwise acted upon.[91] Delays in the FDA's review process have been blamed on several factors, including unclear FDA guidelines that can be interpreted in a variety of ways, disagreements between the FDA and drug manufacturers concerning scientific findings and claims, slowness in agency identification of deficiencies in applications and in industry's efforts to remedy those deficiencies, FDA management and coordination of agency resources, and the length of time taken to review chemical and manufacturing processes involved in drug production.[92]

The FDA has made some attempts to reduce the time involved in evaluating NDAs. In 1977, it began to publish guidelines for use by drug firms in testing and evaluating different classes of drugs. The use of these guidelines is voluntary, but they represent the criteria used by the agency in reviewing the design and analysis of clinical tests used in the drug development process. Clinical tests meeting FDA standards are then more likely to lead to FDA acceptance of the test results and analyses.[93] In 1978, the agency began to schedule conferences with drug firms to review the results of preliminary tests of drugs that appear to have great promise for therapeutic use, in order to clarify agency policy, give guidance, and minimize the length of the review process. These conferences occur before the NDA is submitted to the FDA. In the case of drugs that are considered important and likely to yield significant therapeutic improvements, the agency speeds up the review process by asking for the submission of test data before the NDA is submitted so that FDA review can begin earlier.[94] In late 1984 the FDA also reduced the amount of data drug companies were required to submit in the drug approval process, permitted the use of some foreign clinical studies, and made other changes in the drug approval process that were expected to reduce it by about six months.[95]

Another problem is the lack of review of the safety and efficacy of drugs once they are marketed. Physicians, however, are reluctant to release information, fearing that malpractice suits would result. The lack of a systematic evaluation of actual drug use has made the FDA's premarketing review all the more important.[96] The slowness of the FDA's new drug approval process has been blamed for a reduction in pharmaceutical innovation. It is clear that since the early 1960s there has been a decline in new drugs marketed, and a great increase in the time and costs required to develop and market a new drug. The Reagan administration has begun to reverse this trend; in 1981 and 1982 more new drugs were approved by the FDA than ever before.[97] But it is not clear that the increased FDA regulatory activities have been the cause of the problems of the drug industry, nor is there any general agreement that there have been significant benefits from the FDA's regulatory activities.[98] The extraordinary amount of data to be reviewed for each NDA, the difficulty in attracting high-quality medical and scientific personnel, and overly casual management practices have all weakened the FDA's efforts. Many agency officials are skeptical of the drug industry and assume an adversarial position toward it, thus complicating and delaying approval of new drugs, while other officials seek to work more closely with industry representatives. The fear of approving a drug that later is shown to be dangerous is much greater than the concern that a drug with therapeutic value is not marketed as quickly as it could be.[99]

The frequency of meetings between industry and FDA officials has been the focus of complaints by consumer groups. While FDA officials have argued that manufacturers' representatives rely on factual and reasoned arguments rather than overt pressure, the agency is forced to rely to a great extent on industry data. Court appeals are time-consuming and generally used when drug producers, often joined by the medical profession, seek to halt an agency effort to withdraw a drug already on the market.[100] Yet Congress and consumer groups have also played important roles in the drug regulatory process. In 1979, testifying before a congressional subcommittee, the FDA commissioner described the agency's concern for openness and due process:

Although not peculiar to drug regulation, the emphasis on openness in drug decisions is probably as great as in any other area of public concern. The most obvious manifestations of public demands for openness and due process include: open meeting of FDA drug advisory committees; geometric rise in FDA freedom-of-information requests; mounting numbers of consumer and industry petitions; requests for hearings; law suits demanding action or challenging agency decisions on drugs; and aggressive oversight hearings by the Congress. Although these factors unquestionably militate against speedy drug approval, we generally regard them as healthy trends that produce valuable intangible benefits such as greater public participation and understanding of drug benefits and risks.[101]

Attempts to ban (or failure to approve) popular substances, such as laetrile, have occasionally generated political pressure directed at the FDA through Congress and the courts. Public interest groups have pressed for even stricter enforcement efforts.[102]

The most significant external force shaping FDA actions has been Congress. Congressional oversight hearings in the late 1960s and early 1970s were generally in response to concerns—raised by consumer groups—that the public was not being adequately protected from unsafe drugs. FDA officials indicate that this oversight has led the agency to be more cautious and slow-moving, burying itself in documentary detail in an effort to escape congressional criticism. By the late 1970s, however, Congress had begun to focus on delays in approving new drugs, while consumer groups gradually began to be more concerned with the safety of drugs already on the market. One former FDA commissioner argued that

by far the greatest pressure that the Bureau of Drugs or the Food and Drug Administration receives with respect to the new drug approval process is brought to bear through Congressional hearings. In all our history, we are unable to find one instance where a Congressional hearing investigated the failure of FDA to approve a new drug . . . the message conveyed by this situation could not be clearer. . . . Until perspective is brought to the legislative oversight function, the pressure from Congress for FDA to disapprove new drugs will continue to be felt, and could be a major factor in health care in this country.[103]

ASSESSING THE FDA'S REGULATORY EFFORTS

The procedures by which the FDA makes regulatory decisions are generally informal. They have been developed in response to a perception that the formal rule-making proceedings provided by statute are unworkable. Congress has given little attention to those procedures enacted decades ago. In recent legislation it has often focused, instead, on specific substances in response to public pressures. The food and drug laws are a patchwork of categories with many differing standards and criteria, often neglecting to give guidelines for many of the most difficult choices to be made by the FDA. Economic and scientific analyses have been essential elements of the FDA's regulatory process, but have been of limited use for the most complex issues addressed by the agency, a problem plaguing all health and safety agencies. The FDA has been sensitive to the economic costs posed by regulatory actions when they are widespread and extensive, but has generally acted to protect public safety irrespective of costs imposed on the specific manufacturer involved. Beginning in 1981, however, the agency began shifting away from the latter position, as the Reagan administration's emphasis on regulatory relief began trickling down to FDA officials.

In the end, political forces have battered the FDA from many sides and agency officials have often felt that no matter what decision was made, it would be viewed by powerful political forces as wrong. As a former general counsel of the FDA wrote several years ago:

> In the twenty months that I have held my current position, I cannot recall one major safety decision by the Food and Drug Administration—regardless which way it was resolved—that has failed to provoke prolonged, and at times bitter, public dispute. Moreover, even if we had reached exactly the opposite conclusion on any of those decisions, it is unlikely that there would have been any greater or lesser amount of dispute. In short, public policy design and execution with respect to the safety of food and drugs is highly, and perhaps irretrievably, controversial. It raises up a wealth of subjective and emotional views that often obscure rational analysis and that can severely hinder regulation by scientific decision making.[104]

Part 3

Conclusion

Chapter 9 THE PROSPECTS FOR LIMITING BUREAUCRATIC DISCRETION

Rule making is a central element of the administrative process and represents the most controversial exercise of governmental power by regulatory agencies. While it has been championed for its efficiency and flexibility, for the ability it offers to agencies to regulate a wide range of activity, it has become an extremely slow and cumbersome process. Due to the numerous internal and external reviews and the analyses that must be prepared, rule-making proceedings normally last five years, and may take longer with controversial issues. While rule making has been championed as a way for government to take action more quickly than it could through the legislative process, just the opposite is true—Congress, when it chooses to, can react much more quickly than can agencies by writing new laws or amending existing statutes. The promise offered by administrative discretion—flexibility, adaptability, and expertise—has not been realized, and the capacity of institutions of government to accomplish their policy purposes has been diminished by too much discretion in some cases and too little in others.

Much attention has been directed toward agency rule making by congressional and presidential overseers. In the executive branch, oversight has become routinized. The OMB review process has engendered much frustration in agencies, where regulation writers resent the questioning of their handiwork and bristle at the delays. The review has generally caused agencies to provide more analysis to justify the proposed regulations, and has heightened their sensitivity to the costs they impose on those they regulate. But it has not produced comprehensive presidential control over the substance of regulation, since OMB's resources fall far short of what would be required for such an effort. OMB officials can only give very limited time to reviewing rules that are very complex and run into the hundreds of pages. The review has focused on details, on relatively narrow questions, and has not examined the broader, basic questions of how agencies can best accomplish their statutory purposes and what changes in these laws are needed. The primary effect of the review has been to slow down the issuance of new regulations.[1]

Congressional oversight has been ad hoc and sporadic, unlike the routinized nature of White House oversight. Congress has a variety of tools that permit its members to intervene in agency decisions and apply pressure, and members have generally been able to shape the substance of specific regulations in which they have an interest. Oversight has consisted of examination of specific agency decisions that have raised red flags by affected constituents, rather than a more in-depth and comprehensive study of what agencies are doing. Oversight hearings are especially popular in Congress since they can generate publicity, but they do little to help agencies decide how to allocate their resources and make the difficult choices expected of them. Both congressional and presidential oversight are usually driven by an attempt to respond to constituents who seek to block or slow down agency initiatives. Hence, this oversight reflects the political self-interest of members of Congress and presidents.

Administrative law and procedures have had an important impact on the ability of agencies to accomplish the tasks given them. While substantive concerns are rarely sacrificed for procedural ones (agencies are usually able to find a way to do what they really want to) trial-like procedures have made it even more difficult for agencies to deal with the uncertainty and limited information that characterize their rule-making efforts, and have discouraged efforts at compromise among interested parties. Judicial review has had a major impact on the process of rule making, as the demands of courts for a more detailed rule-making record and extensive supporting analysis for regulations consume a significant share of agency resources. But courts have not determined the content of regulations or helped agencies decide how to accomplish their statutory mandates. They are neither equipped to evaluate and contribute to the analysis that accompanies rules nor to assure that rules benefit from this analysis; assure only that the analysis is done.

Courts have had their most pronounced impact when they have been used by groups who seek to put pressure on agencies to issue rules by invoking statutory provisions that impose deadlines for the issuance of particular rules. Courts can easily enforce these procedural requirements and, as a result, litigation has played a major role in establishing agencies' priorities. Such review clearly limits agency discretion, but in a way that is fragmented and procedurally grounded and does little to guide the substance of agency decisions. Some recent decisions of federal courts have increasingly stressed the statutory limits of agency actions, in contrast to an earlier judicial view of administrative decision making as a political process where all relevant interests must be accommodated.[2] The Supreme Court has also recently ruled that an agency's decisions not to initiate regulatory action cannot be appealed to the federal courts. Justice Rehnquist, in the majority opinion, argued that Congress, not the courts, should decide when an agency's refusal to take action is inappropriate. The decision significantly limits the ability of parties to try and pressure agencies to take actions that they have refused to pursue on their own.[3]

The analytic requirements imposed on agencies have also had a pervasive influence on the process of rule making, but have had a much more modest and limited impact on the substance of rules. There is much less information available to agency officials than is assumed by these decision rules. They are so sensitive to the assumptions underlying them that they can easily be manipulated, and serve political considerations rather than providing a basis for policy choices. The ability to detect extremely small traces of dangerous chemicals outstrips the knowledge of the risks associated with such minute levels of exposure. Statutes requiring the issuance of regulations in absolutist terms ignore reality, and provide little direction for agencies deciding how to allocate costs among the regulated parties.[4] Such rules foster an expectation of expertise and analysis that agencies can rarely satisfy. Rule-making efforts become increasingly expensive and time-consuming and thus result in the issuance of a relatively few regulations, which are then challenged both by those who find that the agency has not gone far enough in eliminating hazards and by those who find the regulations too burdensome. In the process, the discretionary authority of one set of bureaucratic officials has been replaced with that of another set, as professional norms and practices of substantive fields such as occupational health and epidemiology are replaced by economic formulas and analyses. As cost–benefit analysis is extended across agencies and monitored by the OMB, agency discretion is reduced. However, because the use of such formulas and decision rules are so sensitive to the assumptions and values of the analysts that employ them, discretion is increased, while being masked in the vocabulary of objective analysis.

Congress and the Politics of Procedure

Table 9.1 summarizes the legally mandated procedures for the agencies examined here. The differences in the kinds of procedural constraints imposed by Congress demonstrate that there is no clear consensus in Congress concerning what procedural provisions should constitute the rule-making process. And the table itself shows more agreement than really exists, as the actual language varies considerably across the organic acts of agencies. Many of these procedures reflect past congressional compromises, when the weakening of enforcement provisions has allowed regulatory bills to pass.

Congress has imposed on these agencies extremely ambitious objectives to assure the health and safety of workers, consumers, and the public as a whole, while committing only a small fraction of the resources required to accomplish the mandated regulatory agenda. Moreover, in the late 1970s through the early 1980s, Congress began to cut back funding for most regulatory agencies, yet no parallel legislation was enacted reducing these agencies'

Table 9.1. Rule-Making Procedures: A Comparison[a]

Agency/Statute	Advanced notice of proposed rule making	Oral hearings	Cross-Examination	Formal Rule-Making Record	Public Financing of Citizen Participation	Citizen Suits to Force Rule Making
EPA:						
Clean Air		x		x		x
Clean Water						
Safe Drinking Water		x	x			
Hazardous Wastes—Resources Recovery Superfund						
Toxic Chemicals		x	x		x	
Pesticides		x		x		
CPSC	x	x				
OSHA		x				
FDA: Food Safety[b]		x	x	x		
Drug Safety[c]		x	x	x		

[a] Procedures which go beyond minimum requirements of informal rule making—publication of proposed rule, public comment period, publication of final rule, and judicial review to assure that rules are not "arbitrary or capricious"—as required by the Administrative Procedure Act.

[b] Primarily regulations establishing tolerances for environmental and natural food contaminants.

[c] Primarily regulations for the testing of the strength, purity, and quality of drugs.

responsibilities. Public demands for action, budget crises, court orders, and pressure generated from crises such as chemical disasters all come to bear on these agencies, but they get little direction from Congress and the president over how to use their scarce resources rationally. Nor has Congress made an effort to resolve the overlaps, conflicts, and incompleteness among the statutes it has enacted.

The experience of the agencies studied here have been very similar, even though they represent independent commissions, independent agencies in the executive branch, and agencies within cabinet departments. The major elements of rule making—legal procedures and judicial review, analytic requirements, and political oversight—are quite consistent across these agencies. The political environment in which they function has been quite similar, and structural factors are not critical independent variables. The CPSC, for example, has been the most beleaguered of the agencies studied here, with budget and personnel cuts that are proportionately greater than for almost any other regulatory agency. Its independent status has done little to protect it from White House disfavor. The major elements of rule making—legal procedures, analytic requirements, political oversight, and judicial review—are quite consistent across these agencies. While it is true that the CPSC, as an independent agency, is not subject to OMB review, that has not been an important factor, since the commission has issued so few regulations. Much more important has been the power of the president to appoint, in all of these agencies, people who agree to carry out the president's regulatory principles.

Nor have statutory differences been major determinants. The EPA's statutes are much more detailed than those of its sister agencies, but with only a few exceptions, such as those for automobile emissions under the Clean Air Act, the agency is given little guidance about the substance of regulations— how to make the important political and policy choices concerning the distribution of the costs and benefits. The statutory responsibilities dwarf the resources given, and give little guidance for how they should be allocated. EPA statutes include lengthy lists of actions to take and deadlines to achieve that the agency cannot even begin to accomplish. This does little to set priorities or give direction: if everything is a priority then nothing is, and directions are set by the vagaries of judicial review and the deadlines imposed by federal judges.

The substantive standards in these statutes call for zero discharge of pollutants into navigable waters, require that worker health not be impaired, and state that no cancer risks will be permitted. Statutes include such unrealistic promises for understandable political reasons. Enthusiastic support is much more likely to be generated by dramatic promises than by modest, incremental proposals. Agencies find such goals impossible to achieve, since all risks cannot be eliminated and tradeoffs are inevitable, but statutes give little guidance about how these inevitable tradeoffs must be made. Statutes deny that such tradeoffs are necessary; they deny that the costs of compliance will extinguish some industrial and commercial activity; they deny that the marginal benefits, as controls become increasingly strict, may be extremely small, and may not justify the often exponential increase in costs.

Administrative Discretion: Is the Cure Worse than the Disease?

Do administrative agencies have too much or not enough discretion? How much should they have? Are some kinds of discretion more desirable than others? If we mean by discretion that agencies are free to do what they choose, are free to allocate their resources and can exercise their power unencumbered by external checks, then agencies clearly have little discretion. Oversight plays a major role in limiting agencies, prohibiting them from taking actions that are opposed by politically powerful forces. Agencies must move slowly, and are constantly susceptible to external direction and influence. Regulatory agencies are not, in this sense, out of control, although presidents may want more control and feel jealous of the power of congressional committees and subcommittees. Agencies are influenced by the issue networks of congressional committees and interest groups, and restrained significantly by the executive branch budget and regulatory review processes.

Oversight of agencies has largely served to complicate and even obscure the accountability of administrative officials. Agency heads assume public responsibility for administrative actions. It is probably rare that agency heads take significant actions to which they are really opposed; if it becomes clear that they are not able to run their agencies, they are not likely to remain on the job long. Agency decisions about which the administrator does not feel strongly are much more susceptible to the demands of overseers and outside groups. Because these interventions rarely take place in public, agency heads cannot be held strictly accountable for the actions of their agencies. In that sense, agencies may have more discretion than we would find desirable.

If agencies are heavily involved in making basic policy choices, the political tradeoffs and policy calculations that we would like to have made by elected officials rather than unelected bureaucrats, we may also conclude that bureaucratic discretion is excessive. The size of agencies and the complexity of their regulatory tasks dwarf the resources of those who would direct them from the outside. Agencies receive little guidance for the substantive decisions they must make about how to allocate the costs and benefits of their decisions and how to balance competing concerns.

It is clearly not true that agencies are unbridled and unrestrained. Rather, they are subject to an oversupply of procedures and overseers. The problem is twofold. First, these efforts to limit discretion fail to assure accountability and responsibility and involvement of elected officials in making basic policy choices. Despite expansive and simplistic statutes which ignore the political significance of the costs of achieving their goals, agencies cannot escape difficult choices. And oversight, whether by the courts or the more political branches, comes at the wrong end of the decision-making process, reviewing specific agency proposals rather than engaging in a much more efficient effort to determine how regulatory burdens are to be distributed and how to balance regulatory goals with other public purposes.

Second, rule-making procedures make it very difficult for agencies to accomplish the tasks delegated to them and to address the significant environmental and health problems that need attention. The regulations that have been issued have often been so strict that they are unenforced by state and local officials fearful of driving out industry and development. Agency resources have been concentrated in preparing analyses and satisfying extensive procedures for a few regulations, while significant environmental and health risks in many other areas have not been addressed.[5] In some cases there is overregulation, where standards are more strict than is justified by the marginal improvement in protection; in others, the problem is underregulation and a lack of even minimum protection.[6]

The integrity and effectiveness of laws suffer when the expectations they foster cannot be met. The rule of law is a practical, concrete concern. If legal provisions lose their integrity, they lose their ability to command compliance. Incentives are created to fight regulatory efforts rather than comply with them, and those who then comply feel unfairly penalized. Extreme and unrealistic statutory provisions that must be compromised in implementation breed contempt for law and discourage voluntary compliance. The millions and millions of actions taken each day that affect environmental quality and human health cannot be monitored, and thus voluntary cooperation is essential. But when statutory provisions are not enforceable, and are subject to informal interpretations, the power of the rule of law is significantly weakened.

Neither Congress nor the president can possibly make all of the policy choices required to accomplish the public purposes they write into law. There is an inescapable tradeoff between the size and scope of government and the ability of a limited number of elected officials to be responsible for the implementation of public policies. If they (and we) continue to pursue regulatory goals through centralized efforts, then we must be prepared to accept increasingly larger doses of discretion. But if efforts to limit administrative discretion are not more carefully constructed, the capacity of government to accomplish public policies effectively will continue to be threatened.

REMEDIES AND REFORMS

Bureaucratic discretion is an inescapable characteristic of the administrative process. It cannot be eliminated, but it can be balanced more effectively with our other expectations of the exercise of administrative power. Increased awareness of the competing expectations directed at the administrative process, and a commitment to balance these pressures, are much more important than attempts to create new institutions or processes that might somehow escape the competing and contradictory concerns of accountability, the rule of law, due process, expertise, and administrative efficiency.

Current practices and procedures are in place as a result of political incentives that are well understood but difficult to alter. Reforms that better provide for the competing expectations of the regulatory process will not produce major improvement unless these incentives—and the values and priorities underlying them—are replaced by different ones. The analysis and discussion above compels certain suggestions for change. These are explored below, in order to complete our analysis, highlight the most important problems and shortcomings of current arrangements, and give some general direction for reforms. They present an agenda for future study, rather than a politically practical recipe for restructuring administrative power.

Learning from the Experience of Others

We should think more creatively and carefully about how to limit and check administrative discretion without producing the kinds of intended and unintended consequences that cripple effective government. The experience of the other industrialized democracies can be useful in identifying more clearly the shortcomings of the United States approach, and in considering alternative institutional arrangements for rule making in particular and policy implementation in general.

Regulation, for example, is much less centralized in the smaller Western European countries and in Canada than in the United States. Officials in German states can ease environmental standards, for example, when local ecological and economic conditions warrant it. Officials from state and national agencies work together in formulating regulations for chemicals. Local government officials in Britain are also given discretion to relax regulations (unlike in the U.S., where local governments can deviate from national standards only to make them more stringent) which encourages industry–government cooperation and flexibility.[7]

The contrast is striking between the procedural requirements outlined in the Administrative Procedure Act, and other U.S. agency-enabling statutes, and those imposed on government agencies in Europe. In Great Britain, for example, there is much less reliance on formal rules and regulations. Agencies within the Department of the Environment, for example, establish "presumptive standards" for the emission of pollutants, after consultation with representatives of the industries involved. These standards are designed to foster voluntary compliance by specific firms; agency officials and plant managers negotiate emission levels for each facility. Inspectors have flexibility and discretion in seeking compliance, preferring persuasion and negotiation, and use prosecution only as a last resort. Little public information is available concerning these decisions in Great Britain, and there is no provision for general public participation.[8]

German regulatory policy relies much more on written rules and precise standards, in contrast to British informality and negotiation. In the area of occupational safety and health, for example, the Ministry of Labor issues binding standards for exposure to chemicals. Unlike U.S. practices, however, its regulations are formulated out of public view. Chemicals that are suspected of being dangerous are first identified by the German Research Society, comprised of academic and industrial scientists. The Ministry of Labor then convenes a technical advisory body that includes representatives of industry, labor, state and federal agencies, and occupational medicine; that body establishes regulations limiting exposure levels, which then become official standards. As in England, the emphasis is on consensus. Participation is limited to representatives of expert groups and affected parties.

In Sweden, rules are promulgated in a similar fashion with few formal requirements. The National Board of Occupational Safety and Health brings together a small number of representatives from labor and industry to formulate rules for workplace hazards. Proceedings are neither public nor secret, but simply generate little external attention. While the board may circulate proposed rules to outside groups for comment, the emphasis is on negotiation and consensus.[10]

In contrast to the U.S. emphasis on scientific and economic decision rules, rule making in Western European bureaucracies gives little attention to formal decision rules. The statutes under which they function rarely prescribe such standards. The costs and benefits of regulatory options are reflected in the positions and concerns of the parties during rule-making negotiations. Rule making is clearly perceived as a political process, where scientific and economic analyses are not determinative but are only part of a broad, political calculation. In the United States, industry groups use cost-benefit analysis to protect their interests against what they perceive to be hostile regulators; in Germany, Britain, and Sweden, industry representatives are part of the policy-making process, and are expected to incorporate cost considerations in the concerns they raise.[11] Scientific bodies in these countries nominate chemicals and industrial practices for regulatory restrictions; the assessment of risk is clearly separated from policy making.

Given the great concern with internal devices to delimit administrative discretion in U.S. agencies, it is remarkable how much attention is also given to external review of agency actions. The Western European approach is, again, dramatically different. Statutes are most often written by the government and passed with few changes by the parliament, reducing significantly the gap between the legislative and administrative processes. Since the ministries are under the control of the same political party, there are few incentives for members of parliament to launch embarrassing attacks on administrative decisions. The tradition of ministerial responsibility narrows and focuses political accountability. The participation of affected groups in the formulation of rules and the emphasis on consensus results in little interest in reversing these decisions through political intervention.

In Western Europe judicial review is not viewed as permitting interested groups an opportunity to overturn agency actions. Review is generally limited to considerations of individual rights affected by the enforcement of administrative policies, rather than by their formulation. The underlying concept of administrative law is significantly different. In Germany, for example, administrative law is "the law of public administration" oriented toward the management of public institutions and the direction of the bureaucracy, unlike the U.S. approach, which primarily focuses on the rights of private parties affected by administrative action.[12] The structure of judicial review differs significantly, as European nations rely much more on the idea of separative administrative courts to review agency actions. Perhaps most importantly, as with political intervention, consensus and representation in the formulation of rules eliminates incentives to seek judicial reversal.

Institutions and processes, of course, cannot be easily transplanted across political cultures. European bureaucrats are much more accepted and trusted than their American counterparts, and government intervention in economic and social affairs is much more accepted. However, the experience of other countries demonstrates that efforts to limit administrative discretion can be more orderly and restrained.[13] Regulatory negotiations, and other innovations with which U.S. agencies are beginning to experiment, promise to reduce conflict and avoid protracted judicial review, and should be more widely considered.[14] Comparative studies need to explore these and other options in more detail, and consider lessons that can be applied to efforts in the U.S.

Increasing Regulatory Capacity

Public and private institutions need to increase their ability to address threats to human and environmental health more effectively. There is a great need to improve our ability to identify environmental and health hazards, to sort out significant threats from minimal ones and reduce the impact of those that present real danger, and to expand significantly our institutional capacity to respond to and remedy these hazards in a way that is effective, comprehensive, and balanced with concerns of economic activity and growth.

It is not at all clear that rule making by federal agencies is the most appropriate means of addressing these needs. Much work needs to be done to explore the possibilities for less centralized approaches and to reduce the excessive expectations directed at the federal government.[15] It is likely, however, that in many areas, national efforts will be required and rule-making will be central to those efforts. Several changes in the rule-making process could significantly increase its contribution to the effective achievement of public policies.

Agencies should not be expected to eliminate all risks and exposures to dangerous substances, and should allocate their limited resources much more broadly. They should become much more willing and able to set exposure levels on the basis of marginal analyses, where the costs and benefits of increments of increased protection are carefully calculated and compared. They should be free to set more modest restrictions on polluters, so that they can use their limited resources in regulating more sources of pollution.[16] For some substances, where risks are unambiguous and substitutions are readily available and not significantly more expensive, total bans may be appropriate. But such cases are quite infrequent, and are overwhelmed by the vast majority of substances for which there is insufficient information to permit such judgments.

Chemicals, for example, that are proven to be carcinogenic when ingested by laboratory animals could be much more widely regulated than they currently are. Rather than requiring the maximum possible reduction in exposure to humans, however, regulations should be based on a more practical calculation of the costs of reducing succeeding increments of exposure. The belief that there is no safe threshold point for carcinogen exposure leads to demands for extreme levels of protection. While there is little certainty of scientific data here, it does seem clear that all humans are constantly being exposed to natural and artificial carcinogens, and that even if exposure to some chemicals were severely limited, much greater levels of exposure to other chemicals would still occur. The increasing ability to identify traces of chemicals that are measured in parts per billion and smaller may generate demands for regulations that are too extreme, that produce extremely small increases in protection for increasingly large expenditures, and that appear to be unreasonable and supercautious when compared with exposures at much greater levels to natural and other unregulated carcinogens.[17]

Rewriting Regulatory Statutes

The kinds of changes discussed above would, in most cases, require changes in statutes to permit such an incremental analysis of costs and benefits and cost effectiveness, and to provide guidelines for balancing the risks, costs, and benefits to be accommodated. Much more attention and study should be directed toward revision of individual statutes, so that more rational regulatory efforts can be developed.[18] Statute writers should give much more attention to the way in which statutes are to be implemented, and should not permit major provisions to be enacted without first considering carefully how they can be accomplished. Although political incentives may encourage them to do otherwise, legislators who are advocates of environmental and health protection ought to be more aggressive in assuring that the laws they enact are crafted in a way that will increase the likelihood of effective implementation.

The language that is used in the debate over statutory and regulatory actions should reflect a more sober awareness of the difficulties of policy implementation. Arguments that people have a "right" to a pollution-free life, or a completely risk-free workplace, hinder the search for compromise and common ground. Once the idea of rights is invoked, the discussion becomes tied up with absolutes, with single purposes, with no attention given to the costs of satisfying those rights. Indeed, rights are justified as being so important that they cannot be abridged, regardless of the costs. Such concepts are not helpful in achieving the tradeoffs and balances required in regulating environmental and health risks.

Such a shift in regulatory policy ought to be welcomed by environmentalists, public interest groups, and others who champion government efforts to protect the environment and human health; such advocates would find that much more overall environmental and health protection is gained. If regulatory agencies could increase by several times the number of hazards they regulate, at relatively modest levels of protection, the amount of protection provided and risks reduced would be much greater than under the current approach of maximum regulation of only a few substances. Analytic resources could be spread much more broadly in identifying the wide range of hazards that exist, rather than in concentrating on developing justifications for extreme standards. Implementation would be much more immediate and efficient if proposed rules were not immediately challenged in court for failing to provide absolute protection.

Industries would likewise benefit from such a shift in regulations. The uncertainty of a system that involves time-consuming and expensive litigation for virtually every regulation of any consequence makes business planning difficult at best. Industry representatives regularly acknowledge that their primary frustration is with regulatory delay and uncertainty, more than with the substance of regulations. Standards that are seen as reasonable, by those who are expected to comply with them, are much more likely to result in compliance than are those that are widely viewed as unreasonable. Regulations that are clear, consistent, and accepted by industry can be implemented immediately, rather than put on hold until the long legal appeals process runs its course. Expanding the scope of regulation may increase prices for consumers, but if regulations are more efficient, compliance costs will be more likely to reflect the true costs of the prevention and treatment of pollution, and prices will more nearly reflect the real costs of producing and distributing goods.

Statutory reform is also essential in seeking to satisfy the expectation of the rule of law. Statutes that make more explicit choices, that raise the level at which basic policy choices are made and engage elected officials more directly, and that limit discretion by identifying more carefully what agencies are to be doing, how they are to allocate costs and benefits, and how they are to accommodate competing policy goals serve to further the idea of the rule of law. Statutes that are extremely detailed and mandate the issuance of specific rules by deadlines reduce administrative discretion, but in ways that do not lead to efficient and effective achievement of agency goals. Statutes must bridge the widening gap between tasks and resources. The legislative process should include a discussion of priorities, and should develop modest goals consistent with the practical power available to agencies. Statutes should address the imperatives of implementation, and should be carefully crafted to take into account how agencies will execute the authority delegated to them.

The rule of law is no guarantee that statutes will be based on an adequate understanding of the problems they are expected to remedy, or that they respond to broad interests rather than the public interest. Nor are there many political incentives to champion the idea of the rule of law. A constituency must be cultivated—one that demands that laws narrow the gap between responsibilities and resources, that they address the costs and benefits involved, and that they are clear, generalizable and understandable, so that those who are to comply with them can be free to conduct their lives accordingly. The rule of law can and should be championed by those concerned with individual freedom as well as by those who seek effective and aggressive public policies. As the integrity of laws is strengthened and more is attention given to their implementation, policy goals can be more effectively achieved. Statutory reform should proceed on a statute-by-statute basis, as scholars, government officials, politicians, and industry and public interest groups work more directly to balance the competing expectations and concerns. Compromises must not rest on retreat to vagueness, or rely on procedural hobbling of agencies to appease opponents. The temptation to claim political credit for enacting broad statutes, which are aggressive in purpose but crippled in procedures and restrictions, should be resisted.

Deregulating the Regulators

The rule-making process can be significantly streamlined so that more rules can be issued. In part, that will naturally flow from reducing the strictness of regulations and the accompanying analyses that are required. But much can be done to reduce the procedural steps and reviews through which regulations must pass, both within and outside of agencies. As statutes and agency heads give more attention to providing clear guidelines, less review will be needed. The quality of rule making will be enhanced by greater attention to the initial conceptualization and formulation of rules, in contrast to the rejection of specific rules that have been under development for years. The usefulness of judicial and executive review will be enhanced if the policies agencies are expected to pursue are clear, widely understood and accepted. Such external reviews will be much less frequent, and less likely to delay rule implementation or raise concerns that reviewers are usurping agency policy-making authority.

Reductions in judicial challenges to agency decisions and in the role of the OMB in reviewing regulations should be matched by a dramatic decrease in congressional oversight of regulatory activity. Congress ought to direct more of its attention to the beginning of the rule-making process—as it writes statutes, and as agencies set priorities and establish their regulatory agendas—and much less at the end of the process in ad hoc oversight. Congress should become much more willing to delegate responsibility to agencies to issue regulations, and then review those efforts in formal, regularized appropriations and reauthorizations processes. Ad hoc, sporadic hearings and informal interventions of congressional committee members and their staffs interfere with the ability of agencies to accomplish the tasks given them, and should be prohibited. One of the most fundamental of the principles underlying the separation of powers is that there be a separation of the writing and the execution of laws. Members of Congress must be more willing to respect that principle, and to restrain their impulse to intervene in the details of administration. Delegation of broad rule-making power deranges constitutional arrangements and expectations. Much more attention needs to be given to how this gulf between constitutional principle and administrative practice can be narrowed.

The Prospects for Reform

Recommendations that Congress somehow write better laws are frequently offered, and just as frequently dismissed as unlikely and improbable. If Congress spent much less time in oversight, it would have more time and resources to dedicate to statute-writing. Such a change in congressional operations, however, would conflict with the incentives that drive the current system. Members of Congress find it politically profitable to support and enact statutes with broad, all-encompassing, optimistic absolutes, and then intervene on behalf of constituents when the costs are borne close to home. Nevertheless, since the statutes assume such a central role in the regulatory process, reforms that exclude the legislation—the foundation of agency actions—hold little promise for real improvement. The solution to excessive discretion, in the basic policy choices confronting agencies, and the excessive restraints produced by oversight, do not require new institutions or procedures but a rethinking of our acceptance of current practices and a recalculation of their political benefits and incentives.

Such changes in statutes and in the regulatory process would also contribute to increased accountability. The current system produces regulations that are affected directly and indirectly as rule writers anticipate external review— by members of Congress and their staffs, OMB desk officers and their supervisors, federal judges and their clerks, and sometimes even the president and White House officials. While authority for regulations still rests with agency heads, they must bend their decisions to accommodate these other influences, and are thus less responsible for and less in control of their agencies' actions. Giving more independence to agency heads, along with clearer goals and criteria on which their actions will be evaluated, can enhance accountability.

If members of Congress believe that rule making should be viewed as a legislative function and an extension of its law-making power, then they should issue the rules themselves, drafted by their own expanded staffs or those of the regulatory agencies. Some members of Congress have proposed, in response to the Supreme Court's rejection of the legislative veto, that Congress approve all regulations. The advantages of such direct congressional involvement would include a much greater sense of accountability for the exercise of rule-making power and a more politically solid and secure base for regulations. But much more can be gained from increased congressional attention to making new laws: laws that define the key factors to be considered by agencies, consider the anticipated costs and benefits and how they are to be allocated, and provide clear criteria to guide agencies in writing regulations.

If these proposed reforms appear unrealistic, they are nevertheless essential. If they are impossible, then the basic dilemmas of bureaucratic discretion will remain unresolved. If fundamental changes are not feasible, then at least political credit should not be given for efforts that invoke the claim of reform but hold little promise of real change, or for reforms that will only make current problems worse. The solution to the problems associated with administrative discretion will not be cured by more procedural provisions or more reviews. A sense of what needs to happen, a sense of the general direction in which changes ought to go, can be useful in evaluating the regularly offered incremental remedies.

Modest changes in the right direction should be encouraged. Members of Congress can give more attention to the imperatives of implementation and to the questions that are likely to arise once agencies assume responsibility for regulatory tasks. Scholars can study and debate the nature of statutes, and can develop a richer understanding of what kinds of statutory provisions and policy techniques are more or less likely to be successful in accomplishing policy purposes. More effort can be directed to improving individual statutes, or parts of them, rather than placing hopes on more comprehensive efforts.

Outside groups can do much to pressure Congress to write statutes calling for more comprehensive and less strict regulations. If the groups that Congress is trying to satisfy are able to find some common ground and avoid taking extreme positions, statutory provisions can reflect those compromises.

Presidents must also resist the urge to reshape statutes to their ideological liking through informal, managerial means. Administrative efforts that seek to deregulate and minimize the issuance of regulations are likely to be inconsistent with statutes that order agencies to regulate aggressively and reduce risks and hazards. It is one thing to argue that the president can give direction to agencies to issue, within the discretion they enjoy by law, the most cost-effective regulations, and to choose the least burdensome alternatives in writing rules. It is something very different to say that the basic purposes, priorities and direction of statutes should be reversed. According to their authorizing statutes, the agencies studied here should be issuing more regulations. Better ones are certainly needed, but the statutes nonetheless demand an active, regulatory posture. Statutes do sometimes have unreasonable provisions, and the president and his staff can do much to identify those provisions and press for improvements. Regulatory review efforts which, instead of trying to improve the quality of regulations, simply seek to encourage agencies to avoid taking regulatory actions and minimize the likelihood that regulatory burdens will be imposed on industry express contempt for the integrity of statutes, because they disagree with their provisions. Such regulatory reformers run the risk of discouraging compliance with laws, weakening commitment to the rule of law, ignoring the constitutional charge to take care that the laws are faithfully executed, and rejecting the democratic formalities on which the Constitution and the separation of powers rest. Just as Congress squanders its time and effort in ways that—in the name of limiting direction—actually serve to weaken the idea of the rule of law, presidents and their staffs who seek to replace the discretion of agencies with their own brand of bureaucratic discretion do great disservice to the ideal that laws be clear and specific, applied equally and consistently, with minimum administrative manipulation.

The debate over control of the bureaucracy that has characterized the last decade should be balanced with a concern for bureaucratic competence. Bureaucratic discretion cannot be understood apart from the tasks that agencies are delegated to accomplish. Excessive and misdirected actions to reduce discretion reduce the capability of the administrative process to accomplish its delegated tasks.

NOTES AND REFERENCES

Chapter 1. THE PROBLEM OF BUREAUCRATIC DISCRETION

1. National Research Council, *Risk Assessment in the Federal Government: Managing the Process* (Washington, DC: National Academy Press, 1983).
2. Edith Efron, *The Apocalyptics: Cancer and the Big Lie* (New York: Simon and Schuster, 1984).
3. Robert W. Crandall and Lester B. Lave, *The Scientific Basis of Health and Safety Regulation* (Washington, DC: Brookings Institution, 1981).
4. George C. Eads and Michael Fix, *Relief or Reform? Reagan's Regulatory Dilemma* (Washington, DC: Urban Institute Press, 1984).
5. R. Shep Melnick, *Regulation and the Courts* (Washington, DC: Brookings Institution, 1983).
6. Susan J. Tolchin and Martin Tolchin, *Dismantling America: The Rush to Deregulate* (Boston: Houghton Mifflin, 1983).
7. *Two Treatises of Government*, Second Treatise, Sections 160–161.
8. *Federalist Papers*, no. 70, 72.
9. *Works of Alexander Hamilton*, vol. 7 (1851), quoted in Christopher H. Pyle and Richard M. Pious, *The President, Congress, and the Constitution* (New York: Free Press, 1984), p. 56.
10. *The Autobiography of Theodore Roosevelt* (1958), pp. 197–98, quoted in Pyle and Pious, p. 69.
11. *Congressional Government* (1885), quoted in Pyle and Pious, pp. 158–59.
12. "The Study of Administration," *Political Science Quarterly* 2(2) (1887):213; reprinted in Jay M. Shafritz and Albert C. Hyde, eds., *Classics of Public Administration* (Oak Park, IL: Moore, 1978), pp. 3–16.
13. Douglas Yates, *Bureaucratic Democracy* (Cambridge: Harvard University Press, 1982), p. 28.
14. James Landis, *The Administrative Process* (New Haven: Yale University Press, 1938), pp. 16, 46.
15. Eugene Bardach and Robert Kagan, *Going By the Book: The Problem of Regulatory Unreasonableness* (Philadelphia: Temple University Press, 1983).
16. For a very useful discussion of different kinds of administrative discretion, see Martin Shapiro, "Administrative Discretion: The Next Stage," *Yale Law Journal* 92 (1983):1487–1522.
17. See, for example, Kenneth C. Davis, *Discretionary Justice* (Urbana: University of Illinois Press, 1971).
18. For studies of rule making in other policy areas, see Jeffery M. Berry, *Feeding*

Hungry People: Rule Making in the Food Stamp Program (New Brunswick, NJ: Rutgers University Press, 1984); Robert A. Katzmann, *Institutional Disability: The Saga of Transportation Policy for the Disabled* (Washington, DC: Brookings Institution, 1986).

19. 15 U.S.C. Sec. 753(b) (1); see Richard J. Pierce, Jr., Sidney A. Shapiro, and Paul Verkuil, *Administrative Law and Process* (Mineola, NY: Foundation Press, 1985), pp. 44–45.

20. Robert Baldwin and Keith Hawkins, "Discretionary Justice: Davis Reconsidered," *Public Law* (Winter 1984):570–599.

21. Studies of occupational safety and health that compare the experience of the United States and Sweden, for example, argue that the discretionary authority given Swedish inspectors permits them to focus more attention on resolving problems and eliciting employer cooperation and support, whereas in the United States such flexibility and cooperation is not cultivated. Barbara Jo Fleischauer, "Occupational Safety and Health Law in Sweden and the United States: Are There Lessons to be Learned by Both Countries?" *Hastings International and Comparative Law Review* 6 (1983):283–354; Steven Kelman, *Regulating America, Regulating Sweden: A Comparative Study of Occupational Safety and Health Policy* (Cambridge: M.I.T. Press, 1981).

22. Richard Schultz, "Regulatory Agencies and the Dilemmas of Delegation," in *The Administrative State in Canada*, O. P. Dwivdei, ed. (Toronto: University of Toronto Press, 1982), p. 124.

23. David Vogel, "Cooperative Regulation: Environmental Protection in Great Britain," *The Public Interest* 72 (Summer 1983):88–106.

24. See, generally, F. A. Hayek, *The Road to Serfdom* (Chicago: University of Chicago Press, 1944).

25. See Theodore Lowi, *The End of Liberalism*, 2nd ed. (New York: Norton, 1979), pp. 56–63 for a discussion of the idea of pluralism and administrative discretion.

26. Lee Fritschler, *Smoking and Politics* (Englewood Cliffs, NJ: Prentice-Hall, 1984), p. 69.

27. Davis, p. 219.

28. Lowi, pp. 303–304.

29. Lief Carter, *Administrative Law and Politics* (Boston: Little Brown, 1983), p. 15.

30. Norman Ornstein et al., *Vital Statistics on Congress* (Washington, DC: American Enterprise Institute, 1982), p. 138.

31. 1 Stat. 137 (1790); 3 Stat. 26 (1813).

32. Attorney General's Committee on Administrative Procedures, *Final Report*, 1941, chap. 7.

33. Ibid., p. 102, n. 29, 30.

34. Ibid., p. 103.

35. Safety Appliance Act of 1903, 32 Stat. 943.

36. Butterfield v. Stranahan, 192 U.S. 470 (1903).

37. J. W. Hampton, Jr., and Co. v. U.S., 276 U.S. 394 (1928).

38. Panama Refining Co. v. Ryan, 293 U.S. 338 (1935).

39. L. A. Schechter Poultry Corp. v. U.S., 295 U.S. 495 (1935). In the only other case where legislation was struck down, *Carter v. Carter Coal Co.,* the Court rejected a delegation of power to a private commission to write a Bituminous Coal Code, finding that "This is legislative delegation in its most obnoxious form; for it is not even delegation to an official or an official body, presumptively disinterested, but

to private persons whose interests may be and are often adverse to the interest of others in the same business." 298 U.S. 238 (1936).

40. Yatus v. U.S., 321 U.S. 414 (1944).

41. National Cable Television Association v. U.S., 415 U.S. 336 (1974). Justice Rehnquist has recently sought to renew the use of the nondelegation doctrine, arguing in a recent opinion that the Occupational Safety and Health Act of 1970 should be rejected as an unconstitutional delegation of power to an administrative agency. See Justice Rehnquist's dissent in American Textile Manufacturers Institute v. Donovan, 452 U.S. 490 (1981).

42. See Hampton v. Mow Sung Wong, 426 U.S. 88 (1976); Kent v. Dulles, 357 U.S. 116 (1958), where the Court found that statutes could be (but were not in these cases) rejected if due process standards were violated through congressional delegations of authority to administrative agencies.

43. Ronald J. Penoyer, *Directory of Federal Regulatory Agencies—1982 Update* (St. Louis: Washington University, 1981), p. 1–9.

44. See, for example, the Air Cargo Deregulatory Act, PL 95–163; the Airline Deregulation Act, PL 95–504; Railroad deregulation, PL 96–448; and Trucking deregulation, PL 96–296.

45. Robert Hamilton, "Procedures for the Adoption of Rules of General Applicability: The Need for Procedural Innovation in Administrative Rule Making," *California Law Review* 60 (1972):1315; (Opinion by Judge Henry Friendly), Associated Industries v. U.S. Department of Labor, 487 F. 2d 342, 345, n. 2 (2nd Circuit, 1973).

46. See Marver Bernstein, *Regulating Business by Independent Commission* (Princeton: Princeton University Press, 1975); Lloyd Cutler and David Johnson, "Regulation and the Political Process," *Yale Law Journal* 74 (1975):1395.

47. Robert Litan and William Nordhaus, *Reforming Federal Regulation* (New Haven: Yale University Press, 1983).

48. Antonin Scalia, "Vermont Yankee: The APA, the D.C. Circuit, and the Supreme Court," *The Supreme Court Review* (1978), p. 403.

Chapter 2. ADMINISTRATIVE LAW AND ADMINISTRATIVE PROCEDURES

1. Frank Goodnow, *The Principles of Administrative Law in the United States* (New York: Putnam, 1905).

2. John Dickinson, *Administrative Justice and the Supremacy of Law in the United States* (New York: Russell and Russell, 1927).

3. Paul Verkuil, "The Emerging Concept of Administrative Procedure," *Columbia Law Review* 78 (1978):258.

4. S 915, HR 6324, 76th Cong., 1st sess., 1939.

5. Quoted in Verkuil, p. 269, n. 5. This summary relies on an extensive discussion of the bill in Verkuil.

6. Veto message, 8 December 1940, reprinted, in part, in Robert R. Nordhaus, "Regulating the Regulators: A Legal (and Political) History," unpublished manuscript, 1981.

7. Walter Gellhorn, *Administrative Law: Cases and Comments* (Mineola, NY: Foundation Press, 1940), p. 5.

8. S 7, HR 1203, 79th Cong., 1st sess., 1945, 5 U.S.C. 550 et seq.

9. The President's Committee on Administrative Management, *Report with Special Studies* (Washington, DC: Government Printing Office, 1937).
10. 5 U.S.C. 706 (1976).
11. 5 U.S.C. 551 (1976).
12. 5 U.S.C. 554–557 (1976).
13. K. C. Davis, *Discretionary Justice* (Baton Rouge: Louisiana State University Press, 1969).
14. See, for example, Peter Woll, *Administrative Law—The Informal Process* (Berkeley: University of California Press, 1963).
15. See Securities and Exchange Commission v. Chenery Corp., 332 U.S. 194 (1947); NLRB v. Wyman-Gordon, 394 U.S. 759 (1969); U.S. v. Florida East Coast Railway, 410 U.S. 224 (1973). For a general discussion of this see Antonin Scalia, "Vermont Yankee: The APA, the D.C. Circuit, and the Supreme Court," *Supreme Court Review 1978* (1979), pp. 382–383.
16. Frederick F. Blachly, "Critique of the Federal Administrative Procedure Act," in George Warren, ed. *The Federal Administrative Procedures Act and the Administrative Agencies* (New York: New York University School of Law, 1947), pp. 30–50.
17. U.S., House of Representatives, Judiciary Committee, Report on Administrative Procedure Act of 1946 (1947).
18. William H. Rodgers, Jr., "Judicial Review of Risk Assessments: The Role of Decision Theory in Unscrambling the Benzene Decision," *Environmental Law* 11 (1981):301.
19. U.S. v. Storer Broadcasting Co., 351 U.S. 192 (1956); U.S. v. Florida East Coast Railway Co., 410 U.S. 224 (1973).
20. Richard Stewart, "The Reformation of American Administrative Law," *Harvard Law Review* 88 (1975):1712.
21. Some of the more important cases include Portland Cement Association v. Ruckelshaus, 486 F. 2d 375 (D.C. Circ. 1973) and International Harvester Co. v. Ruckelshaus, 478 F. 2d 1238 (D.C. Cir. 1973).
22. Stewart argued that this was in response to complaints that agencies were captured or dominated by the interests they were supposed to be regulating ("Reformation," p. 1728).
23. American Airlines, Inc. v. CAB, 359 F. 2d 624, 632 (D.C. Cir. 1966).
24. 5 U.S.C. 702 (1972).
25. Sierra Club v. Morton, 405 U.S. 727 (1972) at 733.
26. U.S. v. S.C.R.A.P., 412 U.S. 669 (1973).
27. Stewart, "Reformation", p. 1727.
28. Greater Boston Television Corp. v. FCC, 444 F. 2d 841 (1970), at 850 cert. denied 403 U.S. 923 (1971).
29. Ibid., at 181.
30. Overton Park v. Volpe, 401 U.S. 402 (1971).
31. See, for example, Kennecott Copper v. EPA, 462 F. 2d 846 (D.C. Cir. 1972).
32. See Peter Strauss and Cass Sunstein, "The Role of the President and OMB in Informal Rulemaking," *Administrative Law Review* 38 (1986):181–205; Colin S. Diver, "Policymaking Paradigms in Administrative Law," *Harvard Law Review* 95 (1981):393–434.
33. The four case studies presented in chapter 5 through 8 provide some examples of how the courts have affected agency rule making through this means.
34. Merrick Garland, "Deregulation and Judicial Review," *Harvard Law Review* 98 (1985):505–91.

35. Vermont Yankee Nuclear Power Corp. v. Natural Resources and Defense Council, 435 U.S. 519 (1978).
36. The Occupational Safety and Health Act of 1970, 84 Stat. 1590, 29 U.S.C. 651.
37. Michael Levin, "Politics and Polarity—The Limits of OSHA Reform," *Regulation* (November–December 1969):36–37.
38. Consumer Product Safety Act of 1972, 86 Stat. 1207, 15 U.S.C. 2051 (1972).
39. Magnuson-Moss—Federal Trade Commission Improvements Act, 99 Stat. 2193 (1975).
40. See, for example, the Toxic Substances Control Act (1976), 15 U.S.C. 2601; Department of Energy Organization Act (1977), 42 U.S.C. 7101; Financial Institutions Regulatory and Interest Rate Control Act of 1978, 12 U.S.C. 226.
41. In 1977, led by the administration's efforts, Congress passed legislation which removed most of the federal regulations aimed at the air cargo industry. The following year, an airline passenger deregulation law was enacted, which sought to increase competition among airlines and permitted them more flexibility in raising and lowering their fares. In 1980 the railroad industry, which had actively sought deregulation in order to reverse its weakening financial situation, was given more flexibility in setting rates and other incentives to be more competitive. The trucking industry, in contrast, opposed deregulation, since regulations limited new entries and helped to maintain high prices. However, legislation enacted in 1980 permitted more flexibility in setting rates, ended antitrust immunity for the setting of collective rates in some areas, and facilitated entry into the industry by new firms. Other deregulatory proposals considered by the 97th Congress but not enacted would have deregulated the telecommunications industry and the banking industry. See, generally, Martha Derthick and Paul Quirk, *The Politics of Deregulation* (Washington, DC: Brookings Institution, 1985).
42. See Alan Stone, *Regulation and Its Alternatives* (Washington, DC: Congressional Quarterly, 1982).
43. Other kinds of reform have also generated support among members of Congress. Economic-based proposals have been championed by those who favor more efficient and effective administrative efforts. Some proposals would replace detailed administrative standards with free-market approaches, such as tax incentives, which would rely on competitive, nongovernmental pressures to achieve policy objectives, thus minimizing the size of government and its presence in the economy. Effluent taxes on producers of pollutants, or injury taxes on businesses in which employees suffer accidents, are examples of such an approach. Such reforms would, in theory, reduce the complexity of the administrative process and thereby help to "reform" the process, but the taxes and incentives themselves would likely be developed through some kind of rule-making process. Such proposals presuppose an effective rule-making procedure. See, generally, Charles Schultze, *The Public Use of Private Interest* (Washington, DC: Brookings Institution, 1976).
44. See *Regulatory Reform—A Survey of Proposals in the 94th Congress* (Washington, DC: American Enterprise Institute for Public Policy Research, 1976).
45. Other proposals such as "sunset" reforms, which required that agencies be periodically examined by Congress, that conflicting and duplicative rules be eliminated, and that agencies and programs no longer need be abolished, attracted widespread support. See *Regulation and Regulatory Reform: A Survey of Proposals of the 95th Congress* (Washington, DC: American Enterprise Institute for Public Policy Research, 1978).
46. Diane Granat, "Senate Unanimously Passes Broad Regulatory Reform," *Con-

gressional Quarterly Weekly Report (27 March 1982):701–702.

47. 5 U.S.C. 552 (1976).

48. Michael A. Berry, *A Method for Examining Policy Implementation: A Study of Decision Making for the National Ambient Air Quality Standards, 1964–84* (Washington, DC: Environmental Protection Agency, 1984).

49. *Legislative History of the Administrative Procedures Act* (1946); George Warren, ed., *The Federal Administrative Procedures Act and the Administrative Agencies* (New York: New York University School of Law, 1947).

50. Carl McFarland, "Analysis of the Federal Administrative Procedures Act," in Warren, *Federal Administrative Procedures Act*, pp. 16–29.

51. For a discussion of this see Stewart, "Reformation," p. 1669.

52. Quoted in Jerry Mashaw, *Bureaucratic Justice* (New Haven: Yale University Press, 1983).

53. Lawrence Dodd and Richard Schott, *Congress and the Administrative State* (New York: Wiley, 1979).

54. For a discussion of this, see Morris Fiorina, *Congress: Keystone of the Washington Establishment* (New Haven: Yale University Press, 1978).

55. For an elaboration of this argument, see Theodore Lowi, *The End of Liberalism* (New York: Norton, 1979).

56. See Martin Shapiro, "Rules, Discretion, and Reasonableness Under the Constitution," in *The Constitution and the Regulation of Society*, Gary Bryner and Dennis Thompson, eds. (Provo, UT: Brigham Young University Publications, 1987).

57. See Louis Jaffe, "Invective and Investigation in Administrative Law," *Harvard Law Review* 52 (1939):1219.

58. For a discussion of the perceived virtues of the adversary process, see Donald Horowitz, *The Courts and Social Policy* (Washington, DC: Brookings Institution, 1977); Robert Lorch, *Democratic Process and Administrative Law* (Detroit: Wayne State University Press, 1980).

59. See Nathaniel L. Nathanson, "Central Issues of American Administrative Law," *American Political Science Review* 45 (1951):348. This view was eventually challenged in an influential article by Charles Reich, who argued that the rights–privilege distinction as a basis for determining administrative procedures was flawed. See Reich, "The New Property," *Yale Law Journal* 73 (1964):733.

60. See, for example, Douglas Yates, *Bureaucratic Democracy* (Cambridge: Harvard University Press, 1982).

61. Marshall Dimock, *Law and Dynamic Administration* (New York: Praeger, 1981).

62. Lon Fuller, "The Forms and Limits of Adjudication," *Harvard Law Review* 92 (1978):349, 364, 366.

63. Ibid., pp. 367, 400.

64. Quoted in Anne Strick, "What's Wrong with the Adversary System: Paranoia, Hatred, and Suspicion," *Washington Monthly* (January 1977):23.

65. See Anne Strick, *Injustice for All* (New York: Penguin Books, 1977) for a popularized critique of the adversary process.

66. J. Ronald Fox, "Breaking the Regulatory Deadlock," *Harvard Business Review* 59 (September–October 1981):97.

67. For a discussion of the development of the administrative process as a political process, see Stewart, "Reformation," p. 1066.

68. Robert B. Reich, "Regulation by Confrontation or Negotiation?" *Harvard Business Review* 59 (May–June 1981):82–91.

69. Louis L. Jaffe, "The Illusion of the Ideal Administrator," *Harvard Law Review*

86 (1973):1183; Robert Rabin, "Administrative Law in Transition," *Northwestern University Law Review* 72 (1977):120.

70. U.S., Senate, Committee on Governmental Affairs, *Study on Federal Regulation—Principal Recommendations and Findings*, 96th Congress, 1st session, (1979): 25.
71. Ibid.
72. Judy Sarasohn, "Critics Successful in Reducing Funds for Public Participation," *Congressional Quarterly Weekly Report*, 1 November 1981, p. 3273.
73. Mary Thornton, "Money Plug Pulled for Regulatory Witnesses," *Washington Post*, 1 December 1981; Pete Earley, "Rule Makers No Longer Foster Public Input," *Washington Post*, 7 April 1982.
74. Antonin Scalia, "Regulatory Reform—The Game Has Changed," *Regulation* (January–February 1981):13–15.
75. Antonin Scalia, "Back to Basics: Making Law Without Making Rules," *Regulation* (July–August 1981):25–28.
76. Ronald M. Levin, "Judicial Review and the Bumpers Amendment," unpublished report for the Committee on Judicial Review of the Administrative Conference of the United States.
77. Shapiro, "Rules, Discretion, and Reasonableness."
78. Fuller, p. 364.
79. Joint Anti-Fascist Refugee Committee v. McGrath, 341 U.S. 123 (1951).

Chapter 3. SCIENTIFIC AND ECONOMIC ANALYSIS IN ADMINISTRATIVE RULEMAKING

1. 21 U.S.C. 32 (1976).
2. 42 U.S.C. 7401 (1976).
3. Occupational Safety and Health Act of 1970, 29 U.S.C. 553, 651–678.
4. Lester Lave, *The Strategy of Social Regulation* (Washington, DC: Brookings Institution, 1981), p. 14.
5. 42 U.S.C. 6901 (1976).
6. 21 U.S.C. 301 (1976).
7. Lave, ch. 4.
8. 15 U.S.C. 2601 (1976).
9. The order is not binding upon independent regulatory commissions, due to a general perception that these commissions cannot be made subject to executive orders. Commissions are, however, encouraged to comply with the objectives of the Reagan order; thus, since they are largely staffed by Reagan appointees, decision making in these commissions does not differ much from that of executive agencies.
10. Executive Order 12291 (17 February 1981), sec. 2.
11. 42 U.S.C. 300f (1976).
12. Federal Environmental Pesticide Control Act of 1972, 33 U.S.C. 1254 (1976).
13. Consumer Product Safety Act, 15 U.S.C. 2051 (1976).
14. Executive Order 12291 (17 February 1981), sec. 2(b).
15. See, generally, Joseph D. Alviani, "Federal Regulation: The New Regimen," *Environmental Affairs* 9 (1980):285–309; Donald T. Bliss, "Regulatory Reform: Toward More Balanced and Flexible Federal Agency Regulation," *Peppardine Law Review* 8 (1981):619–651; Susan J. Tolchin and Martin Tolchin, *Dismantling America: The Rush to Deregulate* (Boston: Houghton Mifflin, 1983); and

George C. Eads and Michael Fix, *Relief or Reform? Reagan's Regulatory Dilemma* (Washington, DC: Urban Institute Press, 1984).

16. Industrial Union Department v. American Petroleum Institute, 448 U.S. 607 (1980).
17. *Federal Register*, vol. 44, no. 131 (6 July 1979), pp. 39858–79.
18. Philip J. Hilts, "The White House Reversal on Regulating for Cancer," *The Washington Post National Weekly Edition*, 18 June 1984; *Federal Register*, vol. 49, no. 100 (22 May 1984), pp. 21594–661.
19. *Federal Register*, vol. 49, no. 227 (23 November 1984), pp. 46294–331.
20. Executive Order 12291 (17 February 1981), sec. 2.
21. Ibid., sec. 3.
22. See, for example, the "Risk Analysis Research and Demonstration Act of 1981," HR 3441, 97th Congress, (1981).
23. See Bruce Ackerman and William Hassler, *Clean Coal/Dirty Air* (New Haven: Yale University Press, 1981), for one example of the kinds of considerations reflected in environmental legislation enacted by Congress.
24. For a review of these cases, see Devra Lee Davis, "The 'Shotgun Wedding' of Science and Law: Risk Assessment and Judicial Review," *Columbia Journal of Environmental Law* 10 (1985):67–109.
25. Ibid.
26. 15 U.S.C. 2051 (1976).
27. U.S. Environmental Protection Agency, *U.S. Environmental Protection Agency Advisory Committees: Charters, Roster, and Accomplishments* (1984), quoted in Kathy D. Wagner-Johnson, "Making Public Policy with Expert Opinion: Science Advisory Committees in the EPA," paper presented at the annual meeting of the Midwest Political Science Association, Chicago (1985).
28. Clean Air Act Amendments of 1977, 42 U.S.C. 7401.
29. Wagner-Johnson, "Making Public Policy," pp. 13–14.
30. Office of the Federal Register, *The United States Government Manual 1983–84* (Washington, DC: Government Printing Office, 1983), p. 275.
31. National Research Council, *Risk Assessment in the Federal Government: Managing the Process* (Washington, DC: National Academy Press, 1983).
32. See, for example, Food Safety Council, *Proposed System for Food Safety Assessment* (Washington, DC: Food Safety Council, 1980); Baruch Fischoff et al., *Acceptable Risk* (New York: Cambridge University Press, 1980); Sandra Panem, *Public Policy, Science, and Environmental Risk* (Washington, DC: Brookings Institution, 1983); Lave; and Conservation Foundation, *The State of the Environment: An Assessment at Mid-Decade* (Washington, DC: Conservation Foundation, 1984), pp. 261–318.
33. Conservation Foundation, *State of the Environment*, p. 63.
34. Ibid., p. 290.
35. United States Regulatory Council, "A Survey of Ten Agencies' Experience with Regulatory Analysis," (May 1981):19–20.
36. Fisher, "Overview and Evaluation of EPA's Guidelines," in V. Kerry Smith, ed., *Environmental Policy Under Reagan's Executive Order* (Chapel Hill, NC: University of North Carolina Press, 1984).
37. U.S Regulatory Council, pp. 26–27.
38. See, generally, Edith Stokey and Richard Zechhauser, *A Primer for Policy Analysis* (New York: Norton, 1978).
39. William R. Greer, "Value of One Life? From $8.37 to $10 Million," *New York Times*, 26 June 1985; Conservation Foundation, *State of the Environment*, p. 308.

40. See Figure 3.5.
41. Quoted in David Dickson, *The New Politics of Science* (New York: Pantheon, 1984), p. 263.
42. Andrews, "Economics and Environmental Decisions," pp. 61, 78–80.
43. W. Norton Grubb, Dale Whittington, and Michael Humphries, "The Ambiguities of Benefit-Cost Analyses; An Evaluation of Regulatory Impact Analyses Under Executive Order 12291," in V. Kerry Smith, ed., *Environmental Policy Under Reagan's Executive Order* (Chapel Hill, NC: University of North Carolina Press, 1984), pp. 121–64.
44. H. Gerth and C. Wright Mills, *From Max Weber: Essays in Sociology* (New York: Oxford University Press, 1946).
45. See Martin J. Bailey, *Reducing Risks to Life* (Washington, DC: American Enterprise Institute, 1980).
46. Herbert Kaufman, "Emerging Conflicts in the Doctrines of Public Administration," in *The Politics of the Federal Bureaucracy*, Alan Altshuler, ed. (New York: Dodd, Mead, 1968), p. 75.
47. See Stephen Kelman, "Cost-Benefit Analysis—An Ethical Critique," *Regulation* (January–February 1981):33–40.
48. Mark J. Green, "Cost-Benefit Analysis as a Mirage," in *Reforming Regulation*, Timothy E. Clark, Marvin H. Kosters, and James C. Miller, III, eds. (Washington, DC: American Enterprise Institute, 1980).
49. Richard J. DeSanti, "Cost-Benefit Analysis for Standards Regulating Toxic Substances Under the Occupational Safety and Health Act: American Petroleum Institute v. OSHA," *Boston University Law Review* 60 (1980):115.
50. U.S. Regulatory Council, p. 41.
51. Richard N. L. Andrews, "Economics and Environmental Decisions, Past and Present," in *Environmental Policy Under Reagan's Executive Order*, V. Kerry Smith, ed. (Chapel Hill: University of North Carolina Press, 1984), pp. 43–85; W. Norton Grubb, Dale Whittington, and Michael Humphries, "The Ambiguities of Benefit-Cost Analysis: An Evaluation of Regulatory Impact Analyses under Executive Order 12291," in Smith, pp. 121–164.
52. See Green, "Cost-Benefit Analysis;" Michael S. Baram, "Cost-Benefit Analysis: An Inadequate Basis for Health, Safety, and Environmental Regulatory Decision Making," *Ecology Law Quarterly* 9 (1980):473.
53. Edith Stokey and Richard Zeckhauser, *A Primer for Policy Analysis* (New York: Norton, 1978), pp. 134–135.
54. Jeffrey Lewis Berger and Steven D. Riskin, "Economic and Technological Feasibility in Regulating Toxic Substances Under the Occupational Safety and Health Act," *Ecology Law Quarterly* 7 (1978):285; DeSanti.
55. Neil Orloff, "We Scoff at Big Risks and Scotch Small Ones," *Wall Street Journal*, 3 December 1984.
56. Edith Efron, *The Apocalyptics: Cancer and the Big Lie* (New York: Simon and Schuster, 1984).
57. Dickson, *New Politics of Science*.
58. Charles Derrow, *Normal Accidents* (New York: Basic Books, 1984).
59. Philip M. Boffey, "Rise in Science Fraud is Seen; Need to Win Cited as a Cause," *New York Times*, 30 May 1985.
60. Conservation Foundation, *State of the Environment*, p. 291.
61. Orloff, "We Scoff at Big Risks."
62. See, generally, Mary Douglas and Aaron Wildavsky, Risk and Culture (Berkeley: University of California Press, 1982).
63. Orloff, "We Scoff at Big Risks."

64. Ibid.
65. Robert W. Crandall and Lester B. Lave, *The Scientific Basis of Health and Safety Regulation* (Washington, DC: Brookings Institution, 1981), pp. 13, 17.

Chapter 4. POLITICAL OVERSIGHT OF ADMINISTRATIVE RULE MAKING

1. Louis Fisher, *The Politics of Shared Power* (Washington, DC: Congressional Quarterly, 1983).
2. Lloyd Cutler and David Johnson, "Regulation and the Political Process," *Yale Law Journal* 84:1395–1418.
3. U.S. Senate Committee on Governmental Affairs, *Principal Recommendations and Findings of the Study on Federal Regulation* (Washington, DC: Government Printing Office, 1979), p. 13.
4. Richard P. Nathan, *The Administrative Presidency* (New York: Wiley, 1985), p. 72.
5. Dick Kirschten, "Reagan: No More Business as Usual," *National Journal* (21 February 1981), p. 300.
6. George Eads and Michael Fix, *Relief or Reform? Reagan's Regulatory Dilemma* (Washington, DC: Urban Institute Press, 1984).
7. Susan Tolchin and Martin Tolchin, *Dismantling America: The Rush to Deregulate* (Boston: Houghton Mifflin, 1983).
8. Dale Russakoff, "Clark Confirmation Hits Snag in Senate," *Washington Post*, 16 November 1983.
9. Peter Szanton, *Federal Reorganization: What Have We Learned?* (Abatham, NJ: Chatbaum House, 1981).
10. Richard P. Nathan, *The Plot That Failed Nixon and the Administrative Presidency* (New York: Wiley, 1975).
11. Nathan, *The Administrative Presidency*, p. 73.
12. Advisory Commission on Intergovernmental Relations, *Regulatory Federalism: Policy, Progress, Impact and Reform* (Washington, DC: Advisory Commission on Intergovernmental Relations, 1983).
13. Eads and Fix, *Relief or Reform*.
14. Ibid., pp. 191–206.
15. Jonathan Alter, "Ronald Reagan as Mr. Clean," *Newsweek*, 23 July 1984, p. 48.
16. U.S. Senate Committee on Governmental Relations, pp. 2–26, 61–76.
17. John Alviani, "Federal Regulation: The New Regime," *Environmental Affairs* 9 (1980):285–309.
18. Christopher DeMuth, "The White House Review Programs," *Regulation* (January–February, 1980):13–26; Susan Tolchin, "The Politics of RARG," *Regulation* (January–February, 1978):44–49.
19. Sierra Club v. Costle, 406 F. 2d 298, 1981.
20. Office of Vice President George Bush, press release (11 August 1983).
21. Presidential Task Force on Regulatory Relief, "Reagan Administration Regulatory Achievements," (11 August 1983).
22. Ibid., pp. 64, 69–75.
23. Bush, pp. 3–4.
24. *Federal Register*, vol. 50, (8 January 1985), pp. 1036–38; *Weekly Compilation of Presidential Documents*, vol. 21, no. 1, 1985.
25. Lawrence Dodd and Richard Schott, *Congress and the Administrative State* (New York: Wiley, 1979).

26. Motor Vehicle and School Bus Safety Amendments of 1974, 88 Stat. 1470.
27. Frederick Kaiser, "Congressional Action to Overturn Agency Rules: Alternative to the Legislative Veto," *Administrative Law Review* (1980):670.
28. Railroad Revitalization and Regulatory Reform Act of 1976, 90 Stat. 31; Airline Deregulation Act of 1978, 92 Stat. 1705.
29. Education Amendments of 1976, 90 Stat. 2081.
30. Dodd and Schott, *Congress and the Administrative State*, pp. 168–70.
31. Ibid., p. 237.
32. Norman Ornstein et al., *Vital Statistics on Congress* (Washington, DC: American Enterprise Institute, 1984), p. 108.
33. Ibid., p. 120.
34. Robert Klonoff, "The Congressman as Mediator Between Citizens and Government Agencies: Problems and Prospects," *Harvard Journal on Legislation* 16 (1983):701–734.
35. American Enterprise Institute, *Government Regulation: Proposals for Procedural Reform* (Washington, DC: American Enterprise Institute, 1979).
36. See "Statutory Deadlines in Environmental Legislation: Necessary but Need Improvement," (Washington DC: Environmental and Energy Study Institute, 1985).
37. Myron Struck, "White House Has Had Problems Getting Some Nominees Approved," *Washington Post*, 11 November 1983.
38. Dennis DeConcini and Robert Faucher, "The Legislative Veto: A Constitutional Amendment," *Harvard Journal on Legislation* (1984):29–59.
39. Joseph Cooper and Patricia Hurley, "The Legislative Veto: A Policy Analysis," *Congress and the Presidency* (1983).
40. INS v. Chadha, 103 S. Ct. 2764, 1983.
41. Elliott Levitas and Stanley Brand, "Congressional Review of Executive and Legislative Actions after Chadha: The Son of Legislative Veto Lives On," *Georgetown Law Journal* 72 (1984):801.
42. Senate Joint Resolution 134, 98th Cong., 1st Sess., 27 July 1983.
43. DeConcini and Faucher, p. 30.
44. R. Shep Melnick, "The Politics of Partnership," *Public Administration Review*, (November 1985):653–80; Louis Fisher, "Judicial Misjudgments About the Lawmaking Process: The Legislative Veto Case," *Public Administration Review* (November 1985):705–711.
45. *The President, Congress, and the Constitution* (New York: The Free Press, 1984), pp. 156–157.
46. The "take care" clause and with the accompanying power to appoint executive officers (subject to the advice and consent of the Senate unless otherwise provided for by Congress), provide the constitutional base for presidential control of the administrative process. The framers of the Constitution provided little explanation of what that clause actually meant. Much of the discussion in the *Federalist Papers* concerning the executive, for example, focuses on the president's veto power, the election and term of office of the executive, and its military and diplomatic responsibilities. See especially *Federalist 66–77*.
47. U.S. v. Myers, 272 U.S. 52 (1926) at 117.
48. Humphrey's Executor v. United States, 295 U.S. 602 (1935).
49. U.S. v. Nixon, 418 U.S. 683 (1974).
50. Youngstown Sheet and Tube Co. v. Sawyer, 343 U.S. 57 (1952), at 593.
51. Ibid., at 635.
52. Sierra Club v. Costle, 657 F.2d 298 (D.C. Cir., 1981), p. 406.
53. *Federalist 70*.

54. U.S. General Accounting Office, "Improved Quality, Adequate Resources and Consistent Oversight Needed if Regulatory Analysis Is To Help Control Costs of Regulation (1982)."

55. See, generally, Alan Morrison, "OMB Interference with Agency Rulemaking: The Wrong Way to Write a Regulation," *Harvard Law Review* 99 (1986):1059–74; Christopher C. DeMuth and Douglas H. Ginsburg, "White House Review of Agency Rulemaking," *Harvard Law Review* 99 (1986):1075–88; and Peter L. Strauss, "The Place of Agencies in Government: Separation of Powers and the Fourth Branch," *Columbia Law Review* 84 (1984):573–669.

56. Ben A. Franklin, "Administration Revives Rules on Chemical Labels," *New York Times*, 23 March 1982, p. 17.

57. Ben A. Franklin, "Novel Pressures in Toxic Label Case," *New York Times*, 18 March 1982, p. 22.

58. Michael Wines, "Only Themselves to Blame," *National Journal* (21 November 1981):2082.

59. Jonathan Lash, *A Season of Spoils: The Story of the Reagan Administration's Attack on the Environment* (New York: Pantheon, 1984).

60. Garland, "Deregulation."

61. Wines, "Only Themselves to Blame," p. 2082.

62. U.S. Department of Transportation v. State Farm Mutual Automobile Insurance Co., 463 U.S. 29 (1983).

63. Eads and Fix, pp. 237–253.

64. Howard Kurtz, "OMB's Role in Reviewing Federal Rules Under Debate," *Washington Post*, 9 October 1983, p. 8.

65. Quoted in Tolchin and Tolchin, pp. 58–59.

66. Quoted in Lash, pp. 23–24.

67. Michael E. Kraft and Norman J. Vig, "Epilogue," in *Environmental Policy in the 1980s*, Kraft and Vig, eds. (Washington, DC: Congressional Quarterly, 1984), pp. 359–74.

68. General Accounting Office, p. 4.

69. Garland, "Deregulation," p. 540.

70. James L. Sundquist, "The Legislative Veto: A Bounced Check," *The Brookings Review* 2(1) (Fall 1983):13–16.

71. Harold Bruff and Ernest Gellhorn, "Congressional Control of Administrative Regulation: A Study of Legislative Vetoes," *Harvard Law Review 90:1369–1440.*

72. Barton and Gellman, "Hill Is Advised to Rewrite 'Legislative Veto' Laws," *Washington Post*, 20 July 1983; Gellman, "Administration Tiptoes on Legislative Veto," *Washington Post*, 21 July 1983.

73. Antonin Scalia, "The Legislative Veto: A False Remedy for System Overload," *Regulation* (January/February 1979):19–26.

74. Bruff and Gellhorn, pp. 1417–1418, 1420.

75. Robert B. Reich, "Warring Critiques of Regulation," *Regulation* (January/February, 1979):42.

76. Morris Fiorina, "Congressional Control of the Bureaucracy: A Mismatch of Incentives and Capabilities," in *Congress Reconsidered*, Lawrence C. Dodd and Bruce I. Oppenheimer, eds. (Washington, DC: Congressional Quarterly, 1981), p. 335.

Chapter 5. THE ENVIRONMENTAL PROTECTION AGENCY

1. See Reorganization Plan No. 3 of 1970, 3 *Code of Federal Regulations* 1072 (1970).
2. Clean Air Act Amendments of 1970 (84 Stat. 1676, 42 U.S C. 1857b); Clean Air Act Amendments of 1977 (91 Stat. 685, 42 U.S.C. 7401).
3. Water Quality Improvement Act of 1970 (84 Stat. 94, 33 U.S.C. 1251); Marine Protection, Research and Sanctuaries Act of 1972 (86 Stat. 1052, 33 U.S.C. 1401); Federal Water Pollution Control Act Amendments of 1972 (86 Stat. 819, 33 U.S.C. 1254); Safe Drinking Water Act of 1974 (88 Stat. 1661, 42 U.S.C. 300f); The Clean Water Act of 1977 (91 Stat. 1566, 33 U.S.C. 1251).
4. Federal Environmental Pesticide Control Act of 1972 (86 Stat. 975, 7 U.S.C. 135) (Amendment to the Federal Insecticide, Fungicide and Rodenticide Act); Toxic Substances Control Act of 1976 (90 Stat. 2005, 15 U.S.C. 2601).
5. Resource Conservation and Recovery Act of 1976 (90 Stat. 45, 42 U.S.C. 6901); Comprehensive Environmental Response, Compensation and Liability Act of 1980 (84 Stat. 2767, 42 U.S.C. 9601 note).
6. Noise Control Act of 1972 (86 Stat. 1234, 42 U.S.C. 4901); Aviation Safety and Noise Abatement Act of 1979 (94 Stat. 50, 49 U.S.C. 2101).
7. For general discussions of the kinds of tasks confronting the EPA, see Council on Environmental Quality, *Environmental Quality* (Washington, DC: Government Printing Office, 1980); Richard B. Stewart, "Pyramids of Sacrifice: Problems of Federalism in Mandating State Implementation of National Environmental Policy," *Yale Law Journal* 86 (1977):1196; President's Commission for a National Agenda for the Eighties, *Government and the Regulation of Corporate and Individual Decisions in the Eighties* (Washington, DC: Government Printing Office, 1980).
8. Congressional Quarterly, *Environment and Health* (Washington, DC: Congressional Quarterly, 1981), p. 126. The figures here are from the Council on Environmental Quality and represent pre-Reagan Administration calculations and estimates.
9. Under its enabling legislation, the Environmental Protection Agency is also empowered to issue orders prohibiting the discharge of pollutants, to revoke licenses for activities subject to the EPA's jurisdiction, to seize hazardous pesticides, and impose fines of up to $25,000 per day and jail sentences for violations of clean air laws. The procedure, usually mandated by statute for these kinds of actions, involves four steps: (1) the agency issues an order calling on a polluter to cease illegal actions, (2) informal negotiations are held if the action is not voluntarily stopped, (3) oral hearings may then be conducted, and (4) the EPA may initiate a civil proceeding in the federal district courts.
10. 42 U.S.C. 1867b; 42 U.S.C. 740A.
11. 15 U.S.C. 1251.
12. 33 U.S.C. 1251.
13. 42 U.S.C. 300f; 42 U.S.C. 6901. Some observers have emphasized this "action-forcing" characteristic of environmental laws, which goes far beyond the vague "public interest" mandates of many regulatory agencies. See Bruce Ackerman and William Hassler, *Clean Coal/Dirty Air* (New Haven: Yale University Press, 1981); Richard Stewart, "The Development of Administrative and Quasi-Constitutional Law in Judicial Review of Environmental Decisionmaking—Lessons from the Clean Air Act," *Iowa Law Review* 62 (1977):713; William F. Pedersen, Jr., "Formal Records and Informal Rule Making," *Yale Law Journal* 85 (1975):38; Sanford E. Gaines "Decisionmaking Procedures at the Environmental Protection Agency," *Iowa Law Review* 62 (1977):839; National Academy of Science, *Decision Making in the Environmental Protection Agency* (Washington, DC: National Academy of Science, 1977).

14. 91 Stat. 1589–90 (1977).
15. 42 U.S.C. 7607 (1977).
16. 15 U.S.C. 2605 (1976).
17. 42 U.S.C. 6977 (1976).
18. 7 U.S.C. 136W; 42 U.S.C. 9601 note (1976).
19. Quoted in Susan Tolchin, "Presidential Power and the Politics of RARG," Regulation (July/August 1979):47.
20. Important cases include Kennecott Copper Corp. v. EPA, 462 F. 2d 846 (D.C. Cir., 1972); International Harvester v. Ruckelshaus, 478 F. 2d 495 (D.C. Cir., 1973).
21. EPA v. Portland Cement, 486 F. 2d 374 (D.C. Cir., 1973); South Terminal v. EPA, 504 F. 2d 646 (1st Cir., 1974); Ethyl Corp. v. EPA, 541 F. 2d 1 (D.C. Cir., 1976).
22. Stewart, "Judicial Review of Environmental Decision Making," p. 714.
23. See Richard Stewart, "The Reformation of American Administrative Law," Harvard Law Review 88 (1975):1667.
24. See J. Skelly Wright, "The Courts and the Rule Making Process: The Limits of Judicial Review," Cornell Law Review 59 (1974):375; Harold Leventhal, "Environmental Decision Making and the Role of the Courts," University of Pennsylvania Law Review 122 (1974):509.
25. U.S., Senate, Environment and Public Works Committee, Legislative History of the Clean Air Act Amendments of 1977, 95th Cong., 2d sess., 1978, p. 2786.
26. U.S., Senate, Environment and Public Works, Legislative History, p. 2738. See also Stephen Williams, "Hybrid Rule Making Under the Administrative Procedures Act: A Legal and Empirical Analysis," University of Chicago Law Review 42 (1975):401; and K.C. Davis, Administrative Law Treatise (St. Paul, MN: West, 1975).
27. U.S., Senate, Environment and Public Works Committee, Legislative History, p. 2790.
28. Ibid., p. 366.
29. 46 Federal Register 13, 193 (17 February 1981).
30. The discussion in this section relies on National Academy of Science, Decision-making in the Environmental Protection Agency (Washington, DC: National Academy Press, 1977); Environmental Protection Agency, "The Environmental Protection Agency's 1981 Rule Making Handbook," (May 1981); and interviews with EPA officials in early 1982, who generally requested that no comments be attributed to them.
31. Executive Order 12291, 46 Federal Register 2692 (27 April 1981).
32. Ibid. Elements of the proposed rule which require information collection from individuals and organizations, along with copies of the actual forms to be used, are sent to the OMB as required under the Paperwork Reduction Act (94 Stat. 2767, 1980). The OMB has up to 90 days to review these forms and requirements and may hold public hearings on the proposal. If the OMB rejects these forms and requirements, they must be deleted from the proposed rule.
33. 1980 Amendments to the Federal Insecticide, Fungicide and Rodenticide Act, 7 U.S.C. 135. Regulations issued pursuant to the 1980 "Superfund" legislation were to be submitted for congressional review, where, should either chamber pass a resolution of disapproval of the rule within 60 days of its issuance, or both chambers within 90 days, the regulation would not go into effect. All proposed and final rules issued under pesticide laws were to be submitted to the House and Senate Agriculture Committees, although these committees have no formal veto power. Congress as a whole, however, could veto regulations under these laws if

a resolution of disapproval is passed by both houses within 90 days of the issuance of the regulation. The Supreme Court's rejection of the legislative veto, however, eliminated this step of the rule-making process.

34. One recent study found that ozone pollution results in lost agricultural production of $2 billion to $4.5 billion a year, an estimated 5 percent of total agricultural production. See Philip Shabecoff, "Crop Loss Is Laid to Ozone Effects," *New York Times*, (18 February 1982). The case study relies on Lawrence J. White, *Reforming Regulations—Processes and Problems* (Englewood Cliffs, NJ: Prentice-Hall, 1981), pp. 27-70.

35. 42 U.S.C. 1857 (1976).

36. The Clean Air Act of 1976 (42 U.S.C. 1857) provided for two kinds of ambient air quality standards: Primary standards, as described in the text, are currently the basis of pollution-reducing efforts; secondary standards, representing ultimate air quality goals, are expected to "protect the public welfare from any known or anticipated adverse effects associated with the presence of such air pollutant in the ambient air."

37. 36 *Federal Register* 8186 (30 April 1971). See Lester Lave, *The Strategy of Social Regulation* (Washington, DC: Brookings Institution, 1981), p. 105.

38. White, *Reforming Regulation*, p. 54.

39. Lave, *Strategy*, p. 106.

40. White, *Reforming Regulation*, p. 56.

41. Ibid., pp. 56-66.

42. Ibid., pp. 66-67.

43. Ibid., p. 68.

44. 44 *Federal Register* 8202 (1979).

45. See Joanne Omang, "Federal Court of Appeals Upholds EPA Standard on Control of Ozone," *Washington Post*, 15 September 1981, p. A12.

46. Ibid.

47. U.S., Senate, Commerce Committee, *Legislative History of the Toxic Substances Control Act*, 95th Congress, 2d sess., 1978.

48. Philip Shabecoff, "This Sisyphus Rolls a Wooden Stone," *New York Times*, 29 June 1985.

49. Lawrence Mosher, "Will EPA's Budget Cuts Make It More Efficient or Less Effective?" *National Journal* (15 August 1981):1466-69.

50. Ibid., p. 1466.

51. Lawrence Mosher, "Move Over, Jim Watt, Anne Gorsuch Is the Latest Target of Environmentalists," *National Journal* (24 October 1981):1900.

52. National Academy of Science, *Decision Making*, p. 128.

53. Lawrence Mosher, "Reagan's Environmental Federalism—Are the States Up to the Challenge," *National Journal* (30 January 1982):184-88.

54. Robert E. Taylor, "EPA May Curb Small Pollution Sources and Let States Regulate Chemical Plants," *Wall Street Journal*, 8 June 1985.

55. David Burnham, "New EPA Strategy Seeks Shift in Fight on Toxic Air Pollutants," *New York Times*, 5 June 1985.

56. William R. Greer, "Senators to Fight a Change by EPA," *New York Times*, 10 June 1985.

57. Philip Shabecoff, "Pollution Policy Issue in Congress," *New York Times*, 11 June 1985; Robert E. Taylor, "Bill to Broaden Clean Air Mandate of EPA Attached," *Wall Street Journal*, 22 April 1985.

58. "Federal List of Very Toxic Chemicals," *New York Times*, 20 November 1985.

59. Robert Crandall, "Environmental Ignorance Is Not Bliss," *Wall Street Journal*, 22 April 1985.

60. See Stewart, "Pyramids of Sacrifice," p. 1206.
61. Gilbert Omenn and Lester Lave, *Clearing the Air: Reforming the Clean Air Act* (Washington, DC: Brookings Institution, 1981), p. 40.
62. National Academy of Science, *Decision Making*, pp. 41–42.
63. R. Shep Melnick, *Regulation and the Courts: The Case of the Clean Air Act* (Washington, DC: Brookings Institution, 1983).
64. Ibid., pp. 33–34.
65. Lawrence Mosher, "Distrust of Gorsuch May Stymie EPA Attempt to Integrate Pollution Wars," *National Journal* (2 December 1983):322–24.
66. See Allen V. Kneese and Charles L. Schultze, *Pollution, Prices and Public Policy* (Washington, DC: Brookings Institution, 1975).
67. See M. R. Maloney and Bruce Yandle, "Bubbles and Efficiency," *Regulation* (May/June 1980):49–52.
68. Bruce Yandle, "The Emerging Market in Air Pollution Rights," *Regulation* (July/August 1978), p. 21–29.
69. Omenn and Lave, p. 24.
70. "EPA Planning Pollution Tax for Heavy Trucks," *New York Times*, 5 December 1984.
71. Steven Kelman, "Economists and the Environmental Muddle," *Public Interest* (Summer 1981):106–23.
72. William F. Pedersen, "Why the Clean Air Act Works Badly," *University of Pennsylvania Law Review* 129 (1981):1059–1060.
73. See Ackerman and Hassler, *Clean Coal*.
74. See James P. Leape, "Quantitative Risk Assessment in Regulation of Environmental Carcinogens," *Harvard Environmental Law Review* 4 (1980):86.
75. Ibid., p. 99. See also David Doninger, "Federal Regulation of Vinyl Chloride: A Short Course in the Law and Policy of Toxic Substances Control," *Ecology Law Quarterly* 7 (1978):497.
76. Leape, "Quantitative Risks," pp. 98–99.
77. Joanne Omang, "EPA Nominee Favors Changes in Testing," *Washington Post*, 17 October 1981, p. A3.
78. David G. Hoel and Kenny S. Crump, "Waterborne Carcinogens: A Scientist's View," in *The Scientific Basis of Health and Safety Regulation*, Robert W. Crandall and Lester B. Lave, eds. (Washington, DC: Brookings Institution, 1981), p. 200.
79. Cass Peterson, "How Much Risk Is Too Much?" *The Washington Post National Weekly Edition*, 4 February 1985, p. 7.
80. Hoel and Crump, *Waterborne Carcinogens*, p. 202.
81. Quoted in Paul Johnson, "The Perils of Risk Avoidance," *Regulation* (May/June 1980):8.
82. National Academy of Science, p. 22.
83. Lave, p. 14.
84. See Congressional Quarterly, *Environment and Health*, p. 128.
85. Quoted in ibid., p. 25.
86. Jonathan Friendly, "Pesticide Scare Attributed to Gap in Communication," *New York Times*, 12 March 1985.
87. Douglas Costle, "Brave New Chemical: The Future Regulatory History of Phlogiston," *Administrative Law Review* 33 (1981):195.
88. The EPA recently tried a new variant of public meeting: Residents in Tacoma, Washington were asked by agency officials in a town meeting whether or not a local copper smelter should be closed down in order to reduce the threat of arse-

nic pollution to the nearby residents. See Felicity Barringer, "EPA Asks Residents' Advice About Arsenic Plant," *Washington Post*, 14 July 1983.

89. The EPA has had almost no experience with public funding of citizen participation in rule-making hearings except for one hearing under the Toxic Substances Control Act in 1977 where $1,500 was granted to the New York Public Interest Research Group (NYPIRG) to examine the effect of a proposed rule banning PCB use in the manufacture of optical products. One agency official concluded: "For a very small and strategic amount of money we learned something." See Judy Sarasohn, "Critics Successful in Reducing Funds for Public Participation," *Congressional Quarterly Weekly Report* (1 November 1980):3273.

90. National Academy of Science, *Decision Making*, pp. 22, 80.

91. Glenn Frankel, " 'The Tragedy of TOSCA': Chemical Poisoning the EPA Can't Control," *Washington Monthly* (July 1979):42.

92. See Stewart, "Judicial Review of Environmental Decision Making," pp. 750–63; Melnick, *Regulation and the Courts*; Joanne Omang, "Court Orders EPA to Monitor Dams," *Washington Post*, 30 January 1982, p. A10.

93. Glenn Frankel, "Clean Water EPA Rules Are Voided," *Washington Post*, 21 July 1981, p. B1.

94. Lawrence Mosher, "Environmentalists Sue to Put an End to 'Regulatory Massive Resistance,' " *National Journal* (19 December 1981):2234.

95. National Academy of Science, *Decision Making*, p. 93.

96. Philip Shabecoff, "EPA Adrift in Stalemates," *New York Times*, 23 November 1984.

97. Interview with EPA official, 2 February 1982.

98. Interview with EPA officials, 2 February and 25 February 1982.

99. Quoted in Congressional Quarterly, *Environment and Health*, p. 130. (See note 8, this chapter.)

100. Cass Peterson, " 'No Hit Lists' at EPA, Vows Ruckelshaus," *Washington Post*, 5 May 1983, p. A1.

101. Philip Shabecoff, "Office of Environment and Budget," *New York Times*, 19 June 1985.

102. Kathy Koch, "Congress to Review Clean Water Legislation," *Congressional Quarterly Weekly Report* (23 January 1982):124.

103. Comptroller General of the United States, *EPA Is Slow to Carry Out Its Responsibility to Control Harmful Chemicals* (Washington, DC: General Accounting Office, 1980).

104. Kathy Koch, "Cleaning Up Chemical Dumps Posing Dilemmas for Congress," *Congressional Quarterly Weekly Report* (22 March 1980):798; Mosher, "Reagan's Environmental Federalism," p. 187.

Chapter 6. THE OCCUPATIONAL SAFETY AND HEALTH ADMINISTRATION

1. PL 91 595. Sec. 2(b), 84 Stat. 1590 (1970), 29 U.S.C. 553, 651–678.

2. Construction Safety Act (83 Stat. 96. 1969); Longshoremen's and Harbor Workers' Compensation Act (44 Stat. 1444. 1927); Service Contract Act of 1965 (79 Stat. 1034); and the Walsh–Healey Act (49 Stat. 2036, 1936).

3. Congressional Quarterly, *Federal Regulatory Directory* (Washington, DC: Congressional Quarterly, 1981), p. 380.

4. PL 91-595. Sec. 6(c).

5. Steven Kelman, "The Occupational Safety and Health Administration," in *The Politics of Regulation*, James Q. Wilson, ed. (New York: Basic, 1980), p. 259.
6. Congressional Quarterly, *Federal Regulatory Directory*, pp. 380-81.
7. Kelman, "Occupational Safety".
8. Congressional Quarterly, *Federal Regulatory Directory*.
9. Kathy Sawyer and Peter Earley, "OSHA Befriends Industry, but Draws New Fire," *Washington Post*, 15 July 1983.
10. See Philip J. Harter, "In Search of OSHA," *Regulation* (September/October 1977):38.
11. Ibid.
12. Timothy Clark, "The 'Facts' About OSHA's 1,100 Revoked Regulations," *National Journal* (12 August 1978):1298.
13. Ibid.
14. PL 91-596, 84 Stat. 1590 (1970).
15. Ibid., Sec. 7.
16. Ibid., Sec. 7(b).
17. Ibid., Sec. 7(b).
18. Ibid., Sec. 6(b) (6), 6(e).
19. Congressional Quarterly, *Federal Regulatory Directory*, pp. 390-93.
20. Ibid.
21. Interview (not for attribution) with OSHA official, 21 July 1986.
22. Steven Kelman, *Regulating America, Regulating Sweden: A Comparative Study of Occupational Safety and Health Policy* (Cambridge: M.I.T. Press, 1981), p. 10.
23. Thorne G. Auchter, Assistant Secretary of Labor for Occupational Safety and Health, "OSHA Instruction RUL.1," (1 March 1982), p. II-1.
24. Ibid., pp. II-2 to III-3.
25. Ibid., pp. V-8 to V-11.
26. Ibid., pp. III-9;V-2 to V-6.
27. Ibid., pp. V-10 to V-15.
28. Felicity Barringer, "OSHA Chief Charts His Reassured Pace," *Washington Post*, 10 March 1982.
29. 46 *Federal Register* 4078 (16 January 1981).
30. OSHA, "Regulatory Impact and Regulatory Flexibility Analysis for the Hearing Conservation Amendment," August 1981.
31. Interview with Joanne Linhart, Office of Carcinogen Standards, and Mary Ellen Weber, Office of Regulatory Analysis, April 8, 1982.
32. 46 *Federal Register* 4015-18 (16 January 1981).
33. OSHA, "Regulatory Impact," pp. 37, 43.
34. 45 *Federal Register* 5001-296 (22 January 1980).
35. ASARCO, Inc. et al. v. OSHA, no. 78-1959; The Anaconda Co. et al. v. OSHA, nos. 78-2764 and 3039; General Motors et al. v. OSHA, nos. 78-2477 and 2478, Ninth Circuit, 1978.
36. 47 *Federal Register* 15359 (9 April 1982).
37. Ibid., pp. 15360-66.
38. Ibid., pp. 15362-64.
39. Industrial Union Dept. v. American Petroleum Institute, 448 U.S. 607 at 655-6, n. 62 (1980).
40. American Textile Manufacturers Institute v. Donovan, 452 U.S. 490 (1981).
41. 47 *Federal Register* 15365 (9 April 1982).
42. Ben A. Franklin, "Novel Pressures in Toxic Label Case," *New York Times*, 23

March 1982, p. A17; Ben A. Franklin, "Administration Reviews Rules on Chemical Labels," *New York Times*, 18 March 1982, p. A22.

43. Ibid.; Sandra Sugawara, "Workplace Chemicals Settled," *Washington Post*, 18 March 1982, p. A23.
44. "Court Panel Strikes Down Limits on Information on Hazards in Workplace," *New York Times*, 30 May 1985.
45. David Burnham, "Five House Chairmen Assail Budget Office Role," *New York Times*, 29 June 1985; Public Citizens Health Research Group v. Rowland, U.S. Court of Appeals for the District of Columbia, 25 July 1986.
46. Morton Corn, "Cotton Dust: A Regulator's View," in *The Scientific Basis of Health and Safety Regulation*, Robert W. Crandall and Lester B. Lave, eds. (Washington, DC: Brookings Institution, 1981):110.
47. U.S. Department of Labor, "Report to the Congress: Cotton Dust: Review of Alternative Technical Standards and Control Technologies," (14 May 1979):2.
48. "The Cotton Dust Case," *Regulation* (January/February 1981):5.
49. Ibid., pp. 5-6.
50. Myron Struck, "Administration, in Shift, Backs Cotton Dust Curbs," *Washington Post*, 20 May 1983; Cass Peterson, "OSHA to Seek Revisions in Cotton Dust Standard," *Washington Post*, 8 June 1983.
51. Siegfried Heyden and Philip Pratt, "Exposure to Cotton Dust and Respiratory Disease," *Journal of the American Medical Association* 17 (October 1980).
52. Corn, pp. 111-12.
53. Ibid., pp. 113-14.
54. 42 *Federal Register* 27379 (1978).
55. John F. Morrall, III, "Cotton Dust: An Economist's View," in *The Scientific Basis of Health and Safety Regulation*, Robert W. Crandall and Lester B. Lave, eds. (Washington, DC: Brookings Institution, 1981), pp. 102-3.
56. U.S. Department of Labor, *Report To the Congress*.
57. Ibid., pp. 10-11.
58. Ibid., pp. 14-15.
59. Ibid., pp. 49-58.
60. W. Kip Viscusi, "Cotton Dust Regulation: An OSHA Success Story?" *Journal of Policy Analysis and Management*, 4(3) (1985):325-43.
61. U.S. Department of Labor, pp. 9, 10, 60-69.
62. Kenneth B. Noble, "Job-Linked Injuries and Illnesses Rose in 1984," *New York Times*, 14 November 1985.
63. Kenneth B. Noble, "Study Faults U.S. on Safety Effort," *New York Times*, 17 April 1985.
64. See Morrall, "OSHA After Ten Years"; Eugene Bardoch and Robert Kagan, *Going by the Book* (Philadelphia: Temple University Press, 1983).
65. Christopher DeMuth, "The White House Review Programs," *Regulation* (January/February 1980):19.
66. American Textile Manufacturers Institute, Inc. et al. v. Donovan, and National Cotton Council of America v. Donovan, 452 US 490 (1981).
67. Ibid., p. 4732.
68. Ibid., p. 4734.
69. Ibid.
70. Philip Shabecoff, "Safety Agency to Review Standards on Cotton Dust," *New York Times*, 28 March 1981, p. 9.
71. Ibid.
72. Viscusi, "Cotton Dust Regulation".

73. Office of Technology Assessment, *Preventing Illness and Injury*, (Washington, DC: OTA, 1985):14.
74. Ibid.
75. Peter Perl, "Sanitation in the Fields: A Test for Secretary Brock," *The Washington Post National Weekly Edition*, 1 July 1985.
76. Robert Pear, "States Told to Require Toilets for Field Hands," *New York Times*, 19 October 1985.
77. Kenneth B. Noble, "More Jeers by Critics and Cheers by Businessmen," *New York Times*, 6 May 1985.
78. John Mendelhoff, "Does Overregulation Cause Underregulation? The Case of Toxic Chemicals," *Regulation* (September–October 1981):47–52.

Chapter 7. THE CONSUMER PRODUCT SAFETY COMMISSION

1. Center for the Study of American Business, *Directory of Federal Regulatory Agencies* (St. Louis: Center for the Study of American Business, Washington University, 1981), p. 33.
2. Executive Office of the President, Office of Management and Budget, *Budget of the United States Government FY 1986* (Washington, DC: Government Printing Office, 1985), pp. 8–189.
3. Sari Horwitz, "At the CPSC, a New Test of Regulatory Ideology," *Washington Post National Weekly Edition*, 24 December 1984, p. 33.
4. 86 Stat. 1207, 15 U.S.C. 2056(a) (i), 2057 (1972).
5. Richard Merrill, "CPSC Regulation of Cancer Risks in Consumer Products 1972–81," *Virginia Law Review* 67 (1981):1369.
6. PL 97-35, section 9(a), 95 Stat. 703 (1981).
7. Ibid., section 9(c) and (d).
8. Ibid., Section 9(e) and (f).
9. Ibid., Section 9(d); 9(f) (2).
10. Ibid., Section 9(f); 9(g).
11. Ibid., Section 7 (c), (a); 9(f) (3) (c).
12. Ibid., Section 28.
13. Ibid., Section 1207.
14. Richard E. Cohen, "Passing the Buck," *National Journal* (9 July 1983):1461.
15. Philip Shenon, "Formaldehyde: A Workhorse Chemical Faces Ban," *New York Times*, 4 October 1981, p. 4F; Caroline Mayer, "Formaldehyde Foam Insulation Ban Ordered," *Washington Post*, 23 February 1982, p. A1.
16. Edith Barksdale Sloan, "Check Your Facts, Kirkpatrick," *Washington Post*, 14 November 1981, p. A21.
17. Mayer, "Formaldehyde Foam Ban."
18. 46 *Federal Register* 11189-91 (5 February 1981).
19. Ibid., 11193.
20. In 1981, during the confirmation hearings for Nancy Harvey Steorts, President Reagan's nominee to head the CPSC, Senator Robert Kasten, chairman of the Senate Commerce Committee, interpreted congressional intent toward the CPSC this way: "There's a legitimate role for Government and for Government regulation, but maybe . . . the role of the Government ought to be a referee or the role of an umpire to see that the game is played with maximum competition . . . and the government and especially a regulatory agency . . . ought to be in the role of

an umpire or referee, but not in the role of the other team, especially when we're competing with countries like Japan and others who have such a close working relationship between their government and their industry." Ibid., 11193.

21. Ibid., 11195–96.
22. Ibid., 11200.
23. Interview with Michael Brown, former general counsel, CPSC, 16 March 1982; interview with Judith Pitcher, Economic Section, Directorate for Hazard Identification and Analysis, CPSC, 15 March 1982; Congressional Quarterly, *Federal Regulatory Directory 1981-82* (Washington, DC: Congressional Quarterly, 1981), p. 99.
24. Congressional Quarterly, *Federal Regulatory Directory 1981-82*, pp. 101–02; Pitcher interview.
25. Consumer Product Safety Act of 1972, 86 Stat. 1207, PL 92-573, Section 9(c) (1) (D) (1972).
26. Merrill, "CPSC Regulation," p. 1280.
27. Aqua Slide "N" Dive Corp. v. CPSC, 569 F.2d 831 (5th Cir., 1978); see also Merrill, "CPSC Regulation," pp. 1281–82.
28. U.S., Senate, Commerce, Science and Transportation Committee, *Consumer Product Safety Commission Reauthorization*, 97th Congress, 1st sess., 1981, p. 3; Pitcher interview.
29. 45 *Federal Register* 85774–5 (20 December 1980).
30. Ibid.
31. See "Scientific Basis for Identification of Potential Carcinogen and Estimation of Risks," 22 *Federal Register* 60038 (17 October 1979).
32. 45 *Federal Register* 85776 (30 December 1980).
33. Quoted in Congressional Quarterly, *Federal Regulatory Directory 1983-84* (Washington, DC: Congressional Quarterly, 1983), p. 87.
34. See Molly Sinclair, "Safety Watchdog Stays Rocky Course," *Washington Post*, 8 May 1983, p. L1.
35. Press release statement of Sam Zagoria, Commissioner, CPSC, 22 February 1982.
36. Press release statement of Stuart M. Statler, Commissioner, CPSC, 22 February 1982.
37. Quoted in Michael deCourcy Hinds, "Product Safety Agency Bans Use of Formaldehyde Foam Insulation," *New York Times*, 23 February 1982.
38. Gulf South Insulation v. CPSC, no. 82-4218, U.S. Court of Appeals, Fifth Circuit (7 April 1983).
39. Molly Sinclair, "Consumer Product Safety Commission," *Washington Post*, 8 April 1983.
40. Quoted in Congressional Quarterly, *Congressional Quarterly Almanac 1978* (Washington, DC: Congressional Quarterly, 1979), p. 526.
41. Senate Report No. 749, House Report No. 1153, 92nd Congress, 1st sess., 1972.
42. House Report No. 1153, pp. 24–25.
43. Ibid.
44. U.S., House of Representatives, Interstate and Foreign Commerce Committee, *Federal Regulation and Regulatory Reform*, 94th Congress, 2d sess. 1976, p. 201.
45. Ibid., at 201, fn. 38.
46. House Report No. 1153, p. 14.
47. U.S., Senate, Committee on Commerce, Science and Transportation, *Nomination—Consumer Product Safety Commission*, 97th Congress, 1st sess., 1981, p. 17.

48. Senate Report No. 749, p. 12.
49. Antonin Scalia and Frank Goodman, "Procedural Aspects of the Consumer Product Safety Act," *UCLA Law Review* 20 (1972):951-52.
50. U.S., House of Representatives, Interstate and Foreign Commerce Committee, p. 206, fn. 32.
51. PL 94-284, Sec. 14; PL 97-35, Sec. 17.
52. Quoted in Congressional Quarterly, *Congressional Quarterly Almanac 1978*, p. 554.
53. Bureau of National Affairs, *Product Safety and Liability Reporter*, no. 6 (6 February 1981), p. 129.
54. Ibid.
55. Ibid.
56. BNA, no. 12 (20 March 1981), p. 247.
57. BNA, no. 19 (8 May 1981).
58. BNA, no. 22 (29 May 1981), p. 425.
59. BNA, no. 26 (26 June 1981).
60. Merrill, "CPSC Regulation," p. 1267.
61. U.S., House of Representatives, Interstate and Foreign Commerce Committee, p. 238.
62. Horwitz, "At the CPSC."
63. Terrence M. Scanlon and Robert A. Rogowsky, "Back Door Rulemaking: A View from the CPSC," *Regulation* (July-August 1984):27-28.
64. Kip Viscusi, "The Consumer Product Safety Commission," Working Paper on Regulation (Washington, DC: American Enterprise Institute, 1982), p. 3.
65. See, for example, the testimonies in U.S., Senate, Commerce, Science and Transportation Committee, *CPSC Reauthorization*; U.S., House of Representatives, Committee on Energy and Commerce, *CPSC Reauthorization*, 97th Congress, 1st sess. (1981).
66. Viscusi, "The CPSC," pp. 3-5.
67. Consumer Product Safety Commission, *Annual Report 1981*, Appendix, p. 214.
68. See Viscusi, pp. 3-7.
69. U.S. House of Representatives, Interstate and Foreign Commerce Committee, p. 213.
70. Paul Weaver, "The Hazards of Trying to Make Consumer Products Safer," *Fortune*, July 1975, p. 133.
71. Pitcher interview.
72. Brown interview.
73. Ibid.
74. Ibid.
75. Commissioner Stuart Statler, quoted in Merrill, "CPSC Regulation," p. 1371.
76. 46 *Federal Register* 11200 (5 February 1981).
77. Ibid., 11201.
78. Ibid., 11202.
79. CPSC Memorandum, "Briefing Package on Urea-Formaldehyde (U.F.) Foam Insulation," 29 January 1982, pp. 2, 63.
80. 46 *Federal Register* 56762-63 (18 November 1981).
81. CPSC Memorandum, 29 January 1982, p. 31.
82. Caroline E. Mayer, "Formaldehyde Firms Try to Head Off Ban," *Washington Post*, 11 February 1982, p. C1.
83. Statement of Nancy Harvey Steorts, Chairman, CPSC, 22 February 1982.
84. Michael deCourcy Hinds, "Budget Cuts Imperil Consumer Agency," *New York Times*, 4 October 1981.

85. Press release, statement of Edith Barksdale Sloan, Commissioner, CPSC, 22 February 1982.
86. Press release, statement of R. David Pittle, Commissioner, CPSC, 22 February 1982.
87. Scanlon and Rogowsky, "Back Door Rulemaking," p. 27.

Chapter 8. THE FOOD AND DRUG ADMINISTRATION

1. Food and Drugs Act of 1906 (34 Stat. 768, 21 U.S.C.); Food, Drug and Cosmetic Act of 1938 (52 Stat. 1040, 21 U.S.C. 301); Delaney Amendments of 1958 (72 Stat. 1784, 21 U.S.C. 321); Color Additive Amendments of 1960 (74 Stat. 397, 21 U.S.C. 321); Medical Device Amendments of 1976 (90 Stat. 534, 21 U.S.C. 321); Drug Listing Act of 1972 (86 Stat. 559, 21 U.S.C. 360); Fair Packaging and Labeling Act of 1966 (80 Stat. 1296, 15 U.S.C. 1451); Filled Milk Act of 1923 (42 Stat. 1486, 21 U.S.C. 61); Infant Formula Act of 1980 (94 Stat. 1190, 21 U.S.C. 301 note); Public Health Service Act of 1944 (58 Stat. 682, 42 U.S.C. 201); Radiation Control for Health and Safety Act of 1968 (82 Stat. 1173, 43 U.S.C. 263b); and Federal Hazardous Substances Act of 1960 (74 Stat. 372, 15 U.S.C. 1261).
2. Congressional Quarterly, *Federal Regulatory Directory 1981-82* (Washington, DC: Congressional Quarterly, 1981), pp. 306-07.
3. This classification relies on a study by the FDA's Chief Counsel from 1975 to 1977, Richard A. Merrill. See Merrill, "Regulating Carcinogens in Food: A Legislator's Guide to the Food Safety Provisions of the Federal Food, Drug, and Cosmetic Act," *Michigan Law Review* 77 (1978):171.
4. Food, Drug and Cosmetic Act of 1938, 21 U.S.C. 342(a) (1).
5. Merrill, "Regulating Carcinogens," pp. 187-89.
6. 2 U.S.C. 342(a) (1938).
7. U.S. v. Lexington Mill and Elevator Co., 232 U.S. 399 (1914) at 411. See Merrill, "Regulating Carcinogens," pp. 192-93.
8. 21 U.S.C. 346 (1938).
9. Ibid.; compare with Section 342, discussed above.
10. Merrill, "Regulating Carcinogens," p. 197.
11. Ibid., p. 200.
12. 69 Stat. 54 (1954).
13. 21 U.S.C. 371(e) (1954).
14. See Robert W. Hamilton, "Rulemaking on a Record by the Food and Drug Administration," Administrative Conference of the United States, Report in Support of Recommendation 71-7 (1972), p. 451.
15. 21 U.S.C. 371(e)-(f) (1954).
16. U.S., House of Representatives, Committee on Interstate and Foreign Commerce, *A Brief Legislative History of the Food, Drug, and Cosmetic Act*, 93rd Congress, 2d sess., 1974, pp. 7-8.
17. 72 Stat. 1784.
18. 21 U.S.C. 321 (s) (1958).
19. 34 *Federal Register* 17063 (1969).
20. Merrill, "Regulating Carcinogens," p. 216.
21. Congress also set up a special regulatory scheme for the use of food color additives, generally conforming to the requirements for food additives. The FDA must approve the use of all color additives before they are marketed; such

approval must be based on a finding that the food coloring is safe and does not seek to deceive consumers. Color additives which are found to "induce cancer in man or animal" cannot be approved by the agency. (See 21 U.S.C. 376(b) and 348(c) (1) (A) (1958)).

22. U.S., House of Representatives, Report No. 2284, 85th Congress, 2d sess. 1958, pp. 4–5; U.S., Senate, Report No. 2242, 85th Congress, 2d sess., 1958, pp. 2–3, 6.
23. 21 U.S.C. 348(c) (3) (a) (1958).
24. 21 U.S.C. 348 (c)–(g) (1958).
25. Merrill, "Regulating Carcinogens," p. 209.
26. 21 U.S.C. 321 (s) (1958).
27. Merrill, "Regulating Carcinogens," pp. 225–26.
28. 21 U.S.C. 348(c) (3) (A).
29. Residues of pesticides used in protecting crops from insects and animals were regulated by the FDA until 1970, when that responsibility was transferred to the Environmental Protection Agency. Under the Food, Cosmetic and Drug Act and the Federal Insecticide, Fungicide, and Rodenticide Act (7 U.S.C. 135) (1970), the EPA is required to prohibit the use of pesticides which present "any unreasonable risk to man or the environment, taking into account the economic, social and environmental costs and benefits of the use of any pesticide" (7 U.S.C. 136a(bb)) (1970). Thus, the EPA is empowered to balance the risks and benefits involved in the use of specific pesticides. The procedural steps required of the EPA are the same as those demanded of the FDA for approving food additives, except that in the case of the EPA petitioners may demand that the petition be reviewed by an advisory committee established by the National Academy of Science (21 U.S.C. 346a(d) (3) (5)) (1970).
30. U.S., Senate, S 1442 (HR 4014), 97th Congress, 1st sess., 1981. See also Ann Pelham, "Food Industry Seeks Rewrite of Federal Food Safety Law," *Congressional Quarterly Weekly Report* (9 September 1981):1791–93; Linda E. Demkovich, "The Delaney Clause Comes Under the Gun as Critics Ask, How Safe Is Safe?" *National Journal* (31 October 1981):1950–52; Comptroller General of the United States, *Regulation of Cancer-Causing Food Additives—Time for a Change?* (Washington, DC: General Accounting Office, 1981).
31. U.S., House of Representatives, HR 5491, 97th Congress, 2d sess., 1982.
32. Richard A. Merrill and Michael Schewel, "FDA Regulation of Environmental Contaminants of Food," *Virginia Law Review* 66 (1979):1383.
33. Merrill, "Regulating Carcinogens," pp. 201–02.
34. "Poisonous or Deleterious Substances in Food," 39 *Federal Register* 42746 (1974).
35. 42 *Federal Register* 52814 (1977).
36. Ibid.
37. Merrill and Schewel, "FDA Regulation," p. 1392, n. 131.
38. 21 U.S.C. 346 (1938).
39. Statement by Peter Hutt, former FDA Chief Counsel, in Merrill and Schewel, "FDA Regulation," p. 1392, n. 134.
40. Statement by Donald Kennedy, quoted in ibid., p. 1394.
41. Ibid., pp. 1393–94. (The Delaney Clause applies only to food additives, and not to environmental contaminants.)
42. Ibid., pp. 1395–96.
43. Interview with Robert Lake, Regulations Coordinator, Bureau of Foods, 2 June 1982.

44. "FDA Ordered to Use Tougher Regulation of Food Substances," *Wall Street Journal*, 28 March 1985.
45. Merrill and Schewel, "FDA Regulation," pp. 1410–11.
46. Ibid., pp. 1411–12.
47. Ibid., pp. 1413–14.
48. 44 *Federal Register* 38334 (1974).
49. Lake interview.
50. Ibid.
51. Policy for Regulating Carcinogenic Animals in Food and Color Additives: Advanced Notice of Proposed Rulemaking, 47 *Federal Register* 14464 (1982).
52. Ibid., p. 14468.
53. Ibid., pp. 14468–69.
54. Ibid., p. 14466.
55. Monsanto v. Kennedy, 613 F. 2d 947 (D.C. Cir. 1979), p. 955.
56. 47 *Federal Register* 14466 (1982).
57. Interview with Carl Blozan, FDA, 20 May 1982.
58. "FDA Again Delays Decision on Suspected Cancer-Causing Dyes," *Wall Street Journal*, 4 April 1985.
59. Clifford Grobstein, "Saccharin: A Scientist's View," in *The Strategy of Social Regulation*, Lester Lave and Robert Crandall, eds. (Washington, DC: Brookings Institution, 1981):117–19. Richard Merrill, "Saccharin: A Regulator's View," same volume, pp. 156–57.
60. Merrill, "Saccharin," pp. 157–59.
61. The Saccharin Study and Labeling Act, 81 Stat. 1451 (1977).
62. PL 96-273 (1980); PL 97-42 (1981); *Wall Street Journal*, 8 May 1985.
63. Press release, statement by FDA Commissioner Donald Kennedy, 14 April 1977.
64. Quoted in Merrill, "Saccharin," p. 167.
65. National Academy of Science, "Saccharin: Technical Assessment," pp. ES-4, ES-10; see Grobstein, "Saccharin," p. 123.
66. Merrill, "Saccharin," pp. 155, 167.
67. Congressional Quarterly, *Environment and Health* (Washington, DC: Congressional Quarterly, 1981), p. 79.
68. See Congressional Quarterly, *Congressional Quarterly Almanac 1977* (Washington, DC: Congressional Quarterly, 1978), pp. 495–99.
69. Congressional Quarterly, *Environment and Health* (1981), p. 80.
70. David Shribman, "Senate Continues Block of FDA Ban on Saccharin Use," *Wall Street Journal*, 9 May 1985.
71. Philip M. Boffey, "Cyclamate's Role in Cancer Unclear," *New York Times*, 11 June 1985; Joe Davidson, "Study Finds Cyclamate Role in Cancer May Be Due to Use with Other Substances," *Wall Street Journal*, 11 June 1985; Judith Randall, "Is Aspartame Really Safe?" *The Washington Post National Weekly Edition*, 28 May 1985.
72. Interview with Faye Dworkin, FDA, 20 May 1982.
73. Lake interview.
74. Nora Zamichow, "Six Cancer-Causing Dyes are Still in Food, Drugs and Cosmetics," *The Washington Post National Weekly Edition*, 24 June 1985.
75. Marian Burrows, "Saga of Food Regulation: 25 Years, Still No Decision," *New York Times*, 13 February 1985.
76. Peter Hutt, speech at Brookings Institution Conference on Regulatory Reform, 20 May 1982.
77. Merrill, "FDA Regulation," p. 1423.

78. The 1906 Food and Drug Act, 34 Stat. 768.
79. 52 Stat. 1040 (1938). See generally Peter Temin, *Taking Your Medicine—Drug Regulation in the United States* (Cambridge: Harvard University Press, 1980), pp. 24-29.
80. 65 Stat. 648 (1951).
81. 76 Stat. 780 (1962).
82. 86 Stat. 559 (1972).
83. U.S., Senate, S 1075 (HR 4258), 96th Congress, 1st sess., 1979.
84. Henry G. Grabowski and John M. Vernon, "FDA Regulation of Pharmaceuticals," p. 32.
85. Ibid., pp. 33-35.
86. General Accounting Office, "FDA Drug Approval—A Lengthy Process That Delays the Availability of Important New Drugs," HRD 80-64, 28 May 1980, pp. 12-15.
87. Food and Drug Administration, *FDA Public Advisory Groups* (1980).
88. GAO, "FDA Drug Approval," p. 14.
89. Grabowski and Vernon, p. 41.
90. Paul Quirk, "The Food and Drug Administration," in *The Politics of Regulation*, James Q. Wilson, ed. (New York: Basic, 1981), pp. 200-03.
91. GAO, "FDA Drug Approval," p. 1.
92. Ibid., pp. 12-25.
93. Ibid., pp. 22-23.
94. Ibid., pp. 25-26.
95. Joe Davidson, "Heckler Signs Rules That Reduce Data Needed for FDA Approval of New Drugs," *Wall Street Journal*, 12 December 1984.
96. Ibid., pp. 30-34.
97. Cristine Russell, "Inside: The Food and Drug Administration," *Washington Post*, 28 January 1983.
98. The various studies of the costs and benefits of new drug regulation are reviewed in Grabowski and Vernon, *FDA Regulation*, pp. 44-63.
99. Quirk, "The Food and Drug Administration," pp. 206-10. See also Daniel Seidman, "The Politics of Policy Analysis," *Regulation* (July-August 1977):22-37.
100. Ibid., pp. 211-13.
101. GAO, "FDA Drug Approval," p. 37.
102. Quirk, "The Food and Drug Administration," pp. 213-15.
103. Commissioner Alexander Schmidt, quoted in ibid., p. 216.
104. Peter Barton Hutt, "Safety Regulation in the Real World," *Food Drug Cosmetic Law Journal* (July 1973):460.

Chapter 9. THE PROSPECTS FOR LIMITING BUREAUCRATIC DISCRETION

1. Alan B. Morrison, "OMB Interference with Agency Rulemaking: The Wrong Way to Write a Regulation," *Harvard Law Review* 99 (1986):1059-74; Christopher C. DeMuth and Douglas H. Ginsburg, "White House Review of Agency Rulemaking," *Harvard Law Review* 99 (1986):1075-88.
2. Judges monitor virtually every aspect of the administrative process, and can reverse or remand agency actions for procedural errors as well as substantive

problems. Courts have described their efforts as taking a "hard look" at the substance of agency rules to assure that actions are reasonable and based on evidence generated during the rule-making process. See Merrick B. Garland, "Deregulation and Judicial Review," *Harvard Law Review* 98 (1985):505–89; Philip J. Cooper, "Conflict or Constructive Tension: The Changing Relationship of Judges and Administrators," *Public Administration Review* (November 1985): 643–52.

3. Stephen Wermeil, "High Court Says Some Agency Decisions to Take No Action Can't be Challenged," *Wall Street Journal*, (21 March 1985), p. 8.

4. See David Schoenbrod, "Goals Statutes or Rules Statutes: The Case of the Clean Air Act" *UCLA Law Review* 30 (1983): 740–828.

5. Philip Shabecoff, "To the EPA, Putting First Things First Can Be A Problem," *New York Times*, (1 December 1985), p. 2E; Barry Meier, "Study by EPA Finds Laws May be Insufficient to Protect the Public Against Toxic Chemicals," *Wall Street Journal*, (8 February 1985), p. 4; Robert Crandall, "Environmental Ignorance is not Bliss," *Wall Street Journal*, (22 April 1985), p. 21; Michele Perrault, "Ruckelshaus, Thwarted," *New York Times*, (11 December 1984), p. 21; Cass Peterson, "How Much Risk is Too Much?" *Washington Post National Weekly Edition*, (4 February 1985), p. 7; Office of Technology Assessment, *Preventing Illness and Injury in the Workplace* (Washington, DC: Government Printing Office, 1985).

6. John Mendeloff, "Does Overregulation Cause Underregulation? The Case of Toxic Substances," *Regulation* (September–October 1981): 47–52.

7. Sheila Jasanoff, "Negotiation or Cost-Benefit Analysis: A Middle Road for U.S. Policy?" *The Environmental Forum* (July 1983):37–43.

8. Davic Vogel, "Cooperative Regulation: Environmental Protection in Great Britain," *The Public Interest* (72) (Summer 1983):91–97.

9. Sheila Jasanoff, "Science and the Limits of Administrative Rule Making: Lessons from the OSHA Cancer Policy," *Osgoode Hall Law Journal* 20 (September 1982):536–61.

10. Barbara Jo Fleischauer, "Occupational Safety and Health Law in Sweden and the United States: Are There Lessons to be Learned by Both Countries?" *Hastings International and Comparative Law Review* 6 (1983):295–96.

11. Jasanoff, "Negotiation or Cost–Benefit Analysis."

12. Dieter Lorenz, "The Constitutional Supervision of the Administrative Agencies in the Federal Republic of Germany," *Southern California Law Review* 53 (1980):543–582; and "Commentary" by Hans Linde and Lee Albert, ibid., pp. 583–609.

13. For further reading in this area, see David Vogel, "Cooperative Regulation: Environmental Protection in Great Britain," *The Public Interest* (72) (Summer 1983):88–106; Jasanoff, "Negotiation of Cost-Benefit Analysis"; Vincent Navarro, "The Determinants of Health Policy, A Case Study: Regulating Safety and Health at the Workplace in Sweden," *Journal of Health Politics, Policy and Law* 9 (1984):137–56; David P. Currie, "Air Pollution Control in West Germany," *The University of Chicago Law Review* 49 (1982):355–93; Carolyn J. Tuohy, "Regulation and Scientific Complexity: Decision Rules and Processes in the Occupational Health Arena," *Osgoode Hall Law Journal* 20 (1982):562–609.

14. See, generally, Philip Harter, "Negotiating Regulations: A Cure for Malaise," *Georgetown Law Journal* 71(1) (October 1982):1–118; Lawrence Susskind and Alan Weinstein, "Towards a Theory of Environmental Dispute Resolution," *Environmental Affairs* 9 (1980):311–357; Allan R. Talbot, *Settling Things: Six Case Studies in Environmental Mediation* (Washington, DC: Conservation

Foundation, 1983); Robert B. Reich, "Regulation by Confirmation or Negotiation?" *Harvard Business Review* (May–June 1981):82–91; Gail Bingham, *Resolving Environmental Disputes: A Decade of Experience* (Washington, DC: Conservation Foundation, 1986).

15. See, generally, Steven Breyer, *Regulation and its Reform* (Cambridge: Harvard University Press, 1983).

16. See Mendelhoff, "Overregulation."

17. For an introduction to this debate, see Office of Technology Assessment, *Assessment of Technologies for Determining Cancer Risks From the Environment* (Washington, DC: Government Printing Office, 1981); Leslie Roberts, *Cancer Today: Origins, Prevention, and Treatment* (Washington, DC: National Academy Press, 1984).

18. For examples of such efforts, see Lester Lave and Gilbert Omenn, *Clearing the Air* (Washington, DC: Brookings Institution, 1982); American Enterprise Institute, *The Clean Air Act: Proposals for Revisions* (Washington, DC: AEI, 1981).

INDEX

AFL-CIO, 134
administrative discretion, 31-32,
208-209, 218; kinds of, 6-7; rule
of law, 8; and theory of, 3-6;
Administrative Procedure Act, 14, 19-31,
33-34, 86, 210
adversary process, 32-39, 115
Amalgamated Clothing and Textile
Workers, 137
American Bar Association, 30, 33
American Conference of Government
Industrial Hygienists, 119
American Health Foundation, 190
American National Standards
Institute, 119
American Petroleum Institute, 108
American Textile Manufacturers Institute,
134
Auchter, Thorne, 127

best available technology, 26, 41
Brennan, William, 138
Brookings Institution, 51
Bumpers amendment, 29
Burford, Anne, 69, 109, 117
Burger, Warren, 139
Bush, George, 72

Canada, regulation in, 210
Carter, Jimmy, 67-68, 71, 115, 121, 134,
137-138
Chemical Institute for Toxicology, 158
chemicals, health effects of, 60
Civil Aeronautics Board, 70
Clark, William P., 67
Collins, Cardiss, 133
congressional oversight, 73-78, 85-87,

117, 133, 171-172
Congressional Research Service, 50, 52
Consumer Product Safety Commission,
10, 27, 45-46, 49, 52, 97,
146-173, 207
Costle, Douglas, 115
cost-benefit analysis, 14-15, 43, 57-60,
114, 127, 139, 155, 162, 166, 205
cotton dust, 131, 134-141
Council on Environmental Quality, 52
Council on Wage and Price Stability, 70,
137-138

Davis, K.C., 9, 22
Delaney, James, 179
Dickinson, John, 19
Drayton, William, 69
drug regulation, 192-198
due process, 31, 40, 115, 170

Energy, Department of, 160
Environmental Protection Agency, 2, 10,
30, 39, 42, 43, 45-46, 49, 52, 67,
83-84, 91-118, 156, 207
Erlichman, John, 70
Executive Order 11821, 47
Executive Order 12044, 47
Executive Order 12291, 47-48, 72, 98,
139, 188, 191
Executive Order 12498, 71-72

Federal Aviation Administration, 55
Federal Communications Commission, 12
Federal Trade Commission, 9, 12, 27-28,
97, 193
Fiorina, Morris, 87
Food and Drug Administration, 10,

42-45, 50, 52, 174-199
Food Safety Council, 51
food safety regulation, 175-192
Ford, Gerald, 70
Ford, Wendell, 171
Formaldehyde Institute, 158
Frankfurter, Felix, 40
Fuller, Lon, 35

General Accounting Office, 52, 82,
    84, 111
Goodnow, Frank, 19
Gray, C. Boyden, 84
Great Britain, regulation in, 210

Hamilton, Alexander, 4, 81-82
Hardesty, Robert, 120
Harvard University School of Public
    Health, 190
Health and Human Services, Department
    of, 52
Heckler, Margaret, 191
Heritage Foundation, 146
Hernandez, John W., Jr., 109
Hodgson, James, 120
Hoover, Herbert, 85

Immigration and Naturalization Service v.
    Chadha, 77
Interagency Regulatory Liaison Group,
    46, 156
Interstate Commerce Commission, 11

Jackson, Robert, 80
Johnson, Lyndon B., 120
judicial review of administrative actions,
    24-29, 38-40, 48-49, 65, 116-
    117, 131-132, 138, 170, 204

Kahn, Alfred, 107
Kaufmann, Herbert, 57
Keyworth, George, 56

Labor, Department of, 120, 133
Landis, James, 5
legislative veto, 75-78
Levitas, Elliott, 77

Locke, John, 3
Lowi, Theodore, 10

Marshall, Ray, 120-121
McFarland, Carl, 30
Miller, James C. III, 84
Muskie, Edmund, 97

National Academy of Sciences, 50, 110,
    113, 149, 159
National Cable Television Association v.
    U.S., 12
National Cancer Institute, 190
National Highway Traffic Safety
    Administration, 10, 55
National Industrial Recovery Act, 11
National Institute of Health, 50
National Institute of Occupational Safety
    and Health, 50, 119, 122
National Insulation Certification Institute,
    160, 163
National Science Foundation, 50
National Toxicology Program, 158
Natural Resources Defense Council, 108
Nixon, Richard, 68
Nuclear Regulatory Commission, 10, 83

Office of Management and Budget,
    15-16, 29, 47-48, 52, 57, 67,
    82-87, 117-118, 125, 132-133,
    144-145, 203, 216-217
Office of Science and Technology Policy,
    46, 50, 52
Office of Technology Policy, 50
Occupational Safety and Health
    Administration, 27, 42, 44-46, 52,
    67, 82, 119-145, 156
ozone, 105-108

Panama Refining Co. v. Ryan, 11
Pious, Richard, 79
Pittle, R. David, 164
pluralism (and the administrative process),
    32
polybrominated biphenyls (PBBs),
    184-185
Pyle, Christopher, 79

Reagan, Ronald, 66, 68, 71, 85, 98
Regulatory Analysis and Review Group, 71, 107–108
Rehnquist, William, 139, 204
Reich, Robert, 87
reorganization of executive branch, 67
risk assessment, 14, 41–42, 46, 53–55, 115, 130–132, 143–144, 162–165
risk, public perception of, 62–63
Roosevelt, Franklin, 20
Roosevelt, Theodore, 4
Ruckelshaus, William, 69, 117
rule of law, 2, 209, 215

saccharin, 188–190
Schechter Poultry Corp. v. U.S., 11
Schultze, Charles, 137
science advisory bodies, 42, 49
Shapiro, Martin, 39
Shultz, George, 70
Sierra Club v. Costle, 80
Sierra Club v. Morton, 25
Sloan, Edith Barksdale, 164
Statler, Stuart M., 164
Steorts, Nancy Harvey, 163, 165–166
Stewart, Potter, 139
Stockman, David, 171

Sweden, regulation in, 211

Thomas, Lee, 117
de Tocqueville, Alexis, 16

urea-formaldehyde foam insulation, 157–167
U.S. Chamber of Commerce, 143
U.S. v. Nixon, 80
U.S. v. SCRAP, 25

Vice-President's Task Force on Regulatory Relief, 71–72

Walter-Logan Act, 19
Watts, James, 67, 75
Weaver, Paul, 168
Weber, Max, 57
West Germany, regulation in, 211–212
Wiedenbaum, Murray, 157
Wilson, Woodrow, 4

Yakus v. U.S., 12
Youngstown Sheet and Tube Co. v. Sawyer, 80

Zagoria, Sam, 164

 # ABOUT THE AUTHOR

Gary Bryner is currently an assistant professor in the Department of Political Science at Brigham Young University. He received his Ph.D. from the Department of Government at Cornell University. He has been a research fellow and visiting scholar at the Brookings Institution and has directed research projects at the National Academy of Public Administration. In cooperation with a number of colleagues at BYU, he is currently working on a series of books about the United States Constitution.